THE
ATLANTA
DOG LOVER'S
COMPANION

By Marilyn Windle

BOOKS BUILDING COMMUNITY™

ISBN 1-57354-008-0

51795

9 781573 540087

Rights Department
Foghorn Press
555 DeHaro Street, Suite 220
San Francisco, CA 94107
foghorn@well.com

To order individual books, please call Foghorn Press: 1-800-FOGHORN
(364-4676) or (415) 241-9550. Foghorn Press titles are distributed to
the book trade by Publishers Group West, based in Emeryville, California. To contact your local sales representative, call 1-800-788-3123.

Although the author and publisher have made every effort to ensure
that the information in this book was correct at press time, the author and publisher do not assume and hereby disclaim any liability
to any party for any loss or damage caused by errors, omissions, or
any potential travel disruption, whether such errors or omissions
result from negligence, accident, or any other cause.

Library of Congress ISSN Data:
November 1996
The Atlanta Dog Lover's Companion:
The Inside Scoop on Where to Take Your Dog in Georgia
First Edition
ISSN: 1089-2710

The Foghorn Press Commitment

Foghorn Press is committed to the preservation of the environment.
We promote Leave No Trace principles in all of our guidebooks, which
include cleaning up your dog's waste in the Great Outdoors. Addi-
tionally, our books are printed with soy-based inks on 100 percent
recycled paper, which has a 50 percent post-consumer waste content.

Printed in the United States of America

This book is dedicated to my sister,
Patricia Partridge, whose unwavering faith
in me and my abilities gave me the courage to go for it.

In memory of Laddie, who passed away just as this book
went to press and is now in leash-free Heaven.

BE A TRAVEL HOUND

If we've missed your favorite park, shop, hotel, festival, or pooch-permissible activity, please let us know. You'll help countless dogs get more enjoyment out of life in the Atlanta area. We welcome your comments about *The Atlanta Dog Lover's Companion*, too. Please write to: Editor-in-Chief, Foghorn Press, 555 DeHaro Street, Suite 220, San Francisco, CA 94107. You may call us at (415) 241-9550, or send us a fax at (415) 241-9648 or an e-mail at foghorn@well.com.

CONTENTS

ATLANTA AREA
CHAPTER REFERENCE MAP

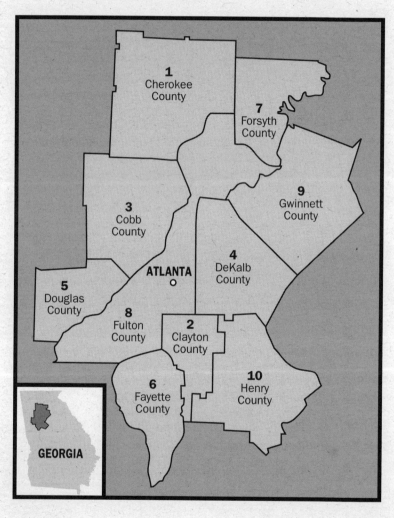

HOW TO USE THIS BOOK

The Atlanta Dog Lover's Companion is conveniently divided into 10 counties, and there is a getaways chapter for dog-friendly places beyond the metropolitan area that are particularly noteworthy. If you know the name of the county, city, park, hotel, or other place you would like to visit, look it up in the index beginning on page 263 and turn to the corresponding page.

Maps

Each chapter begins with a map of the county and features numbers indicating the location of the dog-friendly parks within its borders. Detailed descriptions of places to take your pooch are presented alphabetically after the name of the city in which it's located.

What the Ratings and Symbols Mean

Every park is rated on a scale of one to four paws 🐾. Hydrants 🚒 are reserved for parks that are only worth a squat—in other words, visit these parks only if your dog needs a place to relieve herself. The running dog symbol 🐕 means your pup can romp in leash-free bliss, while the foot 👣 indicates the park is extra special for people, too. For more details on the ratings and symbols, read the introduction starting on page 9.

MAP LEGEND

(95)	Interstate Highway
(1)	U.S. Highway
(814)	State or County Road/Highway
___	Undivided Road/Highway
___	Divided Road/Highway
- - -	State Border
O	City
▢	Highlighted Area
▢	Parks, Bases, and Universities
▢	Land and Islands
▢	Ocean, Lakes, and Rivers

INTRODUCTION

"Now, Charley is a mind-reading dog. There have been many trips in his lifetime, and often he has to be left at home. He knows we are going long before the suitcases come out, and he paces and worries and whines and goes into a state of mild hysteria, old as he is."
From *Travels with Charley,* by John Steinbeck

There was a time when dogs could go just about anywhere they pleased. Well-dressed dogs with embarrassing names attended afternoon teas, while their less-kempt counterparts sauntered into saloons without anyone blinking a bloodshot eye.

No one thought it strange to see a pug-nosed little dog snuggled on his mistress's lap on a long train journey. Equally accepted were dogs prancing through fine hotels, dogs at dining establishments, and dogs in almost any park they cared to visit.

But as the world gets more crowded and patience grows thinner, fewer and fewer places permit dogs. As deep as the human-dog bond goes, people seem to feel increasing pressure to leave their dogs behind when they take to the open road.

The guilt that stabs at you as you push your dog's struggling body back inside the house and tug the door shut can be so painful that sometimes you just can't look back. Even a trip to the grocery store can become a heart-wrenching tale of woe.

Well, feel guilt no longer. You're holding the key to all the dog-friendly parks, shops, lodgings, festivals, and diversions in the Atlanta area. The next time you run out for a paper, pick up this book and select a store where you don't have to tell your pal the dreaded "S" word. Feel like taking a walk? Check out all the pooch-pleasing parks and hiking trails. Ready for an overnight excursion? There are plenty of motels, hotels, and bed-and-breakfast inns where your dog is welcome, too. And when you're after a real adventure with your four-footed friend, turn to the Atlanta Getaways chapter, on page 191.

As any local will tell you, Atlanta is a fabulous city for dogs *and* people. I grew up on an island in Florida and ended up in Atlanta quite by accident in 1974. Shortly thereafter, two unrelated events changed my life. I received a beautiful American Eskimo puppy—Trixie—for Christmas, and I met Betty, who became my dearest human friend. Trixie lived to a ripe old age and is in doggy heaven now, but she'll never be forgotten.

Betty and her daughter, Starr, introduced Trixie and me to hiking. Together, the four of us explored the entire state of Georgia. Trixie loved the woods as much, if not more, than I did, so we spent our weekends checking out the variety of parks and hiking trails from one side of the state to the other.

I now share my life with two dogs who are very different from both Trixie and each other. Laddie, another American Eskimo, is all white and looks like a 25-pound Samoyed. He was a hard-luck case who belonged to one of Betty's neighbors, and though he was about five years old when he came to live with us, he was pretty much untrained. Laddie had spent his life on the tiny, fenced-in patio of a condominium, and was mystified when I asked him if he wanted to go outside. Most dogs learn the "O" word early in life and can't wait to go out at every opportunity. But Laddie wanted to come in. Since our house has a dog door, he can come and go as he pleases and thinks he lives in the best of all possible worlds.

My other pooch, Bandit, is an extremely rambunctious puppy. A cross between a Lhasa apso and a bichon frise, he resembles a 20-pound Old English sheepdog. When I picked him out at the Atlanta Humane Society, he was quiet and cuddly, two very good traits in a puppy. I didn't find out until later that he'd been given his shots that day, which had temporarily calmed down his tornado personality. Everything for Bandit has an exclamation point after it. He races through the house and through life, chewing anything that smells good and chasing anything that moves. When he goes outside, he leaps through the dog door as if there will always be something to chase on the other side. When he comes back in, he races to find me so he can show me whatever wonder he's discovered in the yard. (This is not as popular with me as it is with him.) If I leave the room, he's devastated. Whenever he sees me, whether I've been gone all day or just for a couple of minutes, I get an incredibly joyous greeting.

Laddie and Bandit, being very different in personality, have very different likes and dislikes when it comes to outings. Laddie likes walking downhill, tolerates level ground, and positively abhors walking uphill. If it's supposed to be fun, he seems to say, why is it so hard? Bandit, on the other hand, has lots of energy for hiking, but with his long hair he gets hot very easily. He's happy as long as he's in the shade and has a chance to cool off periodically in a lake or stream. He's the only dog I've ever known who likes to put his head under water and blow bubbles. Bandit enjoys meeting other dogs and their owners, too. Laddie, however, is always worried that people and dogs just want to mess with him, and he'd rather stay as far away from both as possible. A perfect day for Laddie would be an all-downhill trek with lots of food and off-leash romps. I think he'd prefer a ski run where we ride up on a chairlift and then walk down the hill. But Bandit's idea of doggy heaven would include lots of people to fawn over him, and other dogs to play with.

THE PAWS SCALE

I've rated each park and recreation area featured in this book from a dog's perspective. Where Laddie and Bandit differ in their assessment, I've called upon my friend Vickie and her dog, What, to lend a hand (or paw). What is a tiny, five-pound Pomeranian, and she is quite different from Laddie and Bandit. She likes people who make a fuss over her, exploring (and smelling) wildlife, and being carried when she's tired. Other than that, she approaches every situation, person, and animal with a great deal of enthusiasm and a friendly lick. I keep hoping that a little of What will rub off on my Laddie, but I'm still waiting.

The very lowest rating you'll come across in this book is a fire hydrant symbol 🛢, meaning the place is merely worth a squat. Visit one of these parks only if your dog can't hold it any longer, because these parks have virtually no other redeeming qualities for canines.

Beyond that, the paws scale starts at one paw 🐾 and goes up to four paws 🐾🐾🐾🐾. A one-paw park isn't a dog's idea of a great time. When your pooch tells his friends about his weekend, he probably won't mention this park. Maybe it's a tiny place with too many kids running around. Or perhaps it's a magnificent-for-people place that bans dogs from every inch of land except a paved road. A two-paw place is a good park that's worth a drive. And a three-paw park is a great place to spend a day, although your pooch could probably suggest some ways to improve it—perhaps more shade, a place to swim, more space between the picnic tables, or fewer people. Four-paw parks, on the other hand, are just about as pooch-perfect as a place can be. Many have swimming areas or numerous acres for hiking.

Occasionally you'll see the foot symbol 👞, which means the park offers something extra special for the humans in the crowd. You deserve something for being such a good chauffeur.

TO LEASH OR NOT TO LEASH?

This isn't a question that plagues a dog's mind. Ask just about any normal, red-blooded American pooch if she'd prefer to visit a park and be on leash or off, and she'll say "Arf!" No question about it, most dogs would give their canine teeth to be able to frolic about without a cumbersome leash.

Most people I talk to are amazed to learn that Georgia doesn't have a state leash law. But before your dog jumps for joy, I'd better tell you that most counties do. As Atlanta continues to consume formerly rural areas, more and more counties can be expected to have to deal with the canine population explosion.

When you see the running dog symbol 🐕 in this book, you'll know that under certain circumstances, your dog can run around in leash-free bliss. The rest of the parks demand leashes. I wish I could write about the parks where dogs get away with being scofflaws, but those would be the first parks the animal-control patrols would hit. I don't advocate breaking the law by letting your dog off his leash, but if you're going to, please follow your conscience and use common sense. And just because dogs are permitted off leash in certain areas doesn't necessarily mean you should let your dog run free. Show a lot of consideration for the nondog population by making sure your pet is under voice control when he's not tethered to a leash. If he won't come when he's called, he's not a good candidate for a park populated by other people or dogs. Keep in mind that counties make regulations and laws when they get complaints. And it's a lot easier to prevent an anti-dog rule than to get it off the books once it's been passed.

THERE'S NO BUSINESS LIKE DOG BUSINESS

There's nothing appealing about bending down with a plastic bag or a piece of newspaper on a chilly morning and grabbing the steaming remnants of what your dog ate for dinner the night before. It's disgusting. Worse yet, you have to hang on to it until you can find a trash can.

But as gross as it can be to scoop the poop, it's worse to step in it. And have you ever walked into a park where few people clean up after their dog?

Unscooped poop is one of a dog's worst enemies. Like leash laws, pooper-scooper laws are passed because of complaints, and messes are one of the leading causes of ordinances restricting dogs from public areas. Even though scooping is required in only a few areas, I don't want to leave Laddie and Bandit droppings everywhere we go. Do your bit to prevent more cities from outlawing dogs from city parks.

I always carry plastic grocery bags in my car, day pack, and pocket. I scoop up the mess with one bag, tie it off, then drop it in another bag. If there isn't a trash can around, I tie the second bag to my belt.

If you're on a trail and absolutely refuse to pick up your pet's mess, at least flick it off the trail with a stick. One ranger I spoke with told me that the number one complaint she got from more than two million visitors to her park one year was that the trails were littered with dog poop.

LEAVE ONLY FOOTPRINTS

Speaking of messes, it's appalling how much trash is left behind in parks. Whether you're dodging chicken bones in a picnic area or

pulling your pet away from rusty worm cans along the lake, you're sure to find a lot of garbage on your excursions. When you see cans, bottles, cigarette butts, paper, and other trash in a park, pack some of it out. If you're carrying plastic grocery bags for cleaning up after your dog, use one for trash. I keep one bag tied on my belt for dog poop and a second one for trash I find on our outings.

DAY PACK POINTERS

One of the lessons I've learned from my friend Betty is how to be prepared when I hit the trail with my dogs. Although she denies ever being a Girl Scout, she's ready for anything in the woods. The day pack essentials listed below will help prepare you and your dog for most of the problems you might run into, whether you and your pooch are on a day hike on the Appalachian Trail or at Piedmont Park for the afternoon.

Of course, the first essential piece of equipment is the day pack itself. A day pack is a small backpack that will carry anything you might need on a short hike. They're sold in the camping section of most discount and outdoors stores.

The second essential is water—for you *and* your dog. Try carrying your water in a lightweight plastic canteen (some models feature a built-in clip to hang on your belt—very handy when you want to stop for a quick drink). Get a canteen with a screw-off top that's attached to the bottle, so you won't drop it in the horse doo-doo you at your feet. (Trust me, it happens.) You could also buy ...ackaged in small bottles that will fit in your pack.

...about your pet? It's difficult to stop thirsty pooches from ...g out of a stream, but when they do, they risk ingesting G...ia, a nasty little parasite that often lives in the water (see Water Problems on page 255 for more information). If you've ever had food poisoning, you know what I'm talking about. Keep your pup's thirst quenched with the clean water you're carrying. I've found that a lidded plastic bowl makes the best portable doggy water dish. I'm not talking about a reused whipped-topping container, but a Tupperware or Rubbermaid bowl that's guaranteed not to leak. There may be worse things than your dog's water leaking into your pack and down your back, but it's still unpleasant.

To help you and your pooch prepare yourselves for a hike, here is a checklist of day pack essentials:

- Day pack.
- Water for you and your dog.
- Cloth hat for sun protection.
- Bug spray, preferably containing DEET.
- Rain poncho. These are available in the camping section of discount and outdoors stores and come in a variety of unattractive colors. If you're on a hike in the mountains, you'll need something to protect you from sudden downpours.
- Snakebite kit. These are small, lightweight, and available in the camping section of most discount and outdoors stores.
- First aid kit. You can buy these already assembled, but they typically contain products you'll probably never use. I bought a small pouch at a recreational equipment store and stocked it with pain reliever, bandages, antiseptic wipes and cream, rubbing alcohol, cotton balls, hydrogen peroxide, gauze and gauze strips, tape, and since I'm allergic to bee stings, Benadryl tablets. Benadryl can also be given to your dog (see your vet for the right dosage).
- Lots of plastic grocery bags for scooping up poop.
- Dog (and people) treats. Bring your dog's favorite, and your own as well.
- More substantial food for you and your dog if you're going on a long hike.
- A small flashlight—either a penlight or a squeeze light. It's easy to misjudge when darkness will fall.
- A Swiss Army or similar knife. Get the kind with scissors and a saw blade in case you need to cut cloth or tape for bandages.

I carry some other items in the trunk of my car all the time. Plans change, the weather is unpredictable, and a quick drive to the post office can unexpectedly include a stop at a park when one of the boys has a pressing need. Towels are handy for drying off muddy feet before they get on the car seats. A blanket is handy for an impromptu picnic or to cover the backseat when the towels just don't do the job. I also carry extra leashes in the glove box, and a brush and comb, which are handy for removing burrs and checking for ticks. Finally, a small bottle of water and a paper cup are great to have stored in the car in case your dog gets thirsty when you're on the road.

COMMON BEASTIES AND OTHER HAZARDS

When you go into the woods, you're sharing the outdoors with some critters and plants that you wouldn't ordinarily invite into your home. And since you're in their world, it's best to take a few precautions. It's a jungle out there. Please refer to Canine Calamities, beginning on page 253, for more information on the following hazards, as well as other problems your pooch might encounter in the wilderness.

• **Ticks and other bugs.** If you and your dog hike in Georgia, you're going to encounter ticks. The trick is to keep them off you both. For you, I recommend what my sister, Tricia, calls my woodswoman hat. While she assures me it's quite unflattering, it does keep ticks out of my hair, and it comes in handy on miserably hot days. You can soak your hat in a cold stream, wring it out, and use it to cool your head. Also, though I don't like to put poison on my skin, I consider bug spray a necessity during the summer. It helps ward off the flying pests that bite. The best defense against nonflying pests is to keep your eyes open and use common sense. If you're hiking through the woods, watch for spider webs stretching across the trail between the trees.

For your dog, you need to combine whatever flea and tick routine you already have with vigilant searches before getting back into the car. You can reduce your exposure to ticks by staying out of damp, brushy areas, especially near lakes and rivers. While you're not completely out of danger anywhere, the Chattahoochee River Parks seem to be particularly tick infested. I once pulled more than 100 ticks off my two dogs at the end of a four-mile hike in one of these parks. (See Canine Calamities, beginning on page 253, for information about removing ticks and on Lyme disease.)

• **Poison ivy.** This is probably the worst problem you'll encounter in Georgia's parks. Poison ivy is more common than kudzu, which is saying a lot. It grows in a cluster of three leaves. Sometimes the leaves are notched or have a "thumb," but not always. It usually trails along the ground, but can climb trees. Although most dogs aren't sensitive to the sap (probably because it never gets through all that hair to their skin), they can transfer it to you when you touch them. So, unless you keep your dog out of all woods (and my backyard), you're going to be exposed to it occasionally. I could tell you to avoid touching your dog until after you bathe him every time you go in the woods, but how do you keep him from touching you? The best defense is a good offense. You can even get a prescription for a pill that prevents an allergic reaction to the plant.

CROWD CONTROL

Things have changed a lot since Trixie and I first entered the woods together. The population in the Atlanta area has grown dramatically, and the number of people on the trails and attending out-

door events has grown along with it. Over the years, festivals we used to enjoy became more and more crowded, and finally outlawed dogs altogether. The only defense we dog lovers have against public policies restricting dogs is being proactive, which usually comes down to being courteous and using common sense.

For example, think twice about taking your dog into a crowded area, even if she's allowed to be there. She probably won't have a good time. From her vantage point, all she sees are feet—lots of them—and they aren't watching where they're stepping. Also, be aware of who is around you whenever you're out with your dog. Children have a tendency to squeal and pounce on toy-sized pets. Even the calmest dog could bite in those situations, so be ready to scoop up your dog when outstretched hands come reaching for him.

TRAIL MANNERS

Most of the trail rules for dogs are really just common courtesy, mixed with your knowledge of how your dog will respond in a given situation. When we're out hiking and come across other canines, Bandit is delighted, but Laddie bares his teeth and wants nothing more than to get to the other dog. If the other pooch is a little timid, she hides behind her person's leg and makes pitiful sounds. If she's the least bit aggressive, though, her owner and I both have a battle on our hands as we try to control our wild animals.

Since I already know what Laddie's reaction will be, when I spot a group coming with another dog, I call out to them to hold up while I get him off the trail. Though we usually end up standing in poison ivy, I have better control over him.

If your dog is a trifle unfriendly with his own kind, as Laddie is, let the people coming toward you know what you're doing while you move off the trail. I've had some people just keep coming closer with their dog, saying, "Oh, Ginger won't hurt anyone," and then Ginger turns into the Hound of the Baskervilles. But the majority of dog owners are just as eager as I am to avoid confrontations.

If you're on a trail shared with equestrians and you see horseback riders approaching, pull your pooch off the trail and allow them to

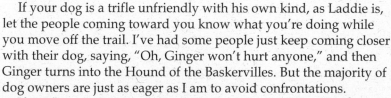

pass. If necessary, put your dog behind you. If she isn't already leashed, snap it on. A dog is no match for a horse.

Likewise, if your dog isn't used to people racing by on bicycles or skates, keep a short leash in all potential problem areas. Although, technically, bikers are supposed to yield to walkers, they may have been absent that day in trail manners class, so avoid confrontations. And if you're sharing a trail with skaters, you're probably on a side-walk or street, which is more their territory than yours. They can build up a pretty good head of steam on such smooth surfaces, so don't force them to take a flying leap into a bush to keep from running you—and Fido—down.

Neither of my dogs would win a speed race in the woods. They're too busy sniffing the smells along the way. When other hikers are outpacing you, pull your pet off the trail to allow them to pass. Many adults are wary of stepping near a dog they don't know, so position yourself between them and your dog.

DINING WITH DOGGY

Unfortunately, it's currently illegal to take Laddie or Bandit with me to eat at a restaurant in Georgia. They can't even curl up under an outdoor table and hope I drop them a bite. According to state regulation: "Live animals, including birds and turtles, shall be excluded from within the food service premises. This exclusion does not apply to edible fish, crustacea, shellfish, or to fish in aquariums. Patrol dogs accompanying security or police officers, or guide dogs accompanying handicapped persons, shall be permitted in dining areas or other public access areas."

Unless you're spending a day with your lobster, this pretty much keeps you and your pet out of any restaurants in this state. I spoke with a very sympathetic individual at the Georgia Department of Human Resources who said the regulation includes outdoor tables and sidewalk benches. He also said the bill was drafted before outdoor dining patios cropped up all over Atlanta, and if there's sufficient interest, he told me the department would consider changing the regulation if it wouldn't endanger human health.

So, here's a chance for you to make a difference. If you would like to be able to take your pet with you when you dine at a sidewalk cafe or on the patio of a restaurant, write a polite letter requesting the department to consider a change to the rules enforced by Chapter 290-5-14, Food Service. If enough dog lovers write, the department will hold a hearing on the rules. Send your letter to: Melinda Scarborough, Department of Human Resources, Division of Public Health, Environmental Health Section, 2 Peachtree Street, Fifth Floor Annex, Atlanta, GA 30303.

HOTEL ETIQUETTE

Happily, the state ban on dogs in restaurants doesn't apply to dogs in many of Georgia's hotels, motels, and bed-and-breakfasts. The decision on whether or not to allow pets in lodgings is up to the establishment's management, and quite a few places in the Atlanta area welcome dogs.

When you stay at a hotel with your pooch, bear in mind that you're sort of an emissary for dog owners everywhere. When a hotel manager has bad experiences with dogs (or, more precisely, dog owners), she's likely to change her pet policy, affecting all of us. You can help prevent that by following some basic hotel etiquette:

• Ask the desk clerk where they'd like you to walk your dog.

• Scoop that poop! Use plastic grocery bags, double bagged if necessary, and securely tie them. Drop them in outdoor trash cans.

• Don't leave your pup unattended in your room—even to dine in the hotel's restaurant. Consider using room service if it's available, otherwise send someone out to get breakfast while one of you stays with the dog or take him with you to a drive-through establishment. Although your dog may not bark while you're gone from home, in a strange place with strange noises, she could get pretty protective and noisy.

If you know you're going to have to leave your pooch alone for a period of time, talk to the desk clerk when you check in. Ask for an end room, as far away from other people as possible. Use the Do Not Disturb sign on the doorknob to spare the housekeeper the scare of his or her life.

• If your puppy isn't housebroken at home, he won't be in someone else's home, either. Don't travel with a piddling pup or one who is still in his chewing stage.

• If your dog sleeps on the bed at home, she probably will at the hotel, too, even if she waits till you go to sleep. Bring a bedspread and put the hotel's spread out of reach.

Until doing the research for this book, I'd given up hope of ever staying at any of the quaint bed-and-breakfasts my friends raved about. Now that I've found delightful, antique-furnished inns where Laddie and Bandit are welcome, I want to continue to enjoy them. Using a little common sense and being respectful of the property of others is the best way to ensure my pets—and yours—will be welcome back.

GENERAL POOCH POINTERS

• Be sure your dog wears his license and identification tag. State law requires that all dogs receive rabies vaccinations and that they wear rabies tags in public.

• Whatever you do when you're out and about with your dog, don't ever leave him in a car with the windows rolled up. Even if you crack the window, a mini-greenhouse is created that can result in heatstroke or death in a surprisingly short period of time. Ever return to the car from the store and find you can't touch the steering wheel because it's too hot? If your dog must stay in the car, park in the shade and have someone stay with him.

• One option when you need to go to a store where your dog isn't allowed is to tie her up outside. It's less likely that she'll overheat if she's outside in the shade than in the car. But choose the location well. Although a light post, mailbox, or sign outside a store may look like a good spot, they may also be too close to car traffic or too exposed to passersby, especially children.

• Don't let your dog ride in the back of a pickup truck unless he's cross-tied.

• While the Metro Atlanta Rapid Transit Authority (MARTA) and Cobb Community Transit (CCT) don't prohibit dogs, they make traveling with one difficult. Only service dogs are allowed to travel on buses and trains uncaged, er, uncrated. Call it what you will, your dog won't like being relegated to a crate to ride on a bus or train.

• If something horrible happens and your dog damages either a person or his property, do the right thing and immediately make whatever restitution is necessary. My dogs aren't angels, and my guess is yours aren't either. The most amazing things seem to happen when you take your dog away from his home base. Laddie tends to spin around in a circle a few times before squatting to do his business. Once he wrapped his leash around three very expensive lily plants, stripping off all signs of green before I could react.

• Don't let your pooch annoy wildlife in the woods. I've been on hikes with other dog lovers who let their pets chase deer. Hazard a guess as to why you can't take your dog on any trail in our national parks. Please don't ruin it for the rest of us by letting him run rampant. Stressed wild animals are more susceptible to disease. They also have to search for every bite of food they eat, and they don't need to waste calories running from your dog. While most wild animals will take off if they hear your dog coming, some won't. I consider myself lucky that I've been dogless each time I've encountered a bear. They're notoriously cranky, don't like being barked at, and will sometimes chase your dog as she runs straight back to you. Skunks don't put up with a lot of abuse before retaliating either.

HE AND SHE

In the spirit of doggy democracy, I've alternated the pronouns "she" and "he" when referring to your pooch. I wouldn't want any dog to feel left out.

STATE PARK PASS

In 1991, the Georgia legislature passed a law requiring state park day users to pay a $2 fee per day per car, or $25 per year. A full 100 percent of the proceeds of this fee are used to pay for park repair and renovation projects.

Day-use and annual passes can be purchased at any state park or historic site. An annual pass (valid from January through December) can also be ordered by sending a check for $26 ($25 for the pass, plus a $1 handling charge), payable to Georgia State Parks, to: Georgia State ParkPass, 205 Butler Street Southeast, Suite 1258 East, Atlanta, GA 30334. Discounts are available for senior citizens and disabled veterans. For more information, call (404) 656-3530.

A DOG IN NEED

If you're thinking about adding another dog to your family, I urge you to consider adopting one through your local animal shelter or humane organization. And be sure to spay or neuter your new buddy to try to lower the number of unwanted dogs. For more information, turn to Pick of the Litter on page 242 for a list of the best places to adopt a dog in the Atlanta area, or contact the National

Humane Education Society (521-A East Market Street, Leesburg, VA 20176), a nonprofit organization that teaches people about the importance of being kind to animals and maintains the Peace Plantation Animal Sanctuary for dogs and cats.

Something else to consider is the value of animal-assisted therapy programs for people in need. You know how your pooch can lift your mood with just a paw in your lap or a lick on your chin, right? Wouldn't it feel good to share some of that love? Through animal therapy programs, dogs can brighten the day of a sick child, an emotionally withdrawn teenager, or an Alzheimer's patient who has retreated into a shell. Pets and especially dogs often have the ability to touch the emotions of some people who have resisted conventional therapy and treatment.

There are different degrees of animal-assisted therapy. Cosby's Therapy Animals evaluates and trains volunteers and their dogs for the Pet Partners hospital visitation program. They can test your dog's temperament and determine if both of you meet the requirements to be effective. Cosby's also raises and trains therapy dogs. The difference between a therapy dog and a Pet Partners pooch is the level of training and commitment involved. Therapy dogs have completed years of training, and work with their handler and a licensed therapist to achieve specific speech or motor improvements in a patient. With Pet Partners, the patient and the dog interact without an outside entity guiding the process. The other service provided by Cosby's Therapy Animals is the training and placement of service dogs. Service dogs assist people with disabilities, such as guide dogs for the blind. In some cases, the disabled individual's own dog can be trained to help them. For more information and to volunteer at the Pet Partners hospital visitation program, call Bill Reynolds, Training Director, at (770) 578-8804.

Another organization that evaluates volunteers and their dogs for hospital and nursing visitations is Happy Tails Pet Therapy. After a dog has passed the

temperament and basic obedience test, volunteers attend a workshop to learn what they should do during a visitation. The $20 annual membership fee is for newsletters and the dog test. At press time, Happy Tails Pet Therapy had 175 dogs, 8 cats, and 2 rabbits on their teams. For more information, contact Happy Tails Pet Therapy at: P.O. Box 767961, Roswell, GA 30076; (770) 740-8211.

BEYOND THE BORDERS

There may be times when you and your dog actually find yourselves leaving the Atlanta area to visit other parts of the United States. Due to the success of *The California Dog Lover's Companion*, Foghorn Press is launching a Dog Lover's series of books for different parts of the country, including Boston, Chicago, Florida, Seattle, Texas, and Washington, D.C. All of the authors are experts in their areas and have adventurous dogs who help them explore and rate various attractions. Keep your eyes peeled for upcoming books, or call Foghorn Press at 1-800-FOGHORN (364-4676) to order yours.

CHEROKEE COUNTY

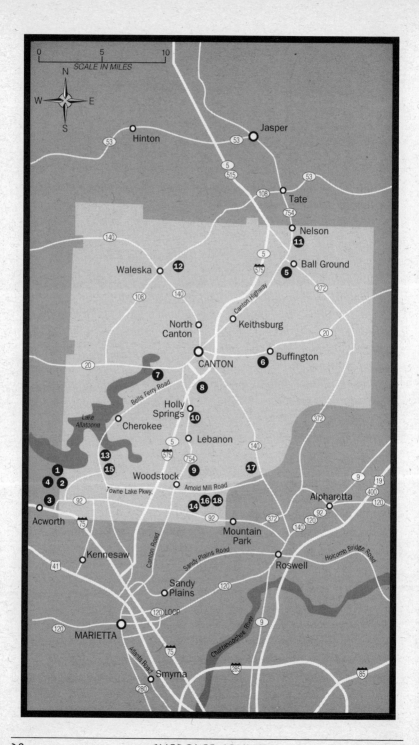

1
CHEROKEE COUNTY

Located about 30 minutes from downtown Atlanta, Cherokee County is a favorite destination for city dwellers in search of peace and quiet in the many parks around Lake Allatoona, an 11,860-acre recreation area. Lucky for dog lovers, pooch-pleasin' places abound—and the news gets even better. While the county does have a leash law, from November through February the Cherokee County Recreation and Parks Department has decreed that dogs are welcome to romp off leash in the fenced ball fields of almost every county park. The only requirements for this rare treat are that the field must be fully fenced, the gate must be kept closed, and you must scoop up after your pet. If someone' else comes into the field to play a game or fly a kite, you must immediately leash your pooch so he doesn't bother any other visitors.

As long as dog owners follow the rules and keep the fields clean, pooches will be able to enjoy this leash-free bliss for years to come. Otherwise, Cherokee County might go the unfortunate way of the city of Canton. After receiving complaint upon complaint about dogs running off leash and getting into trouble, as well as gripes about dog owners who neglected their pooper-scooper duties, the city banned dogs from all parks within city limits. Even wonderful Boling Park, a county facility, is off-limits to your pooch because it's within the city limits of Canton. If you live in Canton, you can lobby the city commissioners to get this ban lifted. But it's a lot easier to prevent an anti-dog ordinance through good behavior than it is to have one repealed.

As you set off for one of the dog-friendly parks in this county, you'll soon discover that some of them are hard to find, with signs in short supply. But with the allure of off-leash joy at most of the county parks in the winter, they're certainly worth the search. Just be sure to bring along this book and a good map. All directions for Cherokee County destinations assume you're traveling on Interstate 575 from Interstate 75. Some of the parks along Lake Allatoona are actually located in Bartow County, but I've included them within this chapter since they're just minutes from the county line.

The parks managed by the United States Army Corps of Engineers system have day-use fees, with a $3 maximum fee per vehicle per day. The boat launch fee is $2 per day, while the swimming beach fee is $1 per person per day. An annual pass can be purchased for $25 per family. Golden Age and Golden Access Passports are half price. Children under 12 are free. Passes can be purchased at the parks. Call (770) 382-4700 for more information.

ACWORTH

Though technically Acworth is in Bartow County, I've included it here because the parks are located right on Lake Allatoona, just across the county line, and are popular destinations from Atlanta. Cobb County dogs will also find Acworth well within reach, since the small town is located just west of Kennesaw.

PARKS AND RECREATION AREAS

• **Bartow Carver Park** 🐾 *See ❶ on page 28.*
Though this park is on Lake Allatoona, access to the water is tough, and you may have trouble containing your leashed pooch (the law here). Much of the lake drops down rapidly from the shore, becoming too deep for smaller dogs like Bandit within inches of the sand. If you can convince your pup to wait for a better spot, walk her past the deep areas and you'll find she can wade and splash without getting in over her head. The picnic area is shaded with large trees, making for a cool spot to relax after a dip in the lake. Watch out for stray chicken bones and other leftovers—the trash cans are underutilized here.

The park is open daily from 8 A.M. to 9 P.M. Take Interstate 75 north from Atlanta to exit 123 (Red Top Mountain Road) and turn right. Go left on Bartow Carver Road, which dead-ends into the park. (770) 387-5149.

• **Clark Creek North Day-Use Area** 🐾 *See ❷ on page 28.*
Good access to Lake Allatoona is the main attraction at this small park. If you have a water-loving dog like my Bandit, you'll be forgiven for a multitude of sins as soon as those pads hit the water. Bandit likes to put his head under and blow bubbles, then leap up and try to pounce on them before they pop. This keeps him entertained for hours, while Laddie looks on in amazement.

On our last visit, we ate lunch at one of the picnic tables right on the lake. But Bandit's attention was focused on the floating wooden loading dock, which he yearned to investigate. When I started to clean up the picnic debris, I tied his leash to the leg of the table to keep him from sneaking away. Laddie always tattles on Bandit when he's doing something the older dog knows he shouldn't do, so I looked up when Laddie gave his "I'm telling" whine, which wanders all up and down the scale. Bandit was gone. I called and called, and finally heard a whine in response, but couldn't see him anywhere. Laddie was looking out at the dock, though I could see no sign of naughty Bandit. Then I noticed a movement near the shore, between the underside of the dock and the water. Bandit had somehow managed to get under the dock. The water level in the lake was only a couple of inches below the bottom of the dock, so Bandit must have ducked his head underwater to reach his hiding place. His only way out was to duck under again, which he hadn't figured out yet. I made my way down to the dock and tried to pull Bandit out, but every time I grabbed for him, he retreated to a back corner in fear. I finally realized there was no way to reach him without going for help.

When I got back to the picnic table, I couldn't tell if Laddie was excited or worried that Bandit was caught in this predicament. I opened the trunk and started to throw the rest of our things in the car so I could drive for help. Then I noticed the treat can in the trunk. The sound of the contents rattling in the can is enough to bring my boys running from the back 40 at our house. It was worth a shot, so I shook the can. Bandit popped out from under the dock and was sitting at my feet within seconds. After I recovered, I put him in the car and took Laddie on a leisurely walk around the wooded area so he could satisfy his urge to sniff for messages from the locals. By the time we got in the car to leave, I was almost calm.

Leashes are required at this park. Next time I'll be sure to hold on to my end.

The park is open daily during daylight hours. This is an Army Corps of Engineers park, so day-use fees apply (see page 30). Take Interstate 75 north from Atlanta to exit 121 and turn right onto Glade Road. The park is on the right just over the bridge, approximately three miles down the road. (770) 382-4700.

• **Old U.S. 41 Park One/Park Two** 🐾🐾 *See* ❸ *on page 28.*

These two day-use areas are connected by a bark-chip path approximately half a mile long. They're right on Lake Allatoona, but the access isn't good except in a few spots. If your dog is anything like Bandit, you might get pulled in before finding one of the decent access areas. The parks are basically undeveloped; they have picnic tables but not a lot of shade. Leashes are required.

The park is open daily from dawn to 9:30 P.M. United States Army Corps of Engineers system fees apply (see page 30 for specifics). From downtown Acworth, go north on Highway 293 a little less than two miles. The two day-use area parks are on the left at the lake. (770) 945-9531.

• **Tanyard Creek Day-Use Area** 🐾 *See* ❹ *on page 28.*

You and your leashed pooch will find limited creek access at this small park, especially during the dry months when the water can be too far down from the bank to reach easily. If you have a water dog like Bandit, he might just take matters into his own paws and jump in—and getting him out becomes your problem! Bring plenty of towels to protect your car. There's a lovely beach for swimming, but unfortunately, it's off-limits to your four-footed pal. The park is heavily wooded with tall pines and offers plenty of cool shade for your pooch to explore.

Hours are daily from dawn to 9:30 P.M. United States Army Corps of Engineers system fees apply (see page 30). From Atlanta, take Interstate 75 north to exit 121 (Glade Road) and turn right. Turn left onto Tanyard Creek Road. The park is on the right. (770) 945-9531.

SHOPPING IN ACWORTH

Beverly's Antiques: An easy way to convince Bandit to be good while shopping is to bribe him with the promise of a lake trip afterward, which is what I do when we visit Beverly's, one of several antique shops in downtown Acworth. Beverly's features lovely furniture as well as candles and Georgia-made gifts. 4835 North Main Street, Acworth, GA 30101; (770) 974-7909.

The Ivy Shop: A combination antique store and florist, The Ivy Shop has something for everyone. The owners are animal lovers who used to have a pet skunk, and they welcome your pup to come on in and shop with you. 4829 South Main Street, Acworth, GA 30101; (770) 974-5576.

Serendipity House: This delightful shop is housed in a beautiful Victorian that was built in the late 1870s, with wide, shady porches along both the front and the back. Your pooch is welcome to join you as you shop for gifts with a Southern flair, including furniture, Heritage Lace curtains and accents, stained glass collectibles, Civil War and *Gone With the Wind* memorabilia, baby gifts, and more. If you don't trust your pup inside, feel free to tie her in the shade on the porch while you shop. 4965 North Main Street, Acworth, GA 30101; (770) 966-1301.

PLACES TO STAY

Best Western Frontier Inn: A long grassy stretch near the children's playground is lit at night for those midnight strolls with your pooch. You won't find a lot of shade around the inn, but there's an area in back with several varieties of wildflowers. Rates are $50, plus $5 per day for your pup. Interstate 75 at Highway 92 Northwest, Acworth, GA 30101; (770) 974-0116.

Days Inn: Better watch your pooch when wandering the large grassy fields and shady spots at this motel—there's a runoff pond on one side. The dog walk area benefits from the parking lot lights at night. Rates range from $38 to $45. 5035 Cowan Road Northwest, Acworth, GA 30101; (770) 974-1700.

Holiday Inn Express: The attractive landscaping at this hotel provides lots of well-maintained grassy areas to stroll with your dog. The hotel allows small to medium pups only. Rates are $59, plus $10 per day for your pooch. 164 Northpoint Parkway, Acworth, GA 30101; (770) 975-9920.

Quality Inn: You can walk your pooch in the grassy areas at this motel, though there's no shade. The room rate is $40, plus $5 per day for your pet. 4980 Cowan Road Northwest, Acworth, GA 30101; (770) 974-1922.

Super 8 Motel: If your pup needs to stretch his legs, head for the wooded area behind this motel. Rates range from $48 to $60, with no charge for your pooch. 4970 Cowan Road Northwest, Acworth, GA 30101; (770) 966-9700.

BALL GROUND
PARKS AND RECREATION AREAS

• **Ball Ground City Park** 🐾 *See* **5** *on page 28.*

Local canines frequent the large trees at this park. Don't be surprised if your male dog spends quite a while catching up on the news. Leashes are mandatory here.

The park is open daily during daylight hours. From Interstate 75, take Interstate 575 to exit 13 and turn right onto Howell Bridge Road. The road changes names to Old Canton Highway at the intersection with Canton Road. Go straight across the intersection onto Old Canton Highway. Turn right onto Gilmer Ferry Road, then left onto Valley Road. The park is on the left a half a block down Valley Road. (770) 735-2123.

CANTON
PARKS AND RECREATION AREAS

• **Buffington Park** 🐾 *See* ❻ *on page 28.*

Located next to an elementary school, small Buffington Park is easy to miss. While kids of the human kind will have fun playing on the swings and slides and climbing on the jungle gym, your leashed canine kids will have to make do with a lot less. There are no trails for canine companions, and though a large, grassy field behind the tennis courts provides a spot for a quick romp with your pooch, the sound of children playing is never far away. Bandit finds this noise very distracting, and he usually can't relax long enough to enjoy himself. He does like nosing around behind the tennis courts in search of a stray ball or two. Deep woods surround the field on three sides. The addition of trails through the woods would improve this park immensely.

Buffington Park is open daily from 7 A.M. to 10 P.M. To reach it from Atlanta, take Interstate 75 north to Interstate 575. Continue on Interstate 575 to exit 10 (Highway 20) and turn toward Cumming. (Since the exit ramp curves around, it's a left turn.) The park is about four miles down the road on the right, next door to Buffington School. Though there's no sign for the park at the entrance to guide you, there is a historic marker at the park entrance in memory of Fort Buffington, the largest holding fort used to contain the Cherokee Indians prior to the infamous Trail of Tears march. (770) 924-7768.

• **Fields Landing Park** 🐾🐾🐾 👣 *See* ❼ *on page 28.*

Bring your lunch and relax at one of the picnic tables or wander down the short gravel trail at this pleasant park with Lake Allatoona access, large trees for shade, and a potpourri of pooch-pleasing smells. Bandit goes nuts over the park's large population of squirrels, while Laddie is in dog-sniffing heaven. Fields Landing Park is one of the biggest county parks in the Atlanta area, with acres of shady woods in addition to nearly a mile of coastline to wander along. Once you're out of the beach area, you and your pup will probably have the shore of the lake to yourselves. Leashes are a must here.

Hours are daily from 6 A.M. to 10 P.M. From Atlanta, take Interstate 75 north to Interstate 575. Take exit 8 (Highway 20) off Interstate 575 and turn left. Go left again onto Fields Landing Court and follow it to the park at the end. (770) 924-7768.

• Kenney Askew Memorial Park 🐾🐾 🐕 🦴
See **8** *on page 28.*

Bandit searched in vain for evidence of other dogs the first time we visited this park. He was pretty disappointed—until he found out that he could run unfettered by the tie that binds in the fenced playing fields. The leash-free life is such a novel activity for city dogs that at first Bandit wouldn't leave my side. When he finally did bound off, he started running rings around Laddie and me, keeping close in case I needed him but loving being beyond the reach of the leash. Remember that dogs are allowed off leash only in the playing fields, and only from November through February. Be sure to leash your pooch if someone else enters the field, and remember to scoop up the you-know-what.

In addition to the ball fields, the four-legged set can also romp on leash around the large grassy fields in the park. Amenities for people include football and baseball fields, basketball and tennis courts, a playground, and picnic pavilions.

Park hours are daily from 7 A.M. to 10 P.M. From Atlanta, take Interstate 75 north to Interstate 575, and get off at exit 7 (Holly Springs). Turn left, toward Canton, then right at the first light onto Univeter Road. (770) 924-7768.

• Lower Cherokee Recreation Association 🐾🐾
See **9** *on page 28.*

At first glance, this park doesn't seem to have much going for it as far as pooches are concerned, with what appears to be just baseball, football, and soccer fields. Take the pretty much unshaded one-mile walk around to the back, though, and you'll come to a creek with good access. Unfortunately, your pup may overheat before she reaches the creek. But if she perseveres, she can cool off in the water before making the trek back to the car. Dogs get thirsty on the hike to the creek, so be sure to bring a bowl and plenty of water to avoid exposing her to Giardia.

Park hours are daily from 7 A.M. to 10 P.M. From Atlanta, take Interstate 75 north to Interstate 575. Get off at exit 5 and turn right on West Mill Street. Turn left onto Canton Road; the park will be on your right when you cross the Little River Mill Creek. (770) 924-7768.

PLACES TO STAY

Sweetwater Creek Campground: This Army Corps of Engineers campground is located on Lake Allatoona at the Etowah River. Your pooch will find easy lake access here, and deep shade at the sites keeps the temperature low in the summer. You won't find any trails, but there are plenty of places around the campground to walk your dog. Sites are $10 to $14, depending on hookups. From Atlanta, take Interstate 75 north to Interstate 575. Take exit 8 (Highway 20) and turn left. Go left on Fields Chapel, then left again on Sweetwater Creek Drive, which leads to the campground. (770) 382-4700.

HOLLY SPRINGS
PARKS AND RECREATION AREAS

• **Holly Springs Park** 🐾 *See ⑩ on page 28.*
Since this park doesn't consist of much more than a baseball field, it's only worth a quick squat. Walk your leashed pooch behind the ball field and be on your way.

The park is open daily during daylight hours. From Atlanta, take Interstate 75 north to Interstate 575. Get off at exit 6 and turn right onto Sixes Road. Go left on Canton Highway (Main Street), then head left on Barrett Road in Holly Springs to the park. (770) 924-7768.

NELSON
PARKS AND RECREATION AREAS

• **Nelson Park** 🐾 *See ⑪ on page 28.*
Although your leashed pooch may enjoy spending a few minutes sniffing around the trees, this park consists of little more than a grassy area and a baseball field lined with trees on one side. It won't take him long to whine for greener pastures.

The park is open daily during daylight hours. From Atlanta, take Interstate 75 north to Interstate 575. Stay on Interstate 575 until it ends, and turn right on Zell Miller Mountain Parkway. Turn left on Ball Ground Highway, right on Baker Street, and then right on School Street to reach the park. (770) 924-7768.

WALESKA
PARKS AND RECREATION AREAS

• **Waleska Park** 🐾🐾 🐕 *See ⑫ on page 28.*
I wasn't at all impressed with Waleska Park on my first visit. It has three baseball fields and some grassy areas for a quick squat, but not enough to go out of your way for a visit—at least at first glance. This was very disappointing, since I'd driven up and down Highway 108 looking for the park in vain. But while I was ready to pack

up and move on, Bandit's radar was working overtime. He led me down a gravel road to a creek, and when I saw how deep the water was, I was amazed that the road continued on the other side. (Perhaps this explains why there are so many four-wheel-drive vehicles in Cherokee County. While Bandit happily blew bubbles, I nervously kept watch for Jeeps.) According to the county, the road is in use, but cars almost never drive on it, so look out for the occasional vehicle and go ahead and let your pooch cool his pads in the water.

From November through February, your dog can also enjoy off-leash bliss on any of the fully fenced ball fields. Be sure to close the gate behind you and pick up after her. The fields are large enough to give any dog's legs a good stretch, and the novelty of being leashless in the Atlanta area is a rare treat.

Park hours are daily from 7 A.M. to 10 P.M. Take exit 8 (Highway 5) from Interstate 575 and turn left. Stay on Highway 5 at the right fork, then turn left onto Highway 140 at the next light, heading toward Waleska. At the four-way stop in Waleska, turn right onto Highway 108, and check your odometer. Exactly eight-tenths of a mile later, turn right into the park. (Pleasant Arbor Road is on your left.) A small house is located right near the entrance to the park, so it'll seem like you're turning into a driveway. Go past the house to reach the park. (770) 924-7768.

WOODSTOCK
PARKS AND RECREATION AREAS

• **Cherokee Mills Day-Use Area** 🐾 *See ⑬ on page 28.*
Unless you're a boat, this park offers little but a place for a quick pooch potty stop. It's mainly a boat launch area, and water access is poor for pups. There is some shade. Leashes are mandatory.

The park is open daily during daylight hours for day use, and until 10 P.M. for boaters. From Atlanta, take Interstate 75 north to Interstate 575. Get off at exit 3 and turn left on Bells Ferry Road. The park is on the left just before the bridge over the lake. (770) 924-7768.

• **Dupree Park** 🐾🐾🐾 🦴 🐕 *See ⑭ on page 28.*
Simply put, Dupree Park is lovely. It's not real big, but it has all the main elements a pooch could want. The small lake has good access for water dogs; the walking trail is short but does offer some opportunity for exercise; and when the sun gets too strong, large trees provide shade and enough doggy smells to set your pup's nostrils atwitter.

Best of all, from November through February, dogs can run leash-free inside the fenced ball fields. As always, be sure to leash your pet if someone else enters the field and to pick up after him. It would be a doggone shame to lose this leashless privilege because of complaints against dog owners.

Park hours are daily from 7 A.M. to 10 P.M. From Atlanta, take Interstate 75 north to Interstate 575. Take exit 5 (Towne Lake Parkway and West Mill Street). Turn right onto West Mill Street, which becomes Arnold Mill Road. Stay on Arnold Mill Road until you reach Neese Road and turn right. The park is on your left. (770) 924-7768.

• **Hobgood Park** 🐾🐾 🐕 *See* **⑮** *on page 28.*

Hobgood Park is the best-kept secret among Cherokee County parks, with a half-mile-long track around the softball complex that's great for stretching your pup's legs. Although shady spots are now in short supply, the Parks Department has planted trees all around the track, so the walk should be Bandit-approved in a few years, when the landscaping matures.

Hobgood is another park blessed with a leash-free area inside the fenced ball fields from November through February. Do scoop the poop, and be sure to leash up if someone else enters the field. Other park amenities include fitness equipment, a picnic area, an amphitheater, and a playground.

Park hours are daily from 7 A.M. to 10 P.M. From Atlanta, take Interstate 75 north to Interstate 575. Take exit 5 (Towne Lake Parkway and West Mill Road). Turn left onto Towne Lake Parkway. Take the right fork, which is still Towne Lake Parkway. Hobgood Park is on the right on Bells Ferry Road. (770) 924-7865.

• **Little River Park** 🚩 *See* **⑯** *on page 28.*

This park has tennis courts, a playground, and a picnic pavilion, but not much in the way of canine entertainment. There must be a river here somewhere, but even Bandit's water radar couldn't find it. Maybe the Little River is similar to Lake Claire in DeKalb County, and just a joke the locals pull on the tourists.

The park is open daily from 7 A.M. to 10 P.M. From Atlanta, take Interstate 75 north to Interstate 575. Turn right at exit 4 onto U.S. 92, then left onto Trickum Road. The park is on the left at Barnes Road. (770) 475-0409.

• **Mountain Road Park** 🐾 🐕 *See* **⑰** *on page 28.*

Located adjacent to Mountain Road Elementary School, this park appears to mainly serve the needs of the school, with baseball and soccer fields, a playground, and a picnic pavilion. My dogs are skittish around this kind of noise and activity level, but yours may love all the commotion.

A big plus here, however, is the leash-free law from November through February, when you can close the gates on any of the fenced playing fields and let your pooch run off leash to his heart's content. Remember to always pick up after your pup and to leash up if someone else enters the field. Complaints could force the Recreation and Parks Department to change the law.

The park is open daily from 7 A.M. to 10 P.M. From Atlanta, take Interstate 75 north to Interstate 575. Turn right at exit 4 onto U.S. 92. Turn left onto Main Street, then right onto Arnold Mill Road. After about seven miles, turn left onto Mountain Road. The park is next to Mountain Road Elementary School. (770) 475-0409.

• **Riverchase Park** 🐾 🐾 *See ⑱ on page 28.*

What's a dog to do? you might ask when you first take stock of this park located in a residential area not far from civilization. The tennis and basketball courts, picnic facilities, children's playground, and leashes-required law are certainly not a pup's cup of kibble. But don't give up too soon. A path from the picnic pavilion leads off to the left, where it winds down to a creek, and sandbars make it easy for water dogs like Bandit to wade in and blow bubbles. You're in full view of the houses across the creek, however, and there are some very vocal dogs living there, which Bandit finds pretty distracting. We discovered this park shortly after Hurricane Opal swept through Atlanta, so when we found trees down on the trail, I thought it was from storm damage. We wandered over and under the trees for quite a distance, having a wonderful time, before I realized I was in someone's yard. The park actually covers just six acres, so the path by the creek quickly meanders beyond the border.

The park is open daily from dawn to dusk. From Atlanta, take Interstate 75 north to Interstate 575. Turn right at exit 4 onto Highway 92. After about five miles, turn left onto West Wylie Bridge Road, then left again on Riverchase Drive into the Riverchase subdivision. The park entrance is the first right turn. (770) 924-7768.

CLAYTON COUNTY

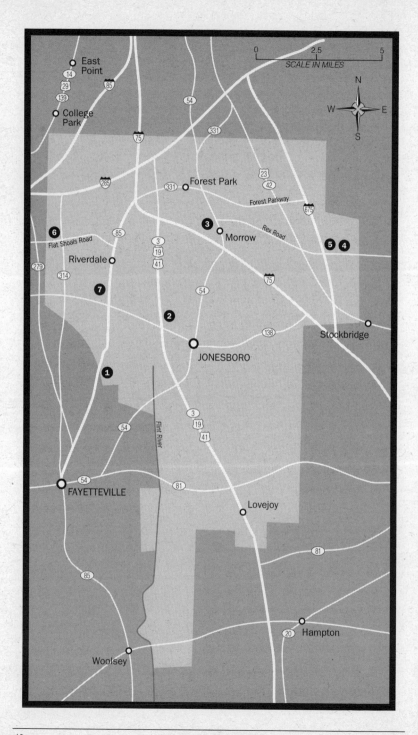

2
CLAYTON COUNTY

Clayton County, just half an hour from downtown Atlanta, has figured prominently in Atlanta's history for two reasons, both concerning the city of Jonesboro. The pivotal Confederate loss of the battle of Jonesboro during the Civil War was followed within 12 days by the fall of Atlanta, due to the capture of the last of the Confederate rail supply lines. Dozens of commemorative markers to critical events in the war are found in the county. Call the Clayton County Chamber of Commerce at (770) 478-6549 if you'd like a map to the historical markers.

Jonesboro was also used by Margaret Mitchell as the historical foundation for *Gone With the Wind*, and this county is the place to find every imaginable type of book, film, and memorabilia on the subject. Many fine antebellum homes and churches from that era still stand. Tours are generally scheduled in the spring and fall and are listed in the *Atlanta Journal and Constitution's* "Saturday Leisure Guide."

Laddie and Bandit simply aren't interested in either the Civil War or this great work of Southern literature, but there's plenty to please them in Clayton County, including the W. H. Reynolds Nature Preserve (see page 45), one of the finest parks in the Atlanta area.

JONESBORO

Jonesboro was the inspiration for Margaret Mitchell's Tara, the fictional home of the O'Haras in *Gone With the Wind*. Tourists still come to Jonesboro to look for Tara, but it only existed on the back lot of a studio in Hollywood. No filming for the movie actually took place here. The famous fire scene in the book, when the Confederate troops burned their supply depots, is historically accurate, patterned after the same occurrence in Jonesboro, just before the Confederates pulled out and surrendered the city to the Union troops. Some 600 Confederate soldiers are buried here. If you're interested in *Gone With the Wind* or Civil War memorabilia, you'll find it in nearly every shop in the city. Your pooch won't be overly impressed by any of the parks in Jonesboro, but they're good for a quick stop when heading for other areas in the county.

PARKS AND RECREATION AREAS

• **Independence Park** 🐾 *See* ❶ *on page 42.*

This large park would be great if it had a path, but instead you and your leashed pooch must walk in the road or strike out on your own through the woods. If you do, be careful not to trip over the tangle of poison ivy and vines along the way. There's plenty of shade, which is much appreciated by longhaired dogs like Laddie and Bandit. Amenities for humans include tennis and basketball courts, baseball fields, picnic pavilions, and a playground if you have tots in tow.

Hours are daily from 8 A.M. to 11 P.M. To get to the park from Atlanta, take Interstate 75 south of Interstate 285 and exit on Highway 85. Turn south on Highway 85. Go left onto the Pointe South Parkway, also known as Flint River Road. Turn right onto Thomas Road, and then left on Independence Road to reach the park. (770) 473-5798.

• **Panhandle Park** 🐾 *See* ❷ *on page 42.*

If nature's calling, go ahead and walk your leashed pooch around the baseball fields in this small park, but that's about all a dog can do here.

Hours are daily from dawn to dusk. To reach the park, take Interstate 75 south of Atlanta to U.S. 41 and turn south. Turn right on Tara Road, then left on Panhandle Road. The park is on your left. (770) 473-5795.

DIVERSIONS

Easter eggs for canines: Why should parents of two-legged children have all the fun when Easter rolls around? Well, the folks at the Atlanta Recreation and Fun Club for Dogs have remedied the situation by hosting an annual canine Easter Egg Hunt. The location for the event varies each year, so give the number below a call a few weeks in advance to find out where to go. The club usually holds the hunt in a fenced field, so your pooch can dash about in leash-free bliss and find the dog-safe treats. These include hard-boiled eggs (decorated with pooch-friendly food coloring) and plastic eggs filled with crunchy dog cookies. You might want to give your pup a head start by introducing him to a hard-boiled egg at home prior to the big event. Laddie wasn't at all interested in eggs until I partially peeled one for him. Once he found out they were food, though, he became an expert at locating the treats. For more information on the Atlanta Recreation and Fun Club for Dogs and the hunt, contact Candy or Daniel Pyron at (770) 961-2435.

MORROW
PARKS AND RECREATION AREAS

• **W. H. Reynolds Nature Preserve** 🐾 🐾 🐾 👣
See ❸ on page 42.

Welcome to one of the best parks in the Atlanta area—and it seems to be our little secret for now. Every time I visit, I wonder why so few people have discovered this gem, which boasts four delightful small lakes, lush gardens, and cool, winding trails through the woods.

You'll find two areas to park at the preserve. Leave the lot by the Nature Center for non-hiking visitors and park by the trailhead.

Take the path from the parking lots across the creek, where water-loving dogs like Bandit are in heaven. The path meets up with the 1.5-mile Brookside Trail, which winds around all of the lakes. Numerous side trails of varying lengths can round out a full afternoon. The park is heavily wooded but still gets pretty muggy in the summer, so I tend to go in the spring and fall. If you and your pup get really hot, cool off in the air-conditioned building at the Nature Center. You can also park in the shade, so you won't be returning to an overheated car.

One of the side trails off the Brookside Trail goes over Black Mountain, the second highest point in Clayton County. Take the Brookside Trail to the right at the entrance for a more gradual climb up to Black Mountain. Laddie doesn't like uphill hikes, and he didn't complain until we backtracked once and took Black Mountain from the other direction. Leashes are required.

Hours are daily from 8:30 A.M. to dusk. From Atlanta, take Interstate 75 south to the Forest Parkway exit (Highway 331), south of Interstate 285. Turn left onto Forest Parkway. Turn right on Dixie Road/U.S. 41, then left on Pineridge Road, which becomes Reynolds Road. The park is on your right. (770) 961-9257.

SHOPPING IN MORROW

Petsmart: Besides offering a wide assortment of pet food and supplies, Petsmart sponsors training classes you and your pooch can attend to pick up basic commands that will make both of you easier to live with. Petsmart has stores all over the city. 1986 Mount Zion Road, Morrow, GA 30260; (770) 478-0860.

PLACES TO STAY

Red Roof Inn South: Room rates are $40 per night, with no extra charge for your pooch. 1348 South Lake Plaza Drive, Morrow, GA 30260; (770) 968-1483.

REX
PARKS AND RECREATION AREAS

• **Rex Horse Ring Park** 🐾 *See ❹ on page 42.*

A myriad of horsey smells are sure to be the main attraction for your leashed pooch at this equestrian park. Just watch where she steps! Treat the horses with the same respect you would accord an 18-wheeler when you're driving a Volkswagen, because your dog will lose any confrontation. Be sure to bring plenty of water for you and your pooch, since it can get very hot and dusty as you walk around the horse rings and in the grassy fields. The park is surrounded by very large trees, but they're all located on the perimeter and provide no shade in the fields.

All the signs at the park claim that it's open daily from 9 A.M. to dusk, but you'll find the gate locked except during scheduled horse shows. It's much more interesting for your dog when the horses are around anyway. From the south side of Interstate 285, take Interstate 675 south toward Macon to exit 3 (Ellenwood, Panola Road, and Forest Parkway). Turn left off the interstate onto Panola Road. Turn right at the four-way stop onto Stagecoach Road. Turn left onto Rex Road, then right onto Wilkerson Road. The park is half a mile down on the left. (770) 474-3635.

• **Walter Estes Rex Park** 🐾🐾 *See ❺ on page 42.*

Any park with a name this grand had better be good, and sure enough, Bandit thinks he's found doggy heaven whenever we pay a visit to Walter Estes Rex Park. The park has two creeks, with fine water access at both. The creek at the back of this large park is more private, and you'll probably be the only ones there as your pooch splashes about. If your dog doesn't like water, take her on a walk in one of the fields or through the wooded area. Your leashed pooch might get lucky and find a stray ball behind the tennis courts, and will certainly enjoy sniffing the trees near the creek. Amenities for the two-legged set include baseball fields, a children's playground, and picnic pavilions and tables.

The park is open daily from 9 A.M. to 11 P.M. From the south side of Interstate 285, take Interstate 675 south toward Macon to exit 3 (Ellenwood, Panola Road, and Forest Parkway). Turn right off the interstate onto Forest Parkway. Turn left onto U.S. 23/Highway 42. After two miles, turn left onto Rex Road. The park is one mile down on the right. (770) 474-3635.

RIVERDALE
PARKS AND RECREATION AREAS

• **Flat Shoals Park** 🐾🐾 *See* ❻ *on page 42.*

There's something for every pooch here, whether she likes to play in the water, sniff in the woods, or run in the fields. As you drive into the park, lower your windows enough for your pup to get a good sniff while you pass through the lovely wooded area. Even Laddie, my wake-me-when-we-get-there dog, sticks his head out and breathes deeply, tail wagging. As you drive past fields and more woods, the road winds to a creek, which leads through the woods to a picnic area, past more fields, and finally to another creek at the end. Watch out for the speed bumps. They're the highest I've seen, and I heard every one of them scrape against the bottom of my Honda. If your car is built lower than average, park your car along the road and walk in. Leashes are required. Also at the park are volleyball nets, lots of baseball fields, football and soccer fields, basketball courts, and picnic areas.

Hours are daily from 8 A.M. to 11 P.M. From Atlanta, take Interstate 85 south past Interstate 285 and exit onto Flat Shoals Road, turning left. The park is on the left, between Highway 279 and Highway 314. (770) 996-3444.

• **Riverdale Park** 🐾🐾 🦴 *See* ❼ *on page 42.*

This small park doesn't get much use, but it has a lot to offer both you and your leashed pooch, including the Lamar Hutcheson Fitness Trail. The half-mile track offers some shade, but Bandit's black coat heats up quickly whenever he gets any sun. Carry water for your dog and he'll be more comfortable. The picnic area is heavily wooded and stays relatively cool even in the summer. Best of all for Bandit is the small creek in the back of the picnic area, which is deep enough for him to cool his pads. Unlike many park creeks, where getting your dog down to the water means taking a bath yourself, this creek has easy access for your pooch. Your human companions can enjoy several baseball fields, a football field, tennis courts, picnic pavilions, and a playground.

Park hours are daily from 8 A.M. to 11 P.M. From Atlanta, take Interstate 75 south of Interstate 285 to the Highway 85 exit. Turn right on Highway 85 and drive into Riverdale. Turn right on Bethsaida Road, and left onto Church Street. The park will be on your right. (770) 997-5945.

COBB
COUNTY

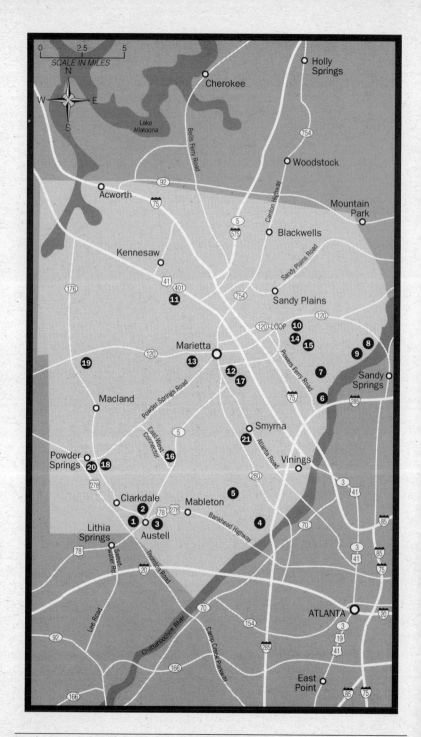

3
COBB COUNTY

Cobb County doesn't pretend to be anything but what it is—a last bastion of independent country in a rapidly encroaching city. Yes, Kennesaw has a gun law (all residents must own a gun), and yes, Cobb was thrown out of consideration as an Olympic venue because of its proclamation against gays. It's not true that there's a law requiring residents to own a pickup truck, but that could change by the time this book goes to press.

More to the point as far as you and your pooch are concerned, Cobb County has many of the best parks in the Atlanta area. Kennesaw Mountain National Battlefield Memorial Park (see page 61) and the various Chattahoochee River National Recreation Areas offer superb hiking trails through cool woods where your leashed pooch can sniff for signs of wildlife or cool off in the water. (While the river parks are great, be forewarned that they are heavily infested with ticks. Wear a hat and check yourself and your dog after your walk.)

The county is also home to a large number of small county and neighborhood parks. Many have "fitness" nature trails, meaning that you'll find multiple stops along the trail with exercise stations. Not only have I never seen anyone using any of the equipment, but Laddie and Bandit steadfastly refuse to do any of the chin-ups or log jumps.

ATLANTA

Just a tiny edge of Cobb County dips down within the city limits of Atlanta. There are a lot of great parks nearby, including several of the Chattahoochee River National Recreation Areas, but none both within the city limits and Cobb County. The bulk of the city lies in Fulton and DeKalb Counties. Refer to those chapters for parks within the Perimeter.

PLACES TO STAY

Hawthorn Suites Hotel: For a $5 per day charge, your pet is as welcome as you are. Room rates are $79 to $169. 1500 Parkwood Circle, Atlanta, GA 30339; (770) 952-9595.

Homewood Suites Hotel: This hotel is conveniently located just two blocks south of the intersection of Interstate 285 and U.S. 41 (Cobb Parkway), making it a good choice for traveling families. There is a $75 nonrefundable pet charge for up to two pets to be used to remove any pet allergens that could affect future guests. Your pooch is also welcome to join you at breakfast unless she bothers other guests. A large field next to the hotel is available for bathroom breaks. Rates are $92 to $102 for a suite, including breakfast. 3200 Cobb Parkway Northwest, Atlanta, GA 30339; (770) 988-9449.

AUSTELL

Sleepy little Austell has two solid parks and a quick stopover for dog lovers, plus the annual Pet Parade held at Six Flags Over Georgia in August (see Diversions, page 53).

PARKS AND RECREATION AREAS

• **Austell Legion Park** 🔥 *See ❶ on page 50.*

This tiny park adjacent to the Austell Senior Center is mostly used for baseball, but if your leashed pooch is whimpering for a quick stop, the park's grassy area will do.

Park hours are daily from 8 A.M. to 11 P.M. From Atlanta, take Interstate 20 west to the Thornton Road exit and turn right. Turn right again onto Bankhead Highway (U.S. 78/278). Turn left on Austell-Powder Springs Road. The park is on the left. (770) 944-4329.

• **Sweetwater Park** 🐾 *See ❷ on page 50.*

If you've been wanting to try one of the fitness courses, the equipment at this small park is in better condition than most. The three-quarter-mile trail is wide, well marked, and covered with pine straw as it winds through deep woods. The cool shade makes this trail especially pleasant for dogs like Laddie who want to take their time and enjoy the smells along the way. Since the path is never far from a picnic pavilion or a baseball field, this might not be a good choice if your pooch is distracted by the shouts of children playing. Laddie ignores all extraneous sounds, but Bandit is constantly looking for a possible playmate. Watch for poison ivy all along the trail. You must leash your dog in this park.

The park is open daily from 7 A.M. to midnight. From Atlanta, take Interstate 20 west to the Thornton Road exit and turn right. Turn right onto Maxham Road, which becomes Austell Road. Turn left onto Clay Road. Turn left into the park, just past Flint Road. (770) 819-3220.

• **Wallace Park** 🐾 🐕 *See* ❸ *on page 50.*

Bandit gives paws-up to the cool, shady trails in the woods at this park. There are also lots of activities to keep your pooch's human companions happy: the wooded trails lead from the parking lots to a variety of fields, picnic pavilions, and play areas for the kids. Leashes are required.

The park is open daily from 8 A.M. to 11 P.M. From Atlanta, take Interstate 20 west to the Thornton Road exit and turn right. Turn right onto Maxham Road, which becomes Austell Road. Turn right on Old Alabama Road. Turn right on Pisgah Road and then left into the park. (770) 528-8807.

PLACES TO STAY

Atlanta West Campground: Your pooch can stay for free at this campground, although he must be on a leash. There are no trails, but he'll enjoy walking along the creek bank. Rates range from about $15 to $21, depending on hookups. 2420 Old Alabama Road, Austell, GA 30001; (770) 948-7302.

La Quinta Inn: All La Quinta Inns allow pets to stay for free, but this one is managed by real dog lovers, Jolane and Loren Brown. Your pooch's tail will wag with glee when he sees the large dog walk area and all the other grassy places he can romp on leash. Be sure to mention your pup when you register, so the Browns can have dog biscuits waiting at the counter. Biscuits occasionally make it to the breakfast buffet as well, when groups with dogs are guests in the hotel. Rates are $50 to $85. 7377 Six Flags Drive, Austell, GA 30001; (770) 944-2110.

DIVERSIONS

Llama walk-o-rama: It's okay to pass turtles on the left at the annual Pet Parade, a one-mile fun walk for all kinds of pets held at Six Flags Over Georgia each August. Dogs and cats promenade with monkeys, turtles—even a pair of llamas. (The llamas live on a farm with several dogs and are quite comfortable walking among them, though uninitiated pooches like Laddie don't know what to think when they first encounter these woolly beasts.) Be sure to keep your pooch under your control since there are distractions aplenty. The event benefits the Atlanta Humane Society. (Since dogs aren't allowed in the park itself, this is the only time you'd want to bring your pooch to Six Flags.) 7561 Six Flags Road Southwest, Austell, GA 30001; (770) 739-3400. For more information about the Pet Parade, call the Atlanta Humane Society at (404) 875-5331.

KENNESAW
SHOPPING IN KENNESAW

Petsmart: Petsmart has elevated shopping with your pet to an art form in Atlanta. Not only does the store have every type of pet food and product imaginable, but items just for fun as well. If you plan to attend the Halloween Party given by the Atlanta Recreation and Fun Club for Dogs (see page 78 in the DeKalb County chapter), you'll want to check out the costumes starting in mid-September. I could never talk Laddie into wearing any of them in the past, but hopefully Bandit can be convinced to go as a ghost or a pumpkin this year. Petsmart is located all over the city. 860 Cobb Place Boulevard, Kennesaw, GA 30144; (770) 424-5226.

Presto Magic Pet Photography, Inc.: Hankering for a coffee cup, T-shirt, Christmas ornament, or calendar adorned with your pooch's own fuzzy portrait? Set up a photo shoot with Jim Presto, who's been specializing in pet portraits since 1992. Presto is known for his beautiful pooch pictures, from wallet-sized to framed oil canvases. He's also very involved in charitable work, with some of the profits benefitting Toys for Tots, local humane organizations, and the homeless. At Christmas, you'll find Presto at work with several grooming salons on his popular Santa pictures with Fido. Best of all, he really loves pets. (He even charmed Laddie.) Call (770) 421-8144 for more information.

PLACES TO STAY

Atlanta North KOA: Rates at this campground are $23 to $27 with full hookups. Best of all, pets stay for free. Your pooch must be leashed while checking out the dog run, and you should bring something to clean up after her. 2000 Old 41 Highway Northwest, Kennesaw, GA 30152; (770) 427-2406.

Rodeway Inn: Rates are $45 to $51, with a fee of $5.65 a day for your pet. You'll find plenty of shade around this inn to keep you cool while your pooch is sniffing out messages left by other canines. There's also a half-mile-long grassy median down Busbee Parkway if you want a longer stroll. 1460 Busbee Parkway, Kennesaw, GA 30144; (770) 590-0519.

DIVERSIONS

Santa Claus is coming to town: Looking for a truly special Christmas card to send to your dog-loving friends? Each year, the Cherokee County Humane Society sponsors a photo shoot featuring your pooch (or other pet) sitting on Santa's lap. Be sure to explain the Santa Claus thing to your pup beforehand ("You better not bark, you better not bite . . .") or Santa may just leave a lump of coal in her doggy stocking. The event is held at the Petsmart store in Kennesaw at 860 Cobb Place Boulevard, Kennesaw, GA 30144; (770) 424-5226. For more information, contact the Cherokee County Humane Society at (770) 928-5115.

MABLETON
PARKS AND RECREATION AREAS

• **Nickajack Park** 🐾🐾 🐾 *See* ❹ *on page 50.*

It won't be hard to convince your human and canine friends to join you for a day here. For the two-legged set, you'll find several ball fields and plenty of picnic pavilions. Your leashed pooch will enjoy the mile-long fitness trail. Skip the exercise stops along the trail as it winds deep into the woods, since you may find yourself getting enough of a workout finding your way out! Because the trail is never far from one of the ball fields, you'll stay in earshot of children playing. Although Bandit normally finds this quite distracting, even he is able to eventually ignore the shouts as they get farther and farther away.

The trail starts out wide and deteriorates into a poorly marked path. Adding blazes to the trees would be a significant improvement. On our first visit, Laddie and I got lost for more than an hour. My friend Vickie and her Pomeranian, What, were with us. Near the back of the park, a footbridge (missing a few planks) led over the creek to a lovely grassy field. I had a hard time negotiating with Laddie to cross the bridge. He approached the gaping holes suspiciously, scowling. My 25-pound pup refused to step over the gaps, and didn't like being carried. What, weighing in at five pounds, calmly started to step over a gap and would have fallen through if Vickie hadn't caught her.

We had a wonderful time in the field on the other side of the bridge until we realized we were on private property. The only access back to the park was over the dreaded bridge, and Laddie wasn't at all happy about facing it again. Once safely off the bridge, we found that the trail had taken a right turn at the bridge. Again, a sign or a blaze would have been very helpful.

Hours are daily from 7 A.M. to midnight. From Interstate 285, take South Cobb Drive north and turn left on Oakdale Road, then right on Nickajack Park Road to reach the park. (770) 696-6767.

• **Thompson Park** 🐾 🐾 🐾 *See* ❺ *on page 50.*

Laddie is partial to parks with lakes, and this one comes complete with ducks. When we visit, he wants nothing more than to stay at the lake and take a nap, one of his favorite hobbies, so he tends to grumble a bit when I'm ready to hit the park's peaceful, half-mile-long nature trail, which winds by Nickajack Creek through dense woods filled with wildflowers and ferns. The path starts at the top of the hill, at the back of the children's play area next to the community center. Although the park is right on Nickajack Road, the trail quickly climbs away from the street, so you'll only occasionally hear a car far below.

This is one of the few Cobb County parks without fitness equipment, which you won't miss a bit, since the hills provide quite an aerobic workout. Laddie, forever dog-dreaming about the lake, doesn't care for aerobic workouts (or fitness equipment, for that matter). On our last hike here, he tried to convince me to go down, rather than up, the trail. I really had to prod him to keep him going in the right direction. At one point he even laid down and rolled over on his side. His tail, usually held curled over his body, was unfurled and dragging the ground as we slowly moved up the hill. As soon as we reached the top, though, the tail was back in position and he trotted quite happily as we made our way down the hill. A fork to the left goes to an outdoor stage where various community programs are held in the spring and summer. A short trail from the back of the concert area leads to railroad tracks scheduled to be closed and converted to a walking and biking trail, as part of the national Rails to Trails Conservancy Project.

Wear long pants to provide some protection from the poison ivy, which grows all along the trail. Your pooch must wear a leash.

The park is open daily from 7 A.M. to midnight. From Bankhead Highway (U.S. 78/278) in Mableton, turn north on Floyd Road. Turn right onto Nickajack Road. The park is just past the railroad tracks. (770) 819-3215.

MARIETTA

Marietta is one of the largest of the cities within the Atlanta metropolitan area that still boasts a town square and many small town activities, most of which can also be enjoyed by your pooch. The variety of city, county, and national parks within Marietta makes it well worth a drive from even the south side of Atlanta. Whether your dog enjoys soaking up culture at one of the concerts in tiny Glover Park (see Diversions, page 68), hiking up Kennesaw Mountain, or splashing in the Chattahoochee River, she'll find more than enough to keep her happy here.

PARKS AND RECREATION AREAS

• **Chattahoochee River National Recreation Area**
(See individual units within the park for ratings and locations.)
If you want to make your dog's tail wag, just tell her you're going to "The River." The Chattahoochee River National Recreation Area consists of 14 separate land areas, called units, along a 48-mile stretch of the Chattahoochee River between Lake Lanier and Peachtree Creek. Four of these land areas are in Cobb County, and they are heaven on earth for city dogs, with an amazing variety of wildlife. Beavers, squirrels, rabbits, opossums, raccoons, herons, hawks, ducks, and kingfishers are abundant. You and your pooch may also find a variety of snakes (including copperheads), in addition to ticks and poison ivy. I once pulled more than 100 ticks off of my two dogs after a four-mile hike, so check your pet carefully before getting into your car. I also recommend protecting yourself by wearing what my sister calls a "woodswoman" hat with a wide brim. It may not be the most stylish attire, but it's effective at keeping creepy-crawlies out of my hair. Be sure to bring along insect repellent, water for you and your dog, and snacks, too. A rain poncho can also come in handy.

Unfortunately, complaints about dogs may force the park service to outlaw pooches from the Chattahoochee parks. I spoke with Field Operations Supervisor Connie Vogel-Brown, who said that the results of a survey of three million Chattahoochee visitors indicated that dogs running off leash and dog poop on the trails are the two biggest complaints about the park.

Off-leash dogs have caused problems not only for other visitors but for themselves. One dog was mauled by a muskrat when he went into a bush to retrieve a ball. In other cases, dogs have been injured when bounding up to greet other park visitors who misinterpreted their overtures as an attack. Some people let their pooches off leash to swim in the river, but dogs can quickly get into trouble in the swift current. You also need to leash your pet to keep him from getting lost. Leashed dogs can't chase after wildlife, such as the deer, red fox, skunk, and beaver found in the park, and end up in the next county or on an expressway. (In some of Georgia's parks, the percentage of lost dogs who are later found is very low—just 50 percent in Red Top Mountain State Park, for instance.)

So, for the sake of all Chattahoochee park–loving pooches and their people, be sure to keep your dog on leash and scoop the poop. Plastic grocery bags work well, and Mutt Mitts are available in Cochran Shoals (see below). The units are all open daily from dawn to dusk. Call the number listed with each park for a map of the unit.

Cochran Shoals Unit 🐾🐾🐾🐾 🦴 *See ❻ on page 50.*

This large, well-maintained unit is one of the more popular of the Chattahoochee River parks due to its convenient location in the heavily populated area near the Cobb cloverleaf. In the morning, joggers and dog walkers share the flat trails that wind in and out of the woods. At lunch, hordes descend from the office parks nearby to eat a sandwich and enjoy the wide river view. After work and on weekends, the parking lots fill up quickly and spill out onto Interstate Parkway as runners, walkers, and their dogs return.

There are two entrances into the unit, one on either side of the river. If you like a wilder, more rugged trail, closer to the river and less populated, try the eastern Cochran Shoals Unit. Even though we run into many more people on the western side, Laddie definitely prefers the wide, sandy, and level trail at this larger entrance, nearest to Powers Ferry. It's as close to perfectly flat as can be found in Atlanta, plus there's easy access to the river for him to wade in and cool his pads. The main trail is three miles long, with many side trails that lead to the Sope Creek Unit and beyond. Dogs are allowed on the 10-mile bike trail, but be sure to keep your pooch leashed and under control. Since mountain bikes have been restricted from most of the other units, there are plenty of them here, most going fast enough to startle even the most stoic of dogs.

The main trail frequently bursts out of the trees to wander along the river. The best access to the water for your pooch is past the rest rooms. Though you may see dogs swimming in the river off leash, it's not recommended—the current can be strong enough to challenge even a Labrador. Cochran Shoals is also quite the social scene for people in the area, dog lovers included. Pooches often sport bandannas in the summer or flashy coats or sweaters in the winter, while their owners wear the latest in exercise apparel.

Be sure to stop by the Mutt Mitts dispenser at the entrance to the trail. These biodegradable plastic gloves enable you to scoop up your dog's mess and deposit it, glove and all, in the nearest trash can. While the Mitts are in use in other parts of the country, they are relatively new to Georgia, and apparently visitors don't know quite what to do with them. A ranger told me that while the Mitts are being removed from the dispenser, the parks staff has not found any used ones, either in the trash or in the woods. Leashes are required.

The Cochran Shoals Unit is open daily from 7 A.M. to dark. It's located on Interstate North Parkway, just off Interstate 285 at Powers Ferry. Unfortunately, this exit is one of the more creative spots in the interstate system. If you're traveling east on Interstate 285 from Interstate 75, take exit 15 (Northside Drive, New Northside Drive, and Powers Ferry Road), and then make a right turn on Northside Drive. Take the first left onto Powers Ferry Road, then the next left onto New Northside Drive and cross back over Interstate 285. (If you're traveling west on Interstate 285, turn right at the exit onto New Northside Drive.) New Northside Drive becomes Interstate North Parkway. The two entrances to the park will be on your right, one on either side of the river. If you're unfamiliar with this interchange, do yourself a favor and take Interstate 75 north to Windy Hill and turn right. Turn right again onto Powers Ferry Road, and left onto Interstate North Parkway. The two parts of the unit will be on your left. (770) 399-8070.

Gold Branch Unit 🐾🐾🐾🐾 🐕 See ➐ on page 50.

The Gold Branch Unit consists of 385 acres of pristine land, with seven miles of hiking trails that range from easy to strenuous. The trails aren't well marked, so be sure to bring along a map. (Call the number below to receive a free trail map in the mail.) Compared to some of the other units in the Chattahoochee system, including Cochran Shoals (see page 58), the trails here are not heavily used, making this a great place to walk a dog like Laddie, who likes his privacy. The wildflowers are spectacular in the spring, and animals such as deer and red foxes are abundant. The park also has a large population of beavers; look for their small dams and evidence of their work on the trees. Bull Sluice Lake, created by Morgan Falls Dam, is stocked with fish.

The park is open daily from 7 A.M. to dark. This unit is on Lower Roswell Road. Take Highway 120 east from the Big Chicken, and turn right on Lower Roswell Road. The park is two miles past Johnson Ferry Road. (770) 394-8324.

Johnson Ferry Unit 🐾🐾 🦴 *See ❽ on page 50.*

The main trail in the Johnson Ferry Unit definitely rates a paws-up from Laddie, since it's fairly level and not very long—about a mile, unless you get lost, like we did on our first visit. The map at the trailhead indicates this is an easy hike—perfect, I thought, for getting a new friend interested in hiking. So three adults and two leashed dogs set off, planning on an enjoyable half hour or so. What the map doesn't mention is that there are numerous side jaunts off the main trail. Neither the main trail nor these side trails are blazed, and the only clues provided along the way are reappearances of the map in three or four places, with little arrows showing your location. At least one of these is mismarked. It's best to ignore the maps, and if the trail becomes strenuous, or even moderate, you've probably wandered off onto one of the side trails and need to backtrack. If you pass a sacred burial ground for old Chevys, you've definitely gone the wrong way. If this weren't a national park, I'd scatter bread crumbs on the trail to help me find my way out, though Laddie would probably just gobble them up.

The main trail follows the river for nearly half a mile, and the combination of deep woods, wildflowers, and peaceful river makes this a very enjoyable walk. Expect your dog to want to linger; there are a lot of interesting smells from the local wildlife.

Since you'll be next to water (either the river, side creeks, or a swamp) during most of the hike, be sure to bring bug repellent. Also take plenty of water and snacks, just in case you make a wrong turn.

The Johnson Ferry Unit is one of the main put-in points for rafting the Chattahoochee. While hiking along the river, you'll occasionally see or hear rafters as they drift by.

The park is open daily from 7 A.M. to dark. Take Highway 120 east from the Big Chicken. Turn right on Johnson Ferry Road. The park is on the left just before the river. (770) 952-4419.

Sope Creek Unit 🐾🐾🐾🐾 🦴 *See ❾ on page 50.*

The Sope Creek Unit has several miles of heavily forested hiking trails, some easy or moderate and others quite strenuous, allowing you to choose the hike that suits you and your leashed pooch. Laddie loves the easy trail around Sibley Pond, which he takes slowly, nose to the ground, sniffing for the wildlife in and around the water. The trail around the pond is also wide, giving you a decent chance of keeping your pet out of the poison ivy.

Sope Creek feeds into the river, and the moderate trail to the ruins of an old paper mill on the creek is lined with wildflowers in the spring. Both Sope Creek and Sibley Pond are open to fishing.

The Sope Creek Unit, open daily from 7 A.M. to dark, is located on Old Paper Mill Road. Take Highway 120 east from the Big Chicken, turn right on Lower Roswell Road, and then right on Old Paper Mill Road. The park is past Terrell Mill Park. (770) 952-4419.

• Fullers Park 😃 🐾 🐾 See ⑩ on page 50.

A one-mile fitness trail winds its way through this park, but with little shade and no water, my leashed dogs only think it's worth a quick stop. You might be tempted to stay longer to enjoy the tennis courts, several ball fields, a playground for the kids, and picnic pavilions.

The park is open daily from 7 A.M. to midnight. To reach it, take Highway 120 (Roswell Road) east from the Big Chicken and turn right onto Robinson Road. Robinson Road intersects Highway 120 twice. If you turn onto Robinson Road at East Gate, west of where Old Canton Road comes into Highway 120, the park will be on your left. The park is closer to the other end of Robinson Road, which is east of the Old Canton Road/Roswell Road intersection. If you take that end of Robinson Road, the park will be on your right. (770) 509-2735.

• Kennesaw Mountain National Battlefield Memorial Park 🐾🐾🐾🐾 🐾 See ⑪ on page 50.

Kennesaw has almost everything a dog could want—a variety of trails to hike, creeks to splash in, horses to investigate, and woods and smells galore from the birds and small mammals who live in the park, not to mention other doggy visitors. (With dogs along, you probably won't actually see anything other than fish and squirrels.) All of my dogs had their first hiking experiences in Kennesaw, both because it's close by and because the park has an assortment of trails, allowing us to choose a length appropriate to the occasion. The park is the historic site of the 1864 Atlanta Campaign of the Civil War, and there are plenty of cannons, monuments, and markers to interest you while your pooch waits impatiently. Dogs are allowed everywhere in the park except in the visitors center, and they must always be kept on leash. (I've seen several owners of off-leash pups being ticketed.)

The trails start at the visitors center. The main loop is a whopping 16 miles long, but you can take smaller loops of two, six, or 10 miles. All of the trails include some moderately steep climbs, particularly the one up Kennesaw Mountain and the one from Kennesaw Mountain to Little Kennesaw Mountain. Because the park crosses several roads, you can enter the trail anywhere along the main loop, allowing you to walk as little or as much as you like.

One of the more popular sections of trail in Kennesaw starts from the entrance on Burnt Hickory Road and heads toward Kolb Farm. Parking is limited along the road, and the area is usually congested with dog lovers and other park visitors, either hiking part of the distance to Kolb Farm or spreading a blanket in one of the grassy fields. There is usually a Frisbee game going on as well.

If you're not up to much of a hike but still want a time-out from city life, take your lunch or a book and park yourself on one of the rocks in the creek at Cheatham Hill. The sound of the water tumbling over the rocks drowns out even the sound of the planes from Dobbins Air Force Base, and your pooch will enjoy playing in the creek or even lying down in the shallow water for some blessed relief from the heat.

For a more extended opportunity to stretch your legs, the 5.5-mile loop from the Illinois Monument at Cheatham Hill to Kolb Farm and back is a relaxing day hike. Bandit loves to splash in the stream that parallels the trail by the monument. This trail is the infamous first hike I made with my dog Trixie, many years ago. I carried nothing but a covered plastic bowl of water for my dog, and while she had a wonderful time, as the day wore on—and heated up—my hiking companions and I were eyeing her water dish. I went out the next day and bought a canteen in the camping department of a local discount store. It was one of those plastic types on a canvas strap to carry over your shoulder, and, remembering my experience the day before, I bought the largest one they had. I have to give my friend Betty a lot of credit for not laughing about that canteen. A teacher in a former life, Betty is extremely patient when dealing with stupidity. When I told her on the phone I had gotten the largest canteen in the store, the gallon size, she said she would hold on while I filled it up and tried it out. After I staggered back to the phone with my gallon jug, Betty suggested I go to an Army/Navy–type store and look for a canteen no bigger than a quart that would clip on my belt. I used that little canteen for years. Now, with bottled water available in so many sizes, I simply throw a bottle or two in my pack. Since the canteen didn't solve the problem of carrying Trixie's water dish, I went back to Betty for advice. She told me to get a day pack, something big enough for my lunch, the water bowl, and a sweater. Although my back protested for the first few miles, it was so much easier to have my hands free that I quickly adjusted. Now, my day pack always contains the items listed in the introduction on page 15. While this may seem like overkill if you're just stopping for a quick squat in a small park, the pack serves as a convenient place to store the things you need on longer hikes in places like Kennesaw.

Gnats and mosquitoes can be a real nuisance at this park late in the summer, so don't forget the insect repellent. Also be sure to bring plenty of water and snacks for both you and your dog. Even if you allow your pooch to drink from the creeks, there are long stretches without water.

The park is open daily from 8:30 A.M. to 7:30 P.M. Stop in at the visitors center for a park map and then plan your day from there. From the Big Chicken, go north on U.S. 41 (Cobb Parkway) and turn left onto Bells Ferry Road. Turn right onto Old U.S. 41 Northwest, then left onto Stilesboro Road. The visitors center will be on your left as you turn onto Stilesboro Road. (770) 427-4686.

• Larry Bell Park 🐾 *See ⑫ on page 50.*

You'll find the standard-issue fitness trail at this park, but without water or much shade, it isn't worth more than a pit stop as far as your leashed pooch is concerned. It does have a running track, though, as well as a playground for the kids, an indoor pool, a gymnasium, several baseball fields, and tennis courts.

The park is open daily from 7 A.M. to midnight. To reach it, go south on U.S. 41 (Cobb Parkway) from the Big Chicken, and turn right on the South Marietta Parkway (the South Highway 120 Loop). The park is adjacent to and behind the Cobb County Civic Center, located on the corner of Fairground Street and South Marietta Parkway. (770) 528-8800.

• Laurel Park 🐾🐾🐾 🦴 *See ⑬ on page 50.*

I love this small park. While Bandit is easy to please and could have a good time in a parking lot, Laddie is very selective about hiking, preferring flat, even terrain and shade. I can please everybody (including myself) at Laurel Park. The paved trail is only one mile long, but it still takes us an hour or so to make our way around it. Ducks and geese populate the two lakes and pond, and, in the spring, there are lots of ducklings.

While I can't stay away from the ducklings that wander around us, Laddie simply ignores them. His interests revolve entirely around food, and he hasn't caught onto the concept of the web-footed variety. My friend Vickie's Pomeranian, What, on the other hand, sees herself as a large predator, so she has a marvelous time straining on the leash (all five pounds of her) to chase after the babies, which are nearly as big as she is. Bandit has an entirely different response. The ducklings had grown a bit the last time I brought him here, and we encountered a noisy group of "adolescents" when we started around the lake. Bandit froze at the sight of them, observed that I wasn't frightened, then surged toward the lake, intent on causing as much puppy damage as possible. (It's a good thing his mandatory leash was firmly fastened.) Most of the ducks reacted instantly, practically standing on the water in their haste to beat a retreat. Bandit skidded to a stop and hid behind my feet, startled by the size of the ducks when they stood up. Although he continued to sneak peeks in their direction as we walked around the lake, he stayed close to my side and out of sight of the large creatures swimming in the water.

Whoever designed Laurel had grandiose plans for a Cobb County park. It has a labeled shade garden—complete with a park bench and azaleas—overlooking a bridge built from recycled plastic bottles. (Actually, it looks just like wood.) You can reserve the large picnic pavilions for a party, or use one of the unprotected tables along the lake and in the woods. With tennis and volleyball courts, you won't get any complaints from your friends if you schedule a gathering here. And is there anyone (except maybe Laddie) who can resist the lure of the ducklings? I'm looking forward to Bandit's reaction in the spring, when the ducks are much smaller again.

The park is open daily from 6 A.M. to 11 P.M. Take Highway 120 (Whitlock Avenue) west from the Marietta Square. Turn left onto Manning Road, a mile and a half past the intersection with the North Marietta Parkway (the Highway 120 Loop). The park is a tenth of a mile down Manning Road on the left. (770) 528-0619.

• Sewell Park 🐾 🐾 🦴 *See* **⑭** *on page 50.*
The main attraction for your leashed pooch at this park is the woods. Dogs aren't allowed in the tennis courts, baseball fields, or pool, but the heavy woods surrounding the park offer cool shade and abundant squirrels and birds. Be sure to wear a hat and check your dog for ticks after your walk. Watch for poison ivy near the fitness trail by the park entrance.

The park is open daily from 7 A.M. to midnight. From Atlanta, take Interstate 75 north to the South Highway 120 Loop and turn right. Turn right onto Lower Roswell Road. The park entrance is on the left about a tenth of a mile down Lower Roswell Road. (770) 819-3220.

• Terrell Mill Park 🐾 🐾 See ⑮ on page 50.

This small park has lots of tennis courts and soccer fields, but just one poorly marked fitness trail for walking your leashed pooch. The exercise stations along the trail have seen better days, but they're frequently the only clue to the trail's location, since it's poorly maintained. Although the soccer fields always seem to be in use whenever Laddie and I visit, we're usually the only ones on the shaded trail—a fact that Laddie loves, since he's not exactly Mr. Sociable when it comes to other canines.

The park is open daily from 7 A.M. to midnight. To reach it from Atlanta, take Interstate 75 north to the Delk Road/Highway 280 exit and turn east. Delk Road becomes Terrell Mill Road. The park will be on your left at the intersection of Terrell Mill Road and Paper Mill Road. (770) 644-2770.

• Tramore Park 🐾 See ⑯ on page 50.

While there are no trails at Tramore Park, which is primarily a series of ball fields, large grassy areas provide a place to walk your leashed pooch if he's desperate. Besides, the park is on the way to almost everything in Cobb.

Tramore Park is open daily from dawn to dusk. From Atlanta, take Interstate 75 north to the Delk Road/Highway 280 exit and turn west. Highway 5 joins in two miles down and runs with Highway 280 for two miles. Follow Highway 5 south and turn right onto Austell Road. Turn right onto the East-West Connector six miles after turning onto Austell Road. The park is one mile down on the right. (770) 528-8892.

• Wildwood Park 🐾 🐾 See ⑰ on page 50.

True to its name, Wildwood Park is home to a labyrinth of trails, where a leashed Laddie and I always seem to lose our way. Be sure to study the map at the trailhead before starting, since it's the only chance you'll have to see one. Although the trails aren't long (they vary in length from a third of a mile to about a mile), be sure to bring water and snacks in case you take a few wrong turns. I've even considered carrying a tent, just in case. The dense woods muffle the sounds from the road, which is actually a disadvantage, since the noise might help us figure out which way to go.

Laddie likes to pretend that he knows exactly where he's going, but he has absolutely no sense of direction. Unfortunately, neither do I. Trixie was able to almost unerringly choose the right path at a fork, but Laddie and I are always at a loss. At Wildwood Park, he starts out full of confidence, but grows increasingly worried every time we cross another trail. By the time we find our way back to the car, which might be a half hour or two hours later, depending on how lost we got, he's a bit wild-eyed and his tail is dragging on the ground. But when he sees the car, he's his old self again, strutting about as if he knew where he was the whole time.

This park was originally designed for the sight impaired, with interpretive signs along the trail in Braille, but they were recently removed.

The park is open daily from dawn to dusk. Take Delk Road/South Cobb Drive west from Interstate 75, and the park will be on your right at Barclay Circle. (770) 528-0615.

SHOPPING IN MARIETTA

Georgia Pets: This small shop carries my dogs' favorite snack—pig hooves stuffed with rawhide. How do they think of this stuff? I try not to watch as the boys eagerly attack the hooves. Bandit, who likes to hide things, has them squirreled all over the house. After the rawhide is gone, he'll continue to chew them up for days. Laddie chews up the rawhide, then abandons the hooves, to Bandit's delight. Georgia Pets always has an interesting mix of animals and merchandise, and the staff is very knowledgeable. Laddie enjoys coming into the store with me to sniff all the strange smells. Bandit is a bit too much of a predator to trust in here. 1150 Powder Springs Street, Marietta, GA 30060; (770) 514-7387.

Mail Boxes Etc.: When the first of these mailing stores opened in Atlanta, I thought I was in heaven. My entire family lives out of state, and I don't like preparing packages to go in the mail. I love turning over this job to someone else. Not only do they do a terrific job, but John Kelley and his staff like dogs and encourage me to bring mine in. What more could I want? 1750 Powder Springs Road, Suite 190, Marietta, GA 30064; (770) 514-7299.

Petsmart: Now that Petsmart has gobbled up Petstuff, its former competitor, Petsmart's stores are the biggest and best places to shop with your pooch. The staff and other customers are all pet lovers. Best of all, Petsmart doesn't sell dogs or cats, believing that there is an overpopulation problem already, but works with area humane societies to sponsor adoptions on its premises. Petsmart is located all over the city. 1285 Johnson Ferry Road Northeast, Marietta, GA 30068; (770) 971-3010.

PLACES TO STAY

Best Inns of America: The best part about staying here may be the location. It's right next to Dave and Buster's, some of the best entertainment around. Unfortunately, Dave and Buster's doesn't allow pets. I don't know what Bandit would think of the pterodactyl in the virtual reality game, anyway. Your pooch is welcome to stay with you. Rates are $48 to $57, with no charge for your pup. 1255 Franklin Road, Marietta, GA 30067; (770) 955-0004 or (800) 237-8466.

La Quinta Inn: All La Quintas seem to be managed by dog lovers, and Marietta's is no exception. Not only do they allow pets, they welcome them. The dog walk area is a large, well-lit grassy field in the back of the property, appreciated by dogs who like their privacy. Rates vary from $63 to $73. 2170 Delk Road, Marietta, GA 30067; (770) 951-0026.

FESTIVALS

Antique leashes, anyone?: The Historic Marietta Antiques Street Festival is held in September each year and is sponsored by the many antique dealers on the Square. Your leashed pooch is welcome to attend. Glover Park, on the Square. (770) 528-0616.

Art in the Park: Each September on Labor Day weekend, this festival draws crowds from all over Atlanta, including the four-legged type. (If your pet doesn't like to be around lots of people, this may not be the place for a doggy outing.) It can get pretty warm at this event, even though it's held in September, but thankfully many of the shops on the Square will let your leashed pet come inside when he starts to get hot. Glover Park, on the Square. (770) 429-1115.

Arts and Crafts: Marietta's Glover Park is the place to be on the first weekend in October for the annual Historic Marietta Arts and Crafts Festival. This show features more than 100 vendors of handmade products, and is a favorite with people and dogs in the area. Laddie hates crowds and prefers to stay at home, but Bandit loves having a fuss made over him by the craftspeople and other visitors. Glover Park, on the Square. (770) 429-1115.

DIVERSIONS

He's making a list: If you've always wanted to have a picture of your pooch on Santa's lap for your Christmas cards, now's your chance. The Cobb County Humane Society sponsors a Santa Paws photo session each November. Besides dogs and cats, Santa has held boa constrictors, iguanas, monkeys, and potbellied pigs at this fun event. You'll want to hang around just to watch. It's held at the Humane Society office, 1060 County Farm Road Southeast, Marietta, GA 30060; (770) 422-8874.

No barks allowed: While you can't bring your dog to the Cobb County Humane Society's annual Silent Auction, it's a great opportunity to pick up some bargains and help Cobb's pets at the same time. You're invited to donate and/or purchase items to benefit this good cause held early in May each year. Call (770) 422-8874 for more information.

Soak up some culture: Bring a blanket, a picnic basket, and your leashed pup and enjoy Concerts on the Square and Brown Bag Concerts, sponsored by the Marietta Visitors Center. The Brown Bag Concerts take place every Thursday at noon during May and again in September, while the Concerts on the Square are held the last Friday of the month from April through August at 8 P.M. Walk your dog before the concert, then stake out your territory with your blanket. These events are popular and can get quite crowded, making them best suited to laid-back pooches. Glover Park, on the Square. (770) 429-1115.

You ought to be in pictures: Who doesn't think their pup has the cutest mug in the dog universe? Well, here's your chance to prove it. Each year, the Cobb County Humane Society sponsors a calendar contest. The winners grace the 12 monthly pages of the calendar, which goes on sale in October. Even if your pooch doesn't win, he'll be featured on a collage page in the front. The calendars make great Christmas gifts. Entry forms can be picked up at many area businesses or at the Humane Society's office at 1060 County Farm Road Southeast, Marietta, GA 30060; (770) 422-8874.

POWDER SPRINGS
PARKS AND RECREATION AREAS

• **Clarkdale Field** 🐾 *See ⓲ on page 50.*

If your dog really must go, walk her—on leash—around the large grassy area here. There are no trails. Amenities for people include a ball field and a community center.

The park is open daily from 7 A.M. to dusk. Heading into Powder Springs on Powder Springs Road from Marietta, turn left on Austell-

Powder Springs Road. The park is located on your immediate left. (770) 528-8890.

• **Lost Mountain Park** 🐾🐾🐾 🐾 *See ⓲ on page 50.*

Lost Mountain got its curious name from the fact that while you can see it from a distance, it disappears as you approach it. But once you locate it, you'll find a delightful park for spending a quiet day with your leashed pooch.

A three-quarter-mile nature walk starts from the picnic pavilion across the road from the parking lot. Though the trail is dry and dusty at first, the fun starts once you hike over a hill and pass a small, sheltered lake. Even though the water looks inviting, keep on going until you get to the second and larger lake, which is surrounded by rolling hills and trees and is a great spot to leave the trail and spread a blanket in the grass. Except for a few people trying their luck fishing the lakes, no one seems to use the trails much, so you and your pooch might just have this peaceful setting all to yourselves. If you wander around either of the narrow lake trails, watch for snakes.

The park is open daily from 7 A.M. to midnight. From the Square in Marietta, drive west on Whitlock Road, which becomes Dallas Highway after crossing over the Highway 120 Loop. The park is on your left just past the intersection of Dallas Highway and Due West Road. (770) 528-8890.

• **Powder Springs Park** 🔥 *See ⓴ on page 50.*

Powder Springs Park is a small, oval-shaped park in town. While it has no trails for walking your energetic pooch, there is plenty of shade, making it a cool place to bring your leashed dog on a sweltering day.

Park hours are daily from 7 A.M. to midnight. From the East-West Connector, turn left onto Powder Springs Road, then left on Brownsville Road at the fork. The park is on the left. (770) 439-3615.

SMYRNA
PARKS AND RECREATION AREAS

• **King Springs Park** 🔥 *See ㉑ on page 50.*

This park has a fitness trail, but with no water or shade, your dog won't like it any more than you will. Leashing is mandatory.

The park is open daily from 7 A.M. to midnight. Take South Cobb Drive north from Interstate 285, then turn right on Magbee Drive. (770) 431-2842.

SHOPPING IN SMYRNA

Petsmart: This huge store is the place to go for pet supplies. Your pooch could be the hit of the next football party in her college or NFL team jersey. Petsmart also carries dog sweaters and backpacks. I bought Laddie a backpack, thinking he could carry his own water and snacks on our hikes. If you need a never-used backpack, let me know. Petsmart is located all over the city. 2540-B Hargrove Road, Smyrna, GA 30080; (770) 432-8250.

PLACES TO STAY

Holiday Inn Express—Cumberland: Your small dog (under 35 pounds) is welcome here as long as you don't leave her unattended in the room. The housekeepers frown on explaining who they are to your pooch while they're trying to do their job. The $20 pet deposit is refundable. Rates are $59 to $61. 1200 Winchester Parkway Southeast, Smyrna, GA 30080; (770) 333-9910.

Red Roof Inn North: Double rooms are $50, and your pooch stays free. You'll get two beds at this price so your malamute won't hog the covers. 2200 Corporate Plaza, Smyrna, GA 30080; (770) 952-6366.

FESTIVALS

Jonquil Festival: Smyrna, the Jonquil City, has two festivals each year to celebrate its flower. The fourth weekend of April marks the height of the bloom season, and the fourth weekend of September the preferred planting time. Each outdoor festival weekend includes more than 150 booths of arts and crafts, as well as music, pony and carnival rides, and, of course, food. The relaxed atmosphere and large numbers of canine visitors is reminiscent of the Piedmont Park Arts Festival, before they outlawed dogs. Keep your pooch on leash and scoop up any reminders of his visit to keep this a dog-friendly festival. On the Village Green; (770) 434-3661.

VININGS

FESTIVALS

Fall Festival: The Vinings Jubilee Fall Festival, which is held in downtown Vinings each October, is popular with area residents and their leashed pups. This Vinings tradition for more than 30 years benefits the historic Pace House. It's held in the parking lot of the Vinings Jubilee Shopping Center. For more information on the festival, call (770) 438-8080.

DeKALB COUNTY

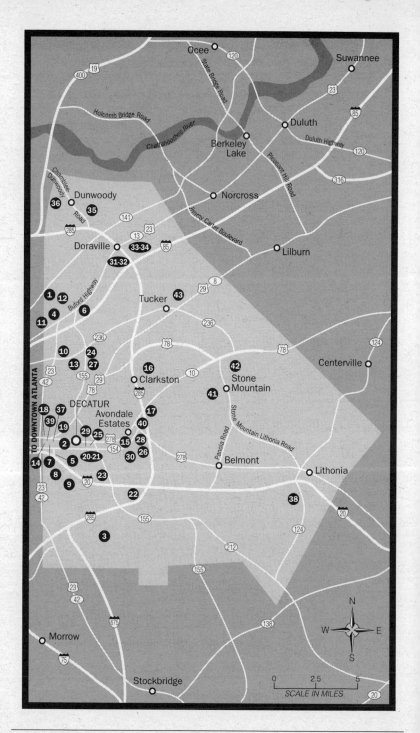

4

DeKALB COUNTY

DeKalb County boasts of being the most ethnically diverse county in the Atlanta area, with Chinese, Hindi, Spanish, and Japanese spoken almost as frequently as English. It also has one of the finest parks around, Stone Mountain Park (see page 90). With miles of trails plus the allure of streams to cross, my dogs always enjoy an outing here. A leash law is in effect for all county parks, and dog owners are also required to scoop up after their pets. Toss a few plastic grocery bags in your pack and you're set.

ATLANTA

The city limits of Atlanta touch several of the metropolitan counties, including DeKalb. If you don't find the park you're looking for here, it's probably in the Fulton County chapter, which begins on page 129.

PARKS AND RECREATION AREAS

• **Ashford Park** 🐾 *See ❶ on page 72.*
This small park doesn't have many of the features your dog would be interested in (just basketball courts, a playground, and a ball field), but it's good for a quick stop if your leashed pooch has to go. Be sure to clean up after your pet.

Hours are daily from 7 A.M. to sunset. Take Peachtree Industrial Boulevard south from Interstate 285, and turn left onto Redding Road. (404) 371-2631.

• **Bessie Branham Park** 🐾 🐾 *See ❷ on page 72.*
My leashed boys love to walk from tree to tree on the perimeter of this large park, making a mandatory pit stop at each trunk. Laddie always strains to add a bit to each message board, and even Bandit, who enjoys "reading" the boards but doesn't usually add a note, grows bored as Laddie checks out the subtle nuances of each tree. It takes us a good hour to make our way around the park. You can also walk your pup through the large open fields, but since there's no water or shade, it can get very hot. The park also has ball fields, playgrounds, and tennis and basketball courts.

Hours are daily from 6 A.M. to 11 P.M. Take the Boulevard exit off of Interstate 20 and turn north. Turn left onto Norwood Avenue Northeast. The park is on the corner of Norwood Avenue and Delano Drive. (404) 371-5010.

• **Bouldercrest Park** 🐾🐾 *See* ❸ *on page 72.*

At 126 acres, Bouldercrest Park is one of the largest parks in DeKalb County, offering plenty of opportunities for your leashed pooch to walk, sniff, and get wet and muddy (plus baseball fields, basketball and tennis courts, and picnic areas if you have people in tow). Bandit uses his water radar to quickly locate the creek, which can be pretty muddy after it rains. Stash a towel in your trunk to take care of any dirty paws. Large oak trees offer plenty of shade. Be sure to clean up after your dog.

Hours are daily from 7 A.M. to sunset. Take the Bouldercrest Road exit off of Interstate 285 and turn outside. The park is on your right. (404) 371-2631.

• **Briarwood Park** 🐾🐾 🦴 *See* ❹ *on page 72.*

You won't have any trouble getting your leashed dog out of the car at Briarwood Park. Like many others in the city, this large park has a deep ravine running through it, and while there isn't any water at the bottom, the heavy woods are still quite attractive to Laddie and Bandit. I think my boys have probably checked out every single tree in the park. There are plenty of attractions for you and your friends as well, including a pool, tennis courts, playgrounds, and picnic areas.

Park hours are daily from 7 A.M. to sunset. Heading south on Buford Highway from the intersection with Clairmont Road, turn right on Drew Valley Road, then left on Briarwood Way. The park is located at the intersection of Briarwood Way and Briarwood Road. (404) 679-5911.

• **DeKalb Memorial Park** 🐾🐾 *See* ❺ *on page 72.*

Both my leashed dogs find plenty to do at this park. Bandit always makes a beeline to the creek, sticks his head under the water, and starts blowing bubbles. Laddie is much more interested in sniffing around the trees. The park also has tennis and basketball courts, a ball field, and a playground.

Hours are daily from 6 A.M. to 11 P.M. From Atlanta, take Interstate 20 east, exiting at Maynard Terrace. Turn left on Maynard Terrace, right on Memorial Drive, then right onto Wilkinson Drive to reach the park. (404) 371-2631.

• Dresden Park 🐾🐾 *See* **6** *on page* 72.

This park is small but has several areas for walking your leashed pooch, and a stream with good doggy access cuts through it. There are some trees for shade, but the park is mainly in the sun, making it a good choice for a cool or cloudy day. Be sure to clean up after your pet. Amenities include three baseball fields, two playgrounds, picnic pavilions, and swings.

Hours are daily from 7 A.M. to sunset. Take Buford Highway/U.S. 23/Highway 13 north from Clairmont Road and turn right onto Dresden Drive. The park is on the right. (404) 371-2631.

• Gilliam Park 🐾 *See* **7** *on page* 72.

Bandit searches in vain for water among the large oak trees in the middle of the long, narrow field of this park, and is disappointed not to find even a drop. Laddie, on the other hand, is happy as can be sniffing all the trees around the perimeter. Remember to keep your pet on a leash at all times in this park.

Hours are daily from 6 A.M. to 11 P.M. To reach the park, go east on Boulevard from Moreland Avenue/U.S. 23. Turn left onto Wyman Street, which ends at the park. (404) 617-6766.

• Glen Emerald Park 🐾🐾 *See* **8** *on page* 72.

Large Glen Emerald Park has a beautiful green lake where your dog can splash along the shore, as well as lots of trees for dogs like Laddie who always have their noses to the ground. I don't recommend one of the long, retractable leashes here; Laddie dashes about and gets me wrapped around the trees. There are paved trails if your pooch will stick to them. Leashes are mandatory, and you must scoop. The park also has tennis and basketball courts, a playground, and many picnic tables and pavilions.

Hours are daily from 7 A.M. to sunset. Take the Flat Shoals Road exit off of Interstate 20, turning left from downtown. Turn right onto Fayetteville Road Southeast, which becomes Bouldercrest Road. The park is on your right. (404) 371-2631.

• Gresham Park and Recreation Center 🐾 *See* **9** *on page* 72.

While this large park has many of the elements my dogs love (sunny fields for a good run, oak trees for shade and sniffing), it's a bit rundown, and we're not entirely comfortable here. Keep an alert eye on your surroundings. Remember to leash your pooch and to clean up after her. Amenities for the two-legged set include a swimming pool, a baseball field, a recreation center, picnic areas, and a playground.

Hours are daily from 7 A.M. to sunset. Take the Gresham Road exit from Interstate 20 and turn south. The park is on your right. (404) 244-4890.

• La Vista Park 🐾🐾 *See ⑩ on page 72.*

Surrounded by woods, this attractive park is long and skinny with a creek running down the middle. Water access is good, meaning that your leashed dog can get in without you taking a plunge, too. The many trees provide shady spots aplenty for you and your pooch to keep your cool in the summer heat. Bandit is fascinated by all the birds that flock to the park, though he seems perplexed when they fly away.

You'll have to park on the street to visit this park. A footbridge leads over the creek to a playground. Bring your lunch and relax at the picnic pavilion while your dog investigates the area. Remember to scoop.

Hours are daily from 7 A.M. to sunset. From downtown Atlanta, take Interstate 85 north to Buford Highway, then exit right onto Cheshire Bridge Road. Turn left onto La Vista Road Northeast, then left on Brookforrest Drive. The park is on the corner of Brookforrest Drive and La Vista Park Road. (404) 244-4890.

• Shady Valley Park 🐾🐾 *See ⑪ on page 72.*

Dog lovers and their leashed pups frequent this heavily used park, with lots of wooded areas and a small creek that's easy for dogs to reach. You and your pooch can choose to socialize or strike out on your own. The personality differences of my two boys become clear here: Laddie prefers the solitude of the woods, while Bandit wants to play in the water and meet other dogs. You'll also find tennis courts, ball fields, playgrounds, and picnic areas.

The park is open daily during daylight hours. From downtown Atlanta, take Interstate 85 north to Buford Highway, and exit left onto North Druid Hills Road. After North Druid Hills becomes Roxboro Road, turn left onto Goodwin Road, then left onto Shady Valley Drive. The park is on the right. (404) 817-6766.

• Skyland Park 🐾 *See ⑫ on page 72.*

Skyland Park, located in the middle of an area known as the Buford Triangle, has tennis courts, ball fields, playgrounds, and picnicking areas for people, but not more than a quick squat's worth of activities for your pooch. Leashing and scooping are required.

Hours are daily from 7 A.M. to sunset. Take Clairmont Road north from the intersection with Buford Highway. Turn left onto Skyland

Road, right onto Stollen Drive, left onto Skyland Terrace, and right onto Skyland Drive. The park is on your left. (404) 371-2631.

• **W. D. Thomson Park** 🐾🐾 *See* ⑬ *on page* 72.

I can please both my dogs at this lovely, shaded park with grass for rolling around in and a creek for splashing about. I've never been here when there weren't several other dogs enjoying themselves, too. The park covers only 29 acres, and the trail here isn't worth mentioning, but you and your canine companion are sure to find plenty to keep you happy. Remember to leash and scoop. A playground, ball fields, pleasant picnic areas, and a basketball court are among the other amenities.

Hours are daily from 7 A.M. to sunset. Take the Clairmont Road exit from Interstate 85 and turn south. Turn left onto Mason Mill Road, just past North Druid Hills Road. (404) 371-2631.

• **Westley Coan Park** 🐾🐾 *See* ⑭ *on page* 72.

Large open fields are bordered by huge oak trees at this pleasant park. The trees always warrant at least a minute's sniffing each by my leashed boys. When Bandit also discovered a creek with good water access, he thought he was in dog heaven. While there aren't any real trails here, it's great to just stroll along the lines of trees. The park also has ball fields, tennis and basketball courts, a community center, and a playground.

Hours are daily from 6 A.M. to 11 P.M. From downtown Atlanta, take Interstate 20 east and exit left onto Maynard Terrace. Turn right onto Memorial Drive, left onto Clay Street Southeast, left onto Boulevard, then left onto Woodbine Avenue Southeast. The park is also bordered by Anniston Avenue Southeast. (404) 817-6766.

SHOPPING IN ATLANTA

Cheshire Pets: This was the first pet store in the Atlanta area to have resident cats and dogs wandering about inside, and to encourage customers to bring in their own for a visit. Although the practice is more common now, at first I would look around furtively whenever I had one of the dogs in tow. Cheshire Pets stocks a full assortment of supplies for dogs, cats, birds, and small animals. The store is located at 2855 North Druid Hills Road Northeast, Atlanta, GA 30329; (404) 325-4945.

Donna Van Gochs, Inc.: Your dog is welcome to come in and help you pick out a cute dog bowl in this fun shop specializing in pottery, jewelry, and arts and crafts. 1651 McLendon Avenue Northeast, Atlanta, GA 30307; (404) 370-1003.

PLACES TO STAY

Emory Inn: Rates are $79 to $82, with a $25 fee per pooch. 1641 Clifton Road Northeast, Atlanta, GA 30329; (404) 712-6700.

DIVERSIONS

Bullyrama: The Bullyrama is a just-for-fun obstacle course that you and your pooch can try to complete together. I know better than to let Bandit bob for wienies—I'd never get him out of the barrel! (Don't worry; only pooches have to do the bobbing.) The yearly event is held by the Bull Terrier Club of Greater Atlanta, a breed club that proves learning can be a lot of fun. Every other month, instead of a regular meeting, they have special events, including hiking trips, an annual Halloween party, and the Bullyrama. Events and meetings are held all over the city. The club is specifically focused on bull terriers, but everyone is welcome, even if you don't share your home with one of these exceptional dogs. For more information, contact Evelin Jackson at (770) 483-1330 or (770) 474-1958.

Trick or Treat: Take your pooch to the Halloween party given by the Atlanta Recreation and Fun Club for Dogs, and you may win one of the costume contests. Ghosts and goblins, devils and angels mingle and compete for such prizes as dog "cookies." The annual event is held at Toco Hills Shopping Center, 1800 Briarcliff Road Northeast, Atlanta, GA 30033. For more information, contact Candy or Daniel Pyron at (770) 961-2435.

AVONDALE ESTATES

Avondale Estates was the first planned community in the South. It's difficult to compare it to Peachtree City (see page 110) without seeing how far we've come, but you can see the beginnings of an attempt to create neighborhoods that worked for all the residents. For dog owners, Peachtree City has done a better job of linking the entire community with nonmotorized vehicle paths, but the village feel is still present in Avondale Estates as you and your pooch wander through the downtown area.

PARKS AND RECREATION AREAS

• **Bess Walker Park** 🐾 🐾 *See* **15** *on page 72.*

Bandit and I spent about an hour playing in the lake at this park, before we found out we were breaking the law. If you live in Avondale Estates, you and your leashed pooch are welcome to wander around Avondale Lake and play in the woods here. You'll have a wonderful time at this lovely, peaceful spot. We certainly did before we found out we were fugitives from justice. A trail goes all the way around the lake, and there are several spots where your pup can wade in and greet the ducks and geese. When Bandit got up close and personal with the birds, he was quite alarmed to find that they were bigger than he was, and felt much more brave when standing behind me. We sat in the gazebo for a few minutes while he got the nerve up to growl threateningly, but they were on to him by that time and completely ignored him.

The park is open daily during daylight hours. Take the Memorial Drive exit off Interstate 285 and turn inside the Perimeter. Take the right fork onto Mountain Drive, then turn left onto Lakeshore Drive to reach the park. (404) 294-5400.

CLARKSTON
PARKS AND RECREATION AREAS

• **Armistead Field/Milam Park** 🐾🐾 👣 *See* **16** *on page 72.*
Milam Park is an enjoyable place to walk your leashed pooch. There are two trails, one of which leads through the woods to Armistead Field, a baseball field dedicated to the memory of Harvey Armistead for his work with youth athletics. The other winds through the park and has exercise stations along the way. But the best part of this park is the creek flowing out of the lake. If your dog likes to play in the water, she'll be a happy pup indeed. Even if she doesn't, she'll find plenty of smells to sniff out along the creek. This is one of those rare parks that pleases both of my boys. A swimming pool, tennis and basketball courts, picnic pavilions, a playground, and baseball fields are among the other highlights.

The park is open daily during daylight hours. Take the Ponce De Leon Avenue exit from Interstate 285 and turn outside the Perimeter. Turn right onto Market Street, left onto Rogers Street, and right onto Norman Road. The park will be on your right. (770) 296-6489.

DECATUR

The city of Decatur, named for Commodore Stephen Decatur, a hero of the War of 1812, contains some of DeKalb County's finest parks. Many of them combine the allure of a cool creek with shade from large oak trees, including Exchange Park (see page 81) and Midway Park (see page 83), or have enough long trails to really stretch your pooch's legs, such as Candler Park (see page 80).

PARKS AND RECREATION AREAS

• **Avondale-Dunaire Park** 🐾 *See* ⓱ *on page 72.*

This park is mainly used for baseball, and the gate is closed when no games are scheduled. If that's the case, you can still park at the gate and walk in with your leashed pooch.

Hours are daily from 7 A.M. to sunset. The park is near the Indian Springs MARTA Station. Take the Memorial Drive exit off Interstate 285 and turn outside the Perimeter. Turn right onto George Luther Drive, which takes you into the park. (404) 371-2631.

• **Candler Park** 🐾🐾 👣 *See* ⓲ *on page 72.*

Located next to a golf course, large, beautiful Candler Park is a real treat for you and your leashed pooch. You can walk along paved trails, through rolling fields, or into the woods. A creek would make this place almost perfect. You'll also find a swimming pool, baseball and soccer fields, basketball and tennis courts, playgrounds, and picnicking areas.

The park is open daily from 6 A.M. to 11 P.M. It's bordered by Candler Park Road and McLendon Avenue Northeast. Take Clifton Road north from DeKalb Avenue, and turn left onto McLendon Avenue. (404) 817-6766.

• **Deepdene Park/Oak Grove Park/Shady Side Park/ Springdale Park/Virgilee Park** 🐾🐾 *See* ⓳ *on page 72.*

Lying along Ponce De Leon Avenue between Decatur and Atlanta, this long series of parks is separated only by side streets. They vary in depth but are generally less than 100 yards across. Your leashed pooch will love these well-kept parks, whether stretching his legs by walking the length of them or sniffing out the trails through the middle. You'll find a variety of wooded and open areas, plus baseball and soccer fields, playgrounds, and benches to stop and watch the squirrels.

Hours are daily from 6 A.M. to 11 P.M. Take Ponce De Leon Avenue east from downtown. The parks will be on both sides of the road after you cross Moreland Avenue. (404) 371-2631.

• **Drew Park** 🐾 *See* ⓴ *on page 72.*

This small park with nothing more than a playground is adjacent to busy Drew Elementary School, making it only worth a pit stop for your leashed pooch.

Hours are daily from 6 A.M. to 11 P.M. Take the Memorial Drive exit from Interstate 285 and turn inside the Perimeter. The park is on your left at East Lake Boulevard. (404) 373-4702.

• **East Lake Park** 🐾🐾 *See* ㉑ *on page 72.*

Large East Lake Park would rate higher if it were better maintained. Water-loving dogs are intrigued by the creek and lake, and your leashed pooch will find lots of room to roam and plenty of trees to sniff. It's a shame the place has a seedy quality. The park also has basketball and tennis courts, a playground, and picnic facilities.

Hours are daily from 6 A.M. to 11 P.M. Take the Memorial Drive exit from Interstate 285 and turn inside. The park is on your left at Green Avenue Southeast. (404) 817-6766.

• **Exchange Park** 🐾🐾 🐾 *See* ㉒ *on page 72.*

With 173 well-maintained acres, Exchange Park is a delightful place for you and your leashed dog to spend an afternoon. You can take the trail around the lake or let your pooch wander into the woods to sniff out all of the messages left by local canines. The creek is deep enough for her to cool her pads on a hot summer day. The baseball fields and tennis courts are separated by open fields for your dog to play in and heavy woods for her to check out. Bring your lunch and stay awhile. Your pooch will not be bored.

Hours are daily from 7 A.M. to sunset. The park is located at Interstate 285 and Columbia Drive. Take the Flat Shoals Parkway exit and turn outside the Perimeter, then left onto Columbia Drive and into the park. (404) 371-2631.

• **Mark Trail Park and Recreation Center** 🐾🐾🐾 🐾
See ㉓ *on page 72.*

The paved trails at this 48-acre park are just one avenue for walking your leashed pooch. Mine prefer the meandering route from tree to tree. There's plenty of room to spread out a blanket and relax for a few hours or even an entire day, since the park also has a swimming pool, basketball and tennis courts, picnic pavilions, a playground, rest rooms, and ball fields.

Hours are daily from 7 A.M. to 11 P.M. Take the Flat Shoals Road exit from Interstate 20 and turn north. Turn right onto Second Avenue, then right onto Tilson Road. The park will be on your left. (404) 244-4891.

• **Mason Mill Park** 🐾 *See* ㉔ *on page 72.*

Although I wouldn't recommend it when a game is in session, leashed dogs love walking around the tennis courts at this park and collecting balls. I once saw a retriever with so many balls stuffed in his mouth that he looked like a cartoon character. He was frantically trying to get one more ball in when he lost them all, resulting in a mad scramble as they flew out in all directions. He kept a wary eye on us while he reclaimed his property. My boys aren't nearly as compulsive about carrying things. Laddie sees no point in it at all, and Bandit will drop whatever is in his mouth to pick up something else. Just be sure you aren't infringing on another pooch's ball territory when you take your pup here. I witnessed a nasty spat between two Lab mixes, even though there are always plenty of balls to keep everyone happy. The park also has ball fields, picnic areas, and a senior citizens center.

Park hours are daily from 7 A.M. to sunset. Take the Clairmont Road exit off of Interstate 85 North and turn right, then left onto McConnell Drive to reach the park. (404) 371-2631.

• **McKoy Park** 🐾 *See* ㉕ *on page 72.*

Though I find this park a peaceful place to eat lunch at one of the picnic pavilions or relax on a bench along the pathway, my dogs seem to be bored here. With no water (except for a swimming pool that's off-limits to them), and nothing interesting to sniff, they don't like staying long. Leashes are required. Other amenities include a baseball field, tennis and basketball courts, and a playground.

Hours are daily from 7 A.M. to sunset. Take the Memorial Drive exit from Interstate 285 and turn inside. Turn right onto Carter Avenue, right onto Fayetteville Road, and right onto Underwood Street, which dead-ends into McCoy Street, where the park is located. (404) 377-3922.

• **Meadowdale Park** 🐾 *See* ㉖ *on page 72.*

Meadowdale Park may be tiny, but it has several grassy areas for you to romp with your leashed pooch, plus a creek with good access if your pup likes to cool off in the water. On one of our visits, a beautiful black Lab was tossing a ball into the water, then chasing after it when the water carried it away. Bandit was fascinated by the movement, but much too shy to approach. The park also has baseball fields, basketball courts, and playgrounds. Pack some plastic grocery bags; the park is managed by the county, so you must clean up after your pet (as you should everywhere).

Hours are daily from 7 A.M. to sunset. Take the Glenwood Avenue exit off Interstate 285 and turn inside. Go right on Hollyhock Terrace, then left onto Larkspur Terrace and into the park. (404) 371-2631.

• **Medlock Park** 🐾🐾 🦴 *See* ㉗ *on page 72.*

This naturalized park in the Emory area has a creek your leashed dog can splash in and trails to wander on through the woods. For your human companions, you'll find a baseball field, tennis and basketball courts, and a playground.

Hours are daily from 7 A.M. to sunset. The park is located on Willivee Drive. To reach it, take Willivee Drive south from North Druid Hills Road, just east of Clairmont Road. (404) 371-2631.

• **Midway Park** 🐾🐾 🐾 *See ㉘ on page 72.*

Besides an assortment of ball fields, tennis courts, a swimming pool, and picnicking facilities, Midway Park has an open field for walking your pooch. The large trees lining the field are a magnet for dogs like Laddie who are ruled by their noses. Bandit, who is bored by all the sniffing, just strains at his leash to get to the creek and blow bubbles, which makes Laddie yawn. I can't always please everybody! Leashing is mandatory, as is cleaning up after your pooch.

Hours are daily from 7 A.M. to sunset, except for the baseball fields, which close at 11 P.M. The park is located on Midway Road, inside Interstate 285 off of Memorial Drive. (404) 286-3328.

• **Oak Grove Park:** See Deepdene Park on page 80.

• **Oakview Park** 🌳 *See ㉙ on page 72.*

This "park," a 12-to-15-foot-wide median strip down the middle of Oakview Road, wouldn't even be worth mentioning if it wasn't so long. Since it continues for 11 city blocks, it's a good place to take your leashed pooch for a pit stop. Some shade is provided by the large oak trees.

Hours are daily from 6 A.M. to 11 P.M. Take the Glenwood Avenue exit off of Interstate 20 and turn east. Turn left onto East Lake Boulevard, then left onto Oakview Road. The park is located along Oakview Road between Boulevard and East Lake Drive. (404) 817-6766.

• **Shady Side Park:** See Deepdene Park on page 80.

• **Shoal Creek Park/Shoal Creek II Park** 🐾🐾
See ㉚ on page 72.

These two large parks on opposite sides of Glenwood Road offer plenty to keep your leashed pooch amused. Laddie prefers nosing around the trees and wandering through the grassy fields, while Bandit sticks to the creek, which means both dogs are blissful part of the time, bored the rest. The park also has tennis and basketball courts, ball fields, playgrounds, and picnic shelters.

Hours are daily from 7 A.M. to sunset, except for the lit ball fields, which close at 11 P.M. Take the Glenwood Avenue exit off of Interstate 285 and turn inside the Perimeter. The parks will be on both sides of Glenwood Avenue just past Hillsdale Drive. (404) 371-2631.

- **Springdale Park:** See Deepdene Park on page 80.
- **Virgilee Park:** See Deepdene Park on page 80.

DIVERSIONS

Calling all bassets: Twice a year, the Basset Hound Rescue of Georgia holds a basset-only reunion picnic. If your buddy is a basset hound, come on down and compete in fun contests for everything from the longest ears to the shortest legs. Everyone has a good time, and donations are accepted for the rescue group. The picnic is held at Candler Park (see page 80). For more information, contact Julie Bradley at (770) 499-1164.

DORAVILLE

PARKS AND RECREATION AREAS

- **Autumn Park** 🐾🐾 *See ㉛ on page 72.*

Small Autumn Park has a pleasant creek flowing through it with easy access for dogs. I like to sit and listen to the water, either at one of the picnic tables or on a blanket on the grass. In the summer, large oaks provide ample shade. It would seem this peaceful spot doesn't get many canine visitors, since Laddie isn't very interested in the trees. Leashes are required.

Hours are daily from 7 A.M. to 11 P.M. You must park on the street. Take Interstate 85 north of Atlanta and exit left onto Chamblee-Tucker Road. Turn right on Bagley Drive, right on Raymond Drive, then right on McClave Drive to reach the park. (770) 936-3850.

- **Brook Park** 🐾 *See ㉜ on page 72.*

This small park offers plenty of trees for shade when taking a leisurely romp with your leashed pooch. Amenities include tennis and basketball courts, a playground, volleyball nets, swings, and picnic tables.

Hours are daily from 7 A.M. to 11 P.M. Take Interstate 85 north of Atlanta and exit left onto Chamblee-Tucker Road. Turn right on Bagley Drive, then right on Raymond Drive. The park is on your left. (770) 936-3850.

- **English Oaks Park** 🚩 *See ㉝ on page 72.*

This park has tennis courts and a playground, but not much for the doggy set. It's long and narrow, so there isn't even much room to walk. Leashes must be worn here.

Hours are daily from 7 A.M. to 11 P.M. To reach this park on English Oak Drive, take Buford Highway north of Interstate 285 and turn right onto Oakcliff Road. Turn left onto Windsor Oak Drive, right onto Moss Oak Drive, then right onto English Oak Drive. The park is on the left. (770) 936-3850.

• Honeysuckle Park 🐾 *See ㉞ on page 72.*

Honeysuckle Park's main claim to fame is basketball, and since neither of my dogs has mastered the game, they're not too impressed. There's a small wooded area where your leashed dog can relax for a few moments.

Hours are daily from 7 A.M. to 11 P.M. Take Buford Highway north of Interstate 285, turn right onto McElroy Road, then left onto Pleasant Valley Drive. The park is on the left. (770) 936-3850.

• Windwood Hollow Park 🐾 *See ㉟ on page 72.*

Tiny Windwood Hollow Park is located within spitting distance of what could be an incredible experience for your pooch. Unfortunately, dogs (and people, too) are restricted from the Twin Lakes, which are part of the Doraville water treatment system. The trail at Windwood Hollow Park is short (the whole park covers just 11 acres). But on the plus side, it does go through heavy woods, so there's plenty to smell along the way. One look at water-loving Bandit's stricken face as we drive by the Twin Lakes is enough to make me not want to come back, though. All that, and he must be leashed, too. Since this park is managed by the county, be sure to clean up after your pooch.

Hours are daily from 7 A.M. to sunset. Take the Peachtree Industrial Boulevard exit off of Interstate 285 and turn outside. Turn left onto Winters Chapel Road, then left onto Peeler Road. Turn right onto Lakeside Drive. The park is on the right. (404) 508-7555.

DUNWOODY
PARKS AND RECREATION AREAS

• Dunwoody Park 🐾🐾🐾 🦴 *See ㊱ on page 72.*

This lovely, heavily wooded park comes complete with a 1.3-mile nature trail loop, which crosses a stream on a footbridge. Another, larger bridge keeps the playground crowd away from my easily distracted Bandit. Wild Cat Creek rushes over big rocks and makes quite a racket. Even though the park is located down a long entrance road off Roberts Road, I'm always amazed that I can't hear Highway 400, which usually drowns out everything for miles around. Dunwoody Park also has a wetlands area. (I like to keep Bandit by the creek and away from the mudlands, er, wetlands.) Part of the park has been landscaped by a garden club and is quite beautiful.

You can pick up maps of the trails at the Nature Center. Dogs must be leashed and the poop must be scooped. Other amenities besides the playground are picnic areas, a nature kiosk with benches, and two baseball fields.

The park is open daily from 7 A.M. to sunset. From Highway 400 going north, get off at Northridge Road and go straight across onto Roberts Road. The park is on your left. (770) 394-3322.

LAKE CLAIRE

Despite the name, there's no lake in the community of Lake Claire, which is quite a joke among the locals. Streets and businesses are named after the nonexistent body of water, and many shops here sell Lake Claire T-shirts and memorabilia. Everyone seems to have a sense of humor, too, if the funny signs posted all around town are any indication. When I pulled into an empty parking lot at a small cafe, I was struck by the number and variety of signs posted there, warning of what would happen if I parked without going in to eat. One of them said, "If your' stupid enough to park here, I'm stupid enough to have you towed." Since one of my passions is finding permanent signs with grammatical errors (I know, my dogs don't understand it either), I had to stop in and see the place. While the boys waited outside, I stood at the counter and ordered a sandwich. Two men were drinking coffee and joking with the woman who owned the cafe, but the three of them kept staring at me as if I had a huge wad of spinach stuck in my front teeth. One of the men wore black leather from head to toe and had silver chains hanging from every possible location. I counted eight earrings in one of his ears and six in the other. His companion wore a skimpy "muscle man" tank top that showed off a lot of skin, most of which was covered with tattoos. Even his neck was tattooed. I was dressed in park attire (a pair of jeans and a T-shirt), and couldn't understand why they were staring at "normal" me. Finally, the owner asked if I lived in the neighborhood. When I told her no, she said, "I didn't think so. You looked strange."

PARKS AND RECREATION AREAS

• **Lake Claire Park** 🐾 *See* ❸❼ *on page* 72.

Bandit isn't amused at the lack of a lake at Lake Claire Park, and quickly gets bored following Laddie from tree to tree in search of canine clues. This park also has tennis courts, a ball field, and a playground. Leashes are a must.

Hours are daily from 6 A.M. to 11 P.M. Take Ponce De Leon Avenue east from Peachtree Street and turn right onto Lake Shore Drive, where the park is located. (404) 817-6766.

LITHONIA
PARKS AND RECREATION AREAS

• **Davidson-Arabia Mountain Nature Preserve** 🐾🐾 🐾
See ❸❽ on page 72.

Ask the park ranger if this is a granite outcrop similar to Stone Mountain, and you'll immediately be corrected. Though granitic, the rock here is classified as Lithonia gneiss (pronounced "nice"). The town of Lithonia was named for the Greek "lithos," which means stone. Lithonia granite or gneiss continues to be mined today, but not in the park.

Whatever the stone is that makes up the mountain, this 498-acre nature preserve is an outstanding place to spend a day with your pooch in the fall and winter months, since it offers a variety of environments and activities—and the rock soaks up the sun's warmth. In the summer, though, it's just too uncomfortable for your dog's tender feet.

There are two main parking areas. The first one you'll come to (on your right on Klondike Road) is near the top of Davidson-Arabia Mountain. Don't climb the mountain from here, but do park here to explore the lake. The trail to the lake starts across Klondike Road from the parking area. The first half mile crosses granite, which can heat up your dog's pads pretty quickly. A one-mile loop trail comes off the back of the granite outcropping. This part of the trail is shady and offers good access to the water as it circles the lake. The first part of this trail, though, is just too unpleasant for my dogs on sunny days. It's all downhill going in and uphill coming out.

The second parking area, about a quarter of a mile farther on Klondike Road, is at the visitors center. The ranger frequently has her dog here, so ask at the door before bringing your pooch in. Pick up some brochures to learn about the very fragile ecosystem found on the mountain. Two types of endangered plants live in the pools on top of the mountain, so be sure to follow the instructions about staying on the trail, leashing your pooch, scooping up her mess, and keeping her out of the pools.

The trail up to the top of the mountain from the visitors center is about three-quarters of a mile long, making a 1.5-mile round-trip without shade or available water. Keep this in mind before taking your dog on this hike, and bring plenty of water for your pooch so he won't be tempted to stop for a drink in the cache pools. The view from the top is spectacular, and the breeze very welcoming after the last 100 yards of fairly strenuous hiking. (The rest of the trail is rated easy.) The parks department is considering restricting dogs from the mountain due to the fragility of the environment, so please follow all of the rules to prevent this as long as possible.

Hours are daily from 7 A.M. to sunset. From Atlanta, take Interstate 20 east to exit 38 (Evans Mill Road) and turn right. Turn right on Klondike Road. The park is less than two miles down Klondike Road. (770) 593-5864.

LITTLE FIVE POINTS

This tiny neighborhood has struggled over the years to maintain its eclectic style and develop a healthy economy. Even in the mid-1980s, Little Five Points had the flavor of the 1960s. You'll still find some hippies in the neighborhood, but many who used to just hang out here have now opened crystal shops and other types of alternative businesses and are trying to make a living.

PARKS AND RECREATION AREAS

• **Goldsboro Park** 🐾 *See* **39** *on page 72.*

This small park has a creek and woods for your leashed pooch to explore, and tennis and basketball courts for human types. It's easy for your dog to get to the water and cool her pads. You must park on the street.

Hours are daily from 6 A.M. to 11 P.M. To reach the park, take Ponce De Leon Avenue east from Peachtree Street. Turn right onto Moreland Avenue, then left onto Euclid Avenue. The park is located at the intersection of Euclid and Moreland Avenues. (404) 817-6766.

SHOPPING IN LITTLE FIVE POINTS

abbadabba's: This eclectic shoe and clothing shop carries Rockports, Birkenstocks, and other trendy footwear. Best of all, pooches are welcome, too. Be sure to take your pup with you if you go into one of the dressing areas. 421-B Moreland Avenue, Atlanta, GA 30307; (404) 588-9577.

Celtic Jamboree: Your pup can shop with you for jewelry, semi-precious stones, scarves, candles, New Age music, and gifts. 1120 Euclid Avenue Northeast, Atlanta, GA 30307; (404) 524-4828.

Crystal Blue: Laddie would plug his nose in this shop if he could, since his tastes are a little more earthy than scented candles and incense. Crystal Blue also carries aromatherapy products, wind chimes, crystals, music, gifts, and jewelry. 1168 Euclid Avenue, Atlanta, GA 30307; (404) 522-4605.

Identified Flying Objects: This is the place to pick up doggy disks, hacky sacks, kites, Frisbee disks, juggling paraphernalia, and everything imaginable dealing with objects in the air. The shop is fascinating, and your pooch is free to browse as well. 1164 Euclid Avenue, Atlanta, GA 30307; (404) 534-4628.

Pink Flamingoes: You and your pooch can stop and shop here for cute clothing and shoes, plus an eclectic assortment of candles, jewelry, cards, and gifts. One section is devoted to collections of salt and pepper shakers. 1166 Euclid Avenue, Atlanta, GA 30307; (404) 577-2025.

SCOTTDALE

PARKS AND RECREATION AREAS

• **Tobie Grant Park** *See 40 on page 72.*

Though this small park does have a creek that's easy for your pup to get to, even Bandit gets bored after an hour here. Humans fare better, with a swimming pool, baseball fields, a playground, picnicking areas, and a recreation center. Take the footbridge over the creek and check out the exercise trail. Leashes are a must, as is cleaning up after your pet.

Hours are daily from 7 A.M. to sunset. Take the Ponce De Leon Avenue exit off of Interstate 285 and turn inside on Church Street, which parallels Ponce De Leon Avenue. Turn left onto Glendale Road, then right onto Parkdale Drive. The park is located on Parkdale Drive, near North Decatur Road. (404) 508-7594.

STONE MOUNTAIN

PARKS AND RECREATION AREAS

• **Hairston Park** *See 41 on page 72.*

When you first arrive at Hairston Park, allow your leashed pooch to play in the creek and then walk him around the two lakes. You'll find plenty of trails for him to explore. The idea is to get him tuckered out so he'll be willing to let you spread a blanket in the large field and eat your lunch. Maybe he'll even enjoy a nap beside you in this peaceful spot, if there isn't a baseball game going on or too many children in the playground.

The woods here are great for cooling off on hot summer days, and the field is sunny when it's brisk out. On our last visit, an older man was teaching three small children to fish at the larger of the two lakes. One little girl was having quite a time trying to get her line in the water, and came close to hooking Laddie as we were trying to get around behind her. On the other side of the lake, he found a lure with dangling hooks in the grass. Watch where you step! Don't forget to clean up after your pooch.

Hours are daily from 7 A.M. to sunset. From Atlanta, take the Memorial Drive exit off of Interstate 285 and turn outside. (It becomes Stone Mountain Highway.) Turn right on Hairston Road, then right into the park. (404) 371-2631.

• Stone Mountain Park 🐾🐾🐾🐾 👣 See ㊷ on page 72.

Stone Mountain is the largest exposed mass of granite in the world, covering 583 acres. Rising more than 800 feet, it contains the largest sculpture in the world (covering three acres) of three Confederate heroes mounted on horseback. The project of carving the picture of General Robert E. Lee, President Jefferson Davis, and General Stonewall Jackson was begun by the Daughters of the Confederacy in 1915, but was not finished until 1970, after the state purchased the mountain and the surrounding area to make a park.

Today, Stone Mountain Park is a popular destination for hiking up the mountain or on the other trails in the park. The Walk-Up Trail to the top is 1.3 miles one way and is rather steep near the end. Neither of my dogs enjoys it, since there's no water, the last portion of the trail is steep, and it's always crowded. But there are other, longer trails through the park that my dogs truly like. The Cherokee Trail (white blazes) is a fairly strenuous, five-mile trail that lets you explore the mountain at a more leisurely pace, and dogs can cool their feet in several streams along the way. If you're not up to the challenge of the Cherokee Trail, try the Nature Gardens Trail. This easy three-quarter-mile path winds through the woods near the Walk-Up Trail. Many joggers and runners take their dogs on the five-mile Robert E. Lee Boulevard loop, but there's insufficient shade for my boys. Be sure to leash your pooch in the park.

Why not stay right at Stone Mountain Park Campground? Your pooch must be on a leash at all times, not tied up unattended, and you must pick up after her. Rates are $15 to $17 depending on hookups. For campground information, call (770) 498-5710.

Whatever you do, don't bring your dog to the park during the Yellow Daisy Festival in September. Although dogs used to be allowed at the festival, it got so crowded that it ceased being fun for them even before they were banned. One beautiful September day, a friend and I headed to Stone Mountain Park with Laddie. As we were approaching the exit off the Stone Mountain Freeway, traffic ground to a halt and crawled for the next half hour. We kept thinking we would pass an accident at any time and the road would free up. It wasn't until we had inched our way into the park that we found Yellow Daisy signs everywhere. We couldn't go to the festival with Laddie along, but we decided to spend the day at the park anyway, as we had planned. It wasn't worth it. Traffic is a mess all over the park on festival day, and many of the roads are closed to cars so the crowds of people can walk to the grounds.

The park is open daily from 6 A.M. to midnight, but the attractions (including the trails) open at 10 A.M. and close at 5:30 P.M. Stone Mountain Park is located off the Stone Mountain Freeway (U.S. 78). From Atlanta, go east on U.S. 78 and follow the signs. There's a per-car parking fee of $5. If you visit the park frequently, you can buy an annual pass for $20. (770) 498-5702.

SHOPPING IN STONE MOUNTAIN

All of the shops listed here are in the quaint shopping district known as Stone Mountain Village, on Main Street in Stone Mountain.

Country Hearts: If you carry your pooch, you can both browse here for teddy bears and antiques. The shop stocks candles and cute gifts as well. 947 Main Street, Stone Mountain, GA 30083; (770) 498-9663.

Lynn's Craft Depot: This shop sells quilts and many Georgia-made items, and welcomes well-behaved pups on leash. Better watch them near the Key Lime Coolers, though. Laddie takes quite an interest in tins of those cookies. 927-B Main Street, Stone Mountain, GA 30083; (770) 498-0495.

Stone Mountain General Store: Even nosy Laddie is welcome to shop in this delightful store, full of such goodies as gadgets, wind chimes, bird feeders, and furniture. 935 Main Street, Stone Mountain, GA 30083; (707) 469-9331.

Stones: The owner of this shop, specializing in handcrafted jewelry, loose beads, and gift items, asks that you carry your pooch if the store is crowded. Otherwise, she's welcome to walk on leash. 955 Main Street, Stone Mountain, GA 30083; (770) 469-5536.

PLACES TO STAY

La Quinta Atlanta Stone Mountain: A double room is $62, with no extra charge for your pooch. 1819 Mountain Industrial Boulevard, Stone Mountain, GA 30084; (770) 496-1317.

Stone Mountain Park Campground: See Stone Mountain Park on page 90.

TUCKER
PARKS AND RECREATION AREAS

• **Henderson Road Park** 🐾🐾🐾 *See ㊸ on page 72.*

If you like hiking with your dog and are looking for an environment similar to what you might find in the north Georgia mountains, Henderson Road Park is for you. This 114-acre park has nearly everything you and your pup could want, even though leashes are required.

There are several trails you can take (some of which are paved) near the soccer fields and tennis courts, but for more of a wilderness feel, head to the lake. The trail doesn't go completely around the lake, unless you're willing to go through some marshy areas, but you'll feel as if you're miles from civilization (my boys and I have even found deer tracks in the marsh). It's easy to get turned around in the marsh and come out at the tennis courts, which means a long walk back. (I speak from personal experience, of course. At least it allowed Bandit time to dry off a bit before we got back to the car.) Wear appropriate footwear and carry water. The park also has playgrounds, ball fields, and picnic shelters.

The park is open daily during daylight hours. To reach the park, take the Chamblee-Tucker Road exit off of Interstate 285 and turn outside the Perimeter. Stay on Chamblee-Tucker Road when it turns 90 degrees at the intersection with Norcross-Tucker Road. Turn right on Livsey Drive, which becomes Henderson Park Road, where the park is located. (404) 371-2631.

SHOPPING IN TUCKER

Cheshire Pets: This store welcomes you and your pooch (and parrot, iguana, or other pet) to shop together. They stock a full assortment of dog, cat, bird, and small animal supplies. 1929 Mountain Industrial Boulevard, Tucker, GA 30003; (770) 934-7682.

Petsmart: I'm always amazed at the variety of animals customers bring into Petsmart, from cats and dogs to members of the reptile family. The store carries supplies for just about every species you can imagine. Petsmart is located throughout the Atlanta area. 4023 Lavista Road, Tucker, GA 30003; (770) 414-5126.

PLACES TO STAY

Ramada Northlake: Rooms go for $65, and dogs stay free. 2180 Northlake Parkway, Tucker, GA 30084; (770) 939-8120.

DOUGLAS COUNTY

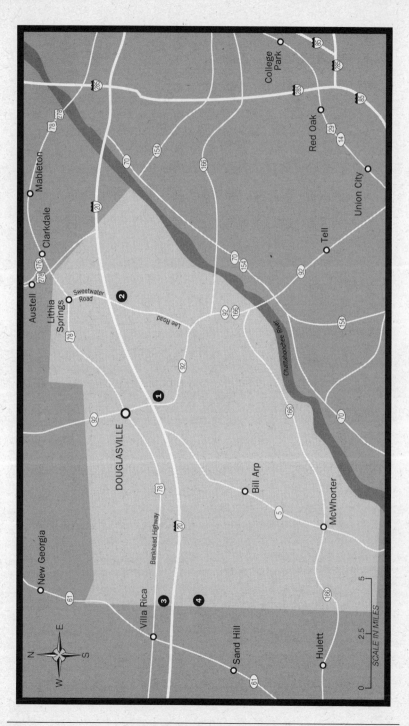

5
DOUGLAS COUNTY

Lithia Springs Mineral Water, bottled since 1887, is this small county's claim to fame. Around the beginning of the century, the rich and famous vacationed here at the "Saratoga Springs of the South." The Sweetwater Hotel in Lithia Springs had indoor spas and steam rooms that were used by the Vanderbilts and other wealthy visitors. But when the hotel burned down in 1912, it wasn't rebuilt, and Lithia Springs faded from the spotlight.

For dog lovers, Douglas County is infamous for its ban on dogs from most city and county parks. That's a real shame, not just because it means you can't take your dog to Hunter Park, Gold Dust Park, or a number of other places, but because of the precedent it sets for other counties in the Atlanta area. Luckily, there are a few good parks in the county that are worth a visit. One county park in Douglasville (Deer Lick Park, page 98) welcomes dogs, at least for the time being. (None of the other county parks have any trails.) You and your pooch can also visit the fabulous Sweetwater Creek State Park (see page 99) in Lithia Springs. But just knowing that 150 acres of parkland in Douglasville are off-limits to Laddie and Bandit bothers me enough to make my visits to the county fairly infrequent. As is the case in most of the metropolitan area, Douglas County has a leash law. You're also required to have your dog's rabies tag affixed to her collar at all times, and to scoop her poop.

AUSTELL

Although part of Austell is in Douglas County, the majority lies within Cobb County. See the Cobb County chapter starting on page 49 for parks and other information.

DOUGLASVILLE

Your worst nightmare is true in Douglasville. Dogs have been banned from all city parks. When I asked the city why this happened, I was told that dog owners were letting their pets run loose and failing to scoop up the poop. After the city council received enough complaints, it passed the "no dogs" ordinance. Douglas

County has grown very rapidly over the past 20 years, and city managers have had to make quick decisions to deal with the encroaching civilization. Obviously, their choices haven't been made with conscientious dog lovers in mind. Douglasville should also serve as a warning to dog owners in every community. It's a lot easier for city councils to just outlaw your pets than to figure out ways to appease both dog owners and everyone else.

If you live in Douglasville, keep after the city council to reconsider the ordinance. I would even think about shopping elsewhere. After all, do you really want your dollars to benefit a city where your best buddy is kept out of sight and out of mind? Some exceptions are the merchants listed here. They welcome your pup to come along as you run your errands.

PARKS AND RECREATION AREAS

• **Deer Lick Park** 🐾 🐾 🐾 *See ❶ on page 96.*

This is the one and only Douglas County park that has a trail—and allows dogs. The paved, half-mile walking and jogging track is for foot traffic only—both the two- and four-footed varieties. There are large pine trees throughout the park, so some of the trail is shaded for part of the day. It's still too hot for Bandit, since his black coat soaks up the heat on the portion without shade. His mood lifts, however, when he gets to the lake and starts blowing bubbles in the water. You can also walk your pooch behind the ball fields, although there's a tight squeeze between a fence and a wall at one end.

The small lake is well stocked with ducks and ducklings in the spring. Fishing is also popular here. But Laddie's favorite feature is the swings. Each one is big enough for two or three adults and their dogs. I lift Laddie in next to me and keep a steadying hand on him while we move slowly back and forth. Leashes and rabies tags are required, and you must pick up anything your pal tries to leave behind. For your noncanine kids, there's a large children's area called Spider Hill.

Hours are daily from 8 A.M. to 11 P.M. Take Interstate 20 west from Atlanta, exit on Fairburn Road, and turn left. After about three miles, turn left on Mack Road. The park is half a mile down on the left. (770) 920-7129.

SHOPPING IN DOUGLASVILLE

Church Street Pharmacy: The great folks at this drugstore love dogs. They make such a fuss over Laddie that he doesn't want to leave. If you're in the downtown area and need a prescription filled, greeting cards, or just a chat with dog-friendly people, stop on by. 6643 Church Street, Douglasville, GA 30134; (770) 942-4982.

Smith and Dabbs Furniture, Inc.: You wouldn't know it from the name of the store, but you'll find a lot more inside than just furniture. This eclectic place is actually a gift shop (Georgia-made peach preserves, anyone?) that also sells some furniture. 6672 Broad Street, Douglasville, GA 30134; (770) 942-2474.

FESTIVALS

Skint Chestnut Fall Festival: Douglasville was originally named Skint Chestnut. (The courthouse sits on the site of a large chestnut tree that was a major landmark to the Cherokee Indians, who skinned off the bark to make it easier to find.) This festival, held each September in Deer Lick Park (see page 98), is a special pet adoption site for the Douglas County Humane Society. Stop by their area and purchase pet supplies or adopt a dog who really needs a home. For more information, call (770) 942-5961.

DIVERSIONS

Have a favorite bone recipe?: Each December, the Douglas County Humane Society publishes its benefit cookbook. Stop by the Douglasville office to pick up a copy, or contact the society early in the year to contribute recipes. 1755 Humane Society Boulevard, Douglasville, GA 30134; (770) 942-5961.

LITHIA SPRINGS

Lithia Springs has had three names. It was originally called Deer Lick by the Cherokee Indians for the deer that frequented the springs. When the first post office was established, the name was changed to Salt Springs. And after lithium was discovered in the water, the town was renamed Lithia Springs. A trip here is like a step back in time. You can buy some of the legendary "love water" from the springs, or stop to visit Frog Rock. Best of all for dog lovers, Lithia Springs has one of the finest parks in the Atlanta area—and dogs are welcome.

PARKS AND RECREATION AREAS

• **Sweetwater Creek State Park** 🐾🐾🐾🐾 🐾
  See ❷ on page 96.

At 2,000 acres, Georgia's third largest park combines all the best elements you and your leashed pooch could want. If you're just after a beautiful place to picnic, stop at the George H. Sparks Reservoir. The view is spectacular, and dogs are even allowed in the picnic pavilion. If you want to hike after lunch, there's a trail leading off the parking area that winds through the thick woods and offers excellent views of the water.

If you continue on Mount Vernon Road past the reservoir, you'll come to the turnoff for the factory run. The red-blazed hiking trail is six-tenths of a mile long, well marked, wide, and Laddie-approved, meaning that it's fairly level. It leads down to the creek and the ruins of the New Manchester Manufacturing Company, a water-powered cotton and yarn factory built in the 1840s. The factory was destroyed by Sherman during the Civil War. My dogs love the side trail onto a small island. There are benches and numbered markers along the trail, so pick up trail information at the bait shop/visitors center.

If you're in the mood for something more strenuous, you'll find several miles of little-used hiking trails along the creek. The steep trail continuing for about a half a mile past the ruins leads to a small waterfall. The blue-blazed trail above the falls leads back to the picnic and parking area, for a round-trip total of a little more than three miles.

This beautiful area has an incredible variety of birds, butterflies, and wildflowers, plus the strangest-looking ants I've ever seen. They're about an inch long and bright red with black markings. (Don't worry; they scurry off when approached.)

Watch for poison ivy on all the trails. Though there isn't a pooper-scooper ordinance, the rangers ask that you at least kick any dog mess off the trail. The visitors center is located in a bait shop by the rest rooms. The park rents canoes and boats, but dogs aren't allowed in any of the state-owned boats. (If you bring your own boat, of course, you can take your dog out on the lake with you.) Dogs aren't allowed in any buildings, including the rest rooms.

As in other state parks, a parking pass is required. You can buy the annual ParkPass for $25 or a day pass for $2 at the bait shop/visitors center. There are also day pass machines located in the parking lots.

The park is open daily from 7 A.M. to 10 P.M. The nature trail road (which goes to the creek and factory trails) closes at dusk. To get to the park, take Interstate 20 west from Atlanta to Lee Road and turn left, then left again at Cedar Terrace. Go straight at Mount Vernon Road to the visitors center, or turn right to get to the factory run. (770) 732-5871.

SHOPPING IN LITHIA SPRINGS

Wyatt's Pharmacy: Stop in this dog-friendly place to fill your prescription or shop without that megastore feel. It's located in Lithia Center. 3750 Bankhead Highway; (770) 948-8825.

DIVERSIONS

"Love water," please?: Lithia Springs Mineral Water was originally hailed as therapeutic, in more ways than one. Among other benefits, it was considered quite an aphrodisiac—hence the name "love water." Although the spa, hotel, and baths no longer exist, a trip to the Springs is like reconnecting with another time. The tiny, one-room museum houses some of the Indian artifacts found here. The mineral water, which contains bicarbonate of lithium, is sold under three labels—Lithia Springs Mineral Water, Love Water, and Deer Lick Spring Water. According to the caretaker, Deer Lick Spring Water is prescribed by area veterinarians for dogs with persistent bladder infections and cats with feline urinary syndrome, since bicarbonate of lithium dissolves uric acid. Take your pet for a drink, then wander over to Frog Rock (see below). 2910 Bankhead Highway, Lithia Springs, GA 30057; (770) 944-3880.

Frog Rock: Located next to the Lithia Springs Mineral Water Company, this natural rock formation does actually resemble a frog perched by the side of the road. There was talk of moving it when Bankhead Highway was widened, but the rock is just the tip of the iceberg—it extends down 10 miles into the earth. Frog Rock is an outcropping of Stone Mountain. Because the roadway was raised when Bankhead Highway was widened, today you won't even see it unless you pull into the Lithia Springs Mineral Water driveway. Don't be surprised if your dog doesn't react to the threat of a giant frog, though. Laddie is not at all impressed by it. A picture of your pet on the frog's nose would make a great Christmas card.

VILLA RICA

If you ask Atlantans where gold was first discovered in Georgia, most of them would think of Dahlonega. It came as a surprise to me that Villa Rica has that distinction. The citizens are quite proud of it, too, judging from the "City of Gold" designations on everything from shops to the city park.

Villa Rica spans both Douglas and Carroll Counties, and includes a good county park, the Clinton Nature Preserve (see page 102). Unfortunately, it also includes Gold Dust Park, which is off-limits to dogs. Bandit just stares forlornly out the window when we drive by the trail, gym, ball fields, and tennis courts. The sign actually says "ABSOLUTELY NO DOGS ALLOWED IN PARK," which quells any temptation to sneak in a small, cute pooch, even one as small and cute as Bandit.

PARKS AND RECREATION AREAS

• **City of Gold Bicentennial Park** 🐾 *See* ❸ *on page 96.*

Although the name is larger than the park itself, it's delightfully lush, green, and shady, with a small creek bubbling through the back. Bandit is very partial to water, and when we come here he immediately lies down in the creek, sticks his head under water, and blows bubbles. There are several picnic tables and a gazebo, and the park gets a lot of use every day of the week, both during the day and in the evening. Remember to leash here.

The unlit park is open 24 hours a day, all year. From Atlanta, take Interstate 20 west to exit 6 (Liberty Road). Turn right on Liberty Road, then left when it dead-ends onto Bankhead Highway (U.S. 78). Turn left onto Leslie Drive, across from the City Hall. The park is on the corner at Bankhead Highway. (770) 459-3656.

• **Clinton Nature Preserve** 🐾🐾 *See* ❹ *on page 96.*

Here are the pooch rules in this park: the walking path in the nature preserve is off-limits to dogs, but your pup is allowed elsewhere in the park, as long as she remains leashed at all times. The nature preserve was created when a woman named Annie Clinton willed half of her 400-acre estate to the county, with the stipulation that it remain protected for the wildlife, mainly deer. I've never seen any deer here, but it isn't very likely since I always have one or both of the dogs with me. There's a pre–Civil War log cabin in the park called the Carnes House, which dates back to 1828 (and looks it). Other amenities are the walking path, rest rooms, and picnic tables.

I was initially annoyed that dogs couldn't go on the walking path, but it's a large oval without any shade, so mine wouldn't like it anyway. Bandit is easily consoled by all the places he finds to sniff around the Carnes House.

The park is open daily from 9 A.M. to dark and closed on Wednesdays. From Atlanta, take Interstate 20 west to exit 7 (Post Road). Turn left onto Post Road, then right onto Ephesus Church Road. The park is on the right after Ephesus Church and before Shiloh Baptist Church. Caretakers live on the property. Their number is (770) 459-6099; the main number for the park is (770) 920-7266.

PLACES TO STAY

Twin Oaks: Villa Rica is home to one of the most delightful bed-and-breakfasts I've found. One of the three ponds on the 23-acre estate is stocked with goldfish and koi. The other two have Canada geese, and both have white and black swans. Owner Carol Turner, whose two dogs like to greet guests, has a suite in her home and two cottages nearby for rent. All of them are quite roomy. The suite in the main house has two bedrooms, a living room, and a kitchen, plus a deck outside. The covered porch by the pool has a gas grill. Scarlett's Cottage is furnished with several *Gone With the Wind* prints and has a sunroom, hot tub, big-screen TV, and a fireplace in the bedroom. Rhett's Cottage (you didn't expect them to stay under the same roof, did you?) has a king-sized bed and whirlpool tub. Carol doesn't allow dogs to spend the night in the cottages, but they both have large covered porches and doghouses. You and your pooch are welcome to roam the 23 acres of woods and pastures during your stay. Rates are $85 to $105, with a $25 refundable deposit for canine guests. 9565 East Liberty Road, Villa Rica, GA 30180; (770) 459-4374.

SEE MAP ON PAGE 96

FAYETTE COUNTY

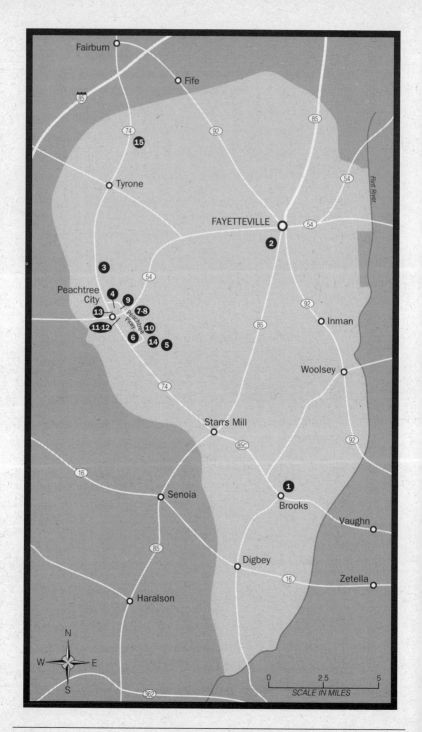

FAYETTE COUNTY

6
FAYETTE COUNTY

Fayette County has taken an interesting approach to controlling the dog population. First, it has a kennel law, which dictates that you can't own more than three dogs unless you have a kennel license, which isn't easy to get. Also, the only dogs at the Fayette County Animal Shelter are strays who have been picked up. The shelter simply doesn't accept dogs turned in by their owners.

I spoke with Bill Newman, director of Animal Control, about this policy. He pulls no punches regarding how he feels about people abandoning their pets. Newman feels you need to have three things before you bring home a pet—finances, facility, and time. Most dogs and cats are adopted with no regard for the cost of proper food and care over the animal's lifetime. According to an article he showed me in the *Atlanta Journal and Constitution,* this care will cost between $12,000 and $13,000 for a dog (over an average of 11 years), and $5,600 for a cat (over an average of 15 years). Newman, long an active player in Atlanta's humane organizations, is currently campaigning for a 2 to 3 percent sales tax on dog and cat food that would be used to provide funds for spaying and neutering.

As for facility, better plan to keep your pet on a leash. The leash law in Fayette County comes with a bite: For the first offense, Animal Control will charge you $150 for picking up your pet. The second offense comes to $250 plus court costs. The third offense is $500 plus court costs. (I didn't have the nerve to ask Newman what would happen on the fourth offense, but I suspect some flesh—yours—is involved.) These hefty fines are just a drop in the bucket compared to what you could end up paying if your pet is found running loose. Insurance companies don't pay for punitive damages against people or dogs, and the courts are awarding hefty damages for negligence if a dog is running loose and bites someone. If it's your dog, you're personally liable. Newman cited a number of recent cases in the county, including one where a small girl was bitten by a Brittany spaniel. Punitive damages in the amount of $100,000 were awarded in addition to money to cover the medical bills for plastic surgery.

SEE MAP ON PAGE 106

If you have the last of Newman's requirements for a dog—time—then you're in luck. Fayette County is one of the best places to live in the metropolitan area if you have a pooch. There are several good county parks, and Peachtree City seems to be designed with dog owners in mind. If you haven't discovered this gem yet, you're in for a treat.

BROOKS

Brooks is a delightful little town set in an agricultural part of Fayette County. If you mention you're from the city here, they'll think you're talking about Peachtree City. Getting to Brooks means driving down country roads, past cow pastures and fields of grain. There isn't much traffic through this area, and the cows seem to be as surprised to see you as you are to see them. Bandit met his first cow here one day when I pulled over on the side of the road to look at my map. Although none of the herd appeared to notice us, they all drifted slowly in our direction. Bandit seemed oblivious to them at first, but then suddenly he dove onto the floor of the backseat. When I looked up from the map, one very large cow was craning her neck toward the car window, which was shut, from at least 10 feet away. Bandit couldn't be coaxed back on the seat until we made our next stop, and even then he paused to look around before getting out of the car.

PARKS AND RECREATION AREAS

• **Aubrey Evans Memorial Park:** See Brooks Park below.

• **Brooks Park/Aubrey Evans Memorial Park** 🐾
  See ❶ on page 106.

Although there are two signs for this pair of parks, consisting mainly of a ball field and picnic pavilion, you'll be hard pressed to say where one stops and the other starts. Bandit's radar targets the small creek in the back. You'll find large fields to walk your pooch in, rife with the smell of cattle across the creek, plus a seldom-used gravel road that runs behind the ball field. Remember to leash your canine companion.

Park hours are daily from dawn to dusk. Take Highway 85 south from Interstate 75, just south of Interstate 285. Follow Highway 85 through Fayetteville to Starrs Mill, and turn left on the Highway 85 Connector. Brooks is about four miles down the road. Turn left just before the railroad tracks, go over several of the worst speed bumps in Georgia, and turn left into both of the parks at 101 Railroad Avenue. (770) 461-9714.

FAYETTEVILLE
PARKS AND RECREATION AREAS

• **Kiwanis Fields** 🐾 *See ❷ on page 106.*

Bandit tried hard to give this park a higher rating. First he discovered the gravel road that leads off the main parking lot. We took off down the road, his tail waving high over his back, but the road disappeared into a gate with Private Property signs all over it. Then he discovered a small bridge in a picnic area and dragged me over to look for water. Alas, the bridge was over a drainage area, not a creek, and it was dry. He did eventually find another ditch and managed to get his nose under water (barely) for a few joyous moments of bubble blowing, but that was the highlight of the park.

Kiwanis Fields is well equipped for your human companions, with ball fields, tennis courts, and picnic tables, but your pooch won't be too impressed. You can get in a good walk around the various playing fields and the parking lots, but don't plan to make a day of it. Leashes are mandatory.

Hours are daily from dawn to dusk. From Atlanta, take Interstate 75 south to Highway 85, just south of Interstate 285. Turn right on Highway 85, which takes you to Fayetteville. Then go right on Beauregard Boulevard, across from the historic City Hall. Beauregard Boulevard turns into Redwine Road. Kiwanis Fields is located on the left after the four-way stop. (770) 461-9714.

• **Meade Field** 🐾 *See ❸ on page 106.*

This small park has several baseball fields and large, grassy areas for walking your leashed pooch. You might feel vulnerable to fly balls if a game is in progress, since you'll be walking literally between the fields. Laddie doesn't seem to mind outside distractions (other than the sound of a can opener), but Bandit just can't ignore all the commotion, and all the activity may prove a bit distracting for your pet, too. The good news is that the park is located on the way to most of what Fayette County has to offer, making it often in the right place at the right time.

Hours are daily from dawn to dusk. From Atlanta, take Interstate 75 south to Highway 85, just south of Interstate 285. Turn right on Highway 85, which takes you to Fayetteville. Go right on Beauregard Boulevard, across from the historic City Hall. Beauregard Boulevard turns into Redwine Road. Redwine Road dead-ends onto Highway 74. Turn right on Highway 74 and drive up to the top of the hill. Turn left on Rockaway Road. The park is at the intersection of Rockaway

Road and Highway 74, across from the Fayette County Animal Control building. (770) 461-9714.

SHOPPING IN FAYETTEVILLE

Petsmart: Some of the friendliest dog lovers in the Atlanta area—both employees and customers—can be found at this store, which carries a wide selection of pet food and supplies, and also offers grooming and training services. Every time I stop by, everyone oohs and aahs over my "kids," while Laddie and Bandit show me what they want in their Christmas stockings. Petsmart stores can be found throughout the metropolitan area. 101 Pavilion Parkway, Fayetteville, GA 30214; (770) 719-4444.

PEACHTREE CITY

I knew nothing about Peachtree City before doing research for this book, so I was amazed at what I found. If more Atlantans were aware of what Peachtree City has to offer, the population would explode. A planned community, the city is laid out in small neighborhoods, with 60 miles of interconnecting paved paths for joggers, cyclists, golf carts, and dog-walkers. Each neighborhood has its own recreational area and is nestled in acres of woodlands and wetlands. Fully 20 percent of all land in the city is preserved as permanent open space. If you feel like a long walk, stop at one of the parks here and set out on the paths as they wind around two 250-acre lakes and a network of ponds and creeks. You could actually sell your car if you lived here, since all shopping and offices are accessible by the paths. Many of the residents own golf carts for getting around.

Bandit and I fell in love with Peachtree City on our first visit. You're never far from accessible water, which he likes, and there are plenty of ducks, green-backed and great blue herons, and other wildlife. I've also seen deer on nearly every trip here.

Peachtree City seems to have provided for all of its residents, with areas specific for children, golfers, senior citizens, nature lovers, and anyone who likes to walk. Dog lovers are plentiful and friendly. What a delightful place to be! The boys and I give this city four paws plus. Even Laddie likes the trails here, since the land is predominantly flat.

After visiting parks all over the Atlanta area and seeing so many underutilized tennis courts and walking trails, it's refreshing to come to Peachtree City and see so many residents and their dogs taking advantage of the parklike environment. As progressive as

Peachtree seems to be, I'm surprised the city doesn't have a dog park that's designated off leash all the time.

To reach Peachtree City from Atlanta, take Interstate 85 south to the Fairburn exit. Turn left onto Highway 74, which leads you through the city. If you're new to the area, stop at the Information Center for a map and a chat. From Highway 74, turn left onto Westpark Drive at the sign.

PARKS AND RECREATION AREAS

While each neighborhood has its own park, these small areas are designed for local use and there's usually not any parking except along the street. But you will find regional recreation facilities that are accessible to visitors. Because of the network of paths, you and your pooch have the potential for a four-paw adventure at any of the following parks.

• **Blue Smoke Recreation Center** 🐾 *See ❹ on page 106.*

This park's main attractions won't appeal to your dog, but there are large grassy fields to walk in. You could always park here to hook up with the network of paved pathways. Other amenities include tennis and basketball courts and a children's play area. Leashing is mandatory.

Hours are daily from dawn to dusk. From Highway 74, turn left on Wisdom Road, left at the dead end onto Rile Parkway, left at the dead end onto Flat Creek Road, left on Golf View Drive, right onto Blue Smoke Trail, and right on Parkgate Lane. The park is on your left. (770) 631-2542.

• **Braelinn Recreation Center** 🐾 *See ❺ on page 106.*

The nice thing about this park, located next to an elementary school, is that the ball fields are separated from each other by large, grassy fields your leashed dog can enjoy. You'll find tennis and basketball courts, fitness equipment, and play areas, too.

Hours are daily from dawn to dusk. From Highway 74, turn left on Crosstown Drive, then right on Loghouse Road. The park is on your left, just past Oak Grove Elementary School. (770) 631-2542.

• **Flat Creek Nature Area** 🐾🐾🐾 🐾 *See ❻ on page 106.*

The wetlands in the Flat Creek Nature Area are home to many species of birds, and you can pick up a brochure at the Recreation Center to help identify what you see and hear. But with my dogs around, all I've ever seen here are the ducks and herons. Every other creature beats a hasty retreat when they hear us coming. What can't get away, though, are the trees and plants. The trail, which leads off of the path to the Frederick J. Brown Jr. Amphitheater, takes you rapidly from uplands-type plants to the boardwalk over the wetlands. As interesting as the wetlands are to me, I have to admit that Bandit and Laddie are unimpressed with the abrupt disappearance of the pines and the arrival of plants that live in water. They like the way the wetlands smell, though, so this short walk (a half mile round-trip) offers something for all of us. Plans are in the works to extend the boardwalk over the next five years, and an observation tower is also being considered.

When you tire of the wetlands, there are more than three miles of paved paths adjacent to the preserve. If you don't feel like walking, check out the William L. Davis BMX Complex. You'll usually find a crowd racing their bikes over the hilly terrain. In addition, this park offers a skateboard area with a half-moon-shaped ramp, a senior center (The Gathering Place), plenty of picnic facilities, and a children's play area. You must leash at this park.

Park hours are daily from dawn to dusk. From Highway 74, turn left on Kelly Drive, then right into the park on McIntosh Trail. (770) 631-2542.

• Glenloch Recreation Center 🐾 *See* ❼ *on page 106.*

This recreation center has just about everything for your human companions, including a pool, soccer fields, tennis and basketball courts, and children's play area, but is only worth a quick stop for your leashed pooch.

Hours are daily from dawn to dusk. From Highway 74, turn left on Highway 54, also known as Floy Farr Parkway. Turn right on Peachtree Parkway, left on Bridlepath, and left on Steven's Entry. The park is on your right. (770) 631-2542.

• Huddleston Pond 🐾🐾 🦴 *See* ❽ *on page 106.*

You'll find one of Peachtree City's small ponds in this delightful park. The trail around the pond is approximately half a mile long and is heavily used by other dog lovers. Stop at the gazebo and watch the ducks. During a half-hour visit, we met one chocolate and one black Labrador retriever and two cocker spaniels, all out walking their people. If you're in the mood for a longer stroll, you can hook up with one of the many paved pathways through the city here. Dogs must wear leashes.

Hours are daily from dawn to dusk. From Highway 74, turn left on Highway 54, also known as Floy Farr Parkway. Turn right on Peachtree Parkway and left on Wingate Road. The park is on your left. (770) 631-2542.

• **Lake Kedron** 🐾 *See* **9** *on page 106.*

The park at Lake Kedron is basically just a parking lot and boat docks. I mention it only because it's a convenient parking spot if you're going to investigate any of the miles of paved pathways in Peachtree City. Dogs must be leashed.

Hours are daily from dawn to dusk. From Highway 74, turn left on Peachtree Parkway, then right into the parking lot. (770) 631-2542.

• **Luther Glass Park/Braelinn Ponds** 🐾🐾🐾
See **10** *on page 106.*

This is Bandit's favorite park. The easily accessible ponds are a short walk down one of the golf cart paths. Surrounded by woods, the paths wind around the ponds and over bridges, connecting with the many miles of paved paths through the rest of the city. You can sit in a shady gazebo and watch your pooch swim or sniff at the ducks, or take a slow, relaxing walk as she checks out the information left by local canines on the trees. Believe it or not, water-loving Bandit is actually more interested in nosing around the trees than jumping in the ponds here. Laddie, of course, is fascinated by them, too, since they seem to be a favorite potty stop for pups.

The boys and I have met many other dog lovers on each visit here. While our pets investigate each other's unmentionable body parts, we humans try not to notice and talk about our favorite places to walk in the area. One resident had to tell me what a small paved area was for (golf cart parking). Another volunteered to demonstrate the fitness equipment when I mentioned I'd never seen anyone using it. Be sure to leash up.

Hours are daily from dawn to dusk. From Highway 74, turn left on Kelly Drive, right on Peachtree Parkway, then left across from Braelinn Green. (770) 631-2542.

• **Pebblepocket Park** 🐾 *See* **11** *on page 106.*

This is a fairly large park with quite a few amenities, including a pool, tennis and basketball courts, a children's play area, and a large shaded area to walk your dog. It hooks up with the paved pathway system, so you and your leashed pooch can walk as long as you like.

The main drawback of this park is that it's a little hard to find (see the directions below).

Hours are daily from dawn to dusk. From Highway 74, turn left on Highway 54, also known as Floy Farr Parkway. Turn right on Willowbend Road and right on Hip Pocket Road. The park is bordered by Hip Pocket Road and Pebblestump Point, hence the odd name. (770) 631-2542.

• **Picnic Park** 🐾 *See* ⓬ *on page 106.*

This small park is on the shore of Lake Peachtree. Besides the obvious appeal of the lake, you'll find nice wooded areas in which to walk your pet on a warm day. You can sit at one of the picnic tables and watch dogs chasing Frisbees or let your pooch join in the fun. If you've the time for a longer walk, you can set off down one of the paved pathways here.

On our first visit, I wasn't sure if the paved pathways met up with the main trail system or led to private homes, so Bandit and I decided to check it out for ourselves. We wandered through what looked like increasingly residential areas for more than an hour. Every few minutes, we would catch sight of a young man walking a rottweiler in the distance. We never got close enough to speak, as we seemed to be heading in different directions, but I would periodically catch a flash of red from his T-shirt and see the large dog. They were moving along at a pretty good speed, and Bandit and I were wandering at his normal, easily distracted pace. I never did figure out how they got out of the residential area Bandit and I seemed to be stuck in, but for the rest of the day, as Bandit and I would drive to a new park and take a walk, we'd catch glimpses of the pair in the distance, still moving with determination. Obviously the interconnected trail system takes a more direct route than the road system. Remember to leash your pooch.

Hours are daily from dawn to dusk. The park is near Pebblepocket Park. From Highway 74, turn left on Highway 54, also known as Floy Farr Parkway. Turn right on Willowbend Road. The park is just past Hip Pocket Road on the right. (770) 631-2542.

• **Riley Field Recreation Area** 🐾 *See* ⓭ *on page 106.*

Many of Peachtree City's parks are located near schools, and Riley Field Recreation Area is no exception. Amenities include football, baseball, and soccer fields, and a children's play area—great for people but not worth much more than a quick stop for leashed pooches.

Hours are daily from dawn to dusk. From Highway 74, turn left on Wisdom Road. The park is on your left, just before Peachtree Elementary School. (770) 631-2542.

• **Rock Spray Pond** 🐾 *See* ⓮ *on page 106.*

This wonderful spot rates only a paw because there's no real parking. You'll have to stop on a cul-de-sac where the paved path comes out of the woods, and walk in to the main path by the pond.

I've never seen anyone else on the paths by this pond, which seems odd since it's in a lovely location, and it also appears larger than the other ponds in the city. Laddie and Bandit haven't found any evidence of other dogs, either, although they have stumbled across several fire ant mounds. This is also the only place where we have encountered poison ivy in Peachtree City. Remember to leash your pooch.

Hours are daily from dawn to dusk. From Highway 74, turn left on Crosstown Drive, right onto Clarin Drive, and left onto Clarin Way to reach the park. (770) 631-2542.

TYRONE
PARKS AND RECREATION AREAS

• **Shamrock Park** 🐾 *See ⓯ on page 106.*

Bandit has a lot of fun at this small park, but that's because his water radar kicks in and he leads us straight to the small lake. He wades in, lies down, and begins his favorite hobby of blowing bubbles. Laddie finds this activity somewhat embarrassing and won't watch, but one time a small crowd gathered to enjoy Bandit's antics. Leashes are required.

While there are no real paths, the park has a long frontage on Senoia Road. Although we haven't run into other dogs here, they must be visiting when we aren't around, since Laddie always has to stop at each tree along the road. Bandit prefers the grassy field in front of the lake, where he promptly forgets his obedience lessons and begins pulling on the leash to get to the water. It's amazing how perfectly he responds to a command if I'm holding his favorite treat. Both my dogs get amnesia as soon as they're in a park.

Hours are from dawn to dusk. Take Interstate 85 south from Atlanta to the Fairburn exit. Turn left on Highway 74, then right on Senoia Road. The park is on the left. (770) 487-4694.

FORSYTH COUNTY

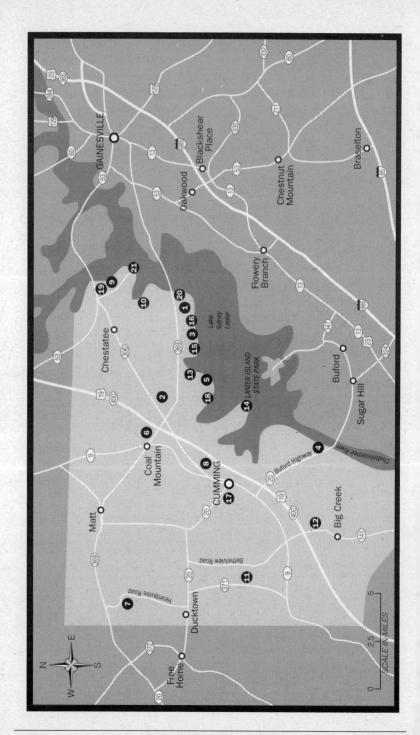

7
FORSYTH COUNTY

Howlelujah! Believe it or not, there's no leash law in Forsyth County. While some of the towns and parks in Forsyth have separate ordinances, as do parks run by the United States Army Corps of Engineers, it's actually possible to let your dog off leash in many areas. The county rule is that pooches must be under your control (by voice or leash) at all times, and since you know your dog best, you'll have to determine what works for you and your pooch. (While voice control worked fine for Trixie, Laddie and Bandit can't always be trusted off leash.)

Many of the great parks in this county are clustered around Lake Sidney Lanier, making them a real treat for water-loving pooches and people. A number of parks rate three paws, but unfortunately many of these are United States Army Corps of Engineers parks, where leashes are a must.

The parks that are part of the United States Army Corps of Engineers system have day-use fees of $3 per vehicle per day. The boat launch fee is $2 per day, and the swimming beach fee is $1 per person per day. An annual pass can be purchased for $25 per family. Golden Age and Golden Access Passports are half price. Children under 12 and dogs of all ages are free.

CUMMING
PARKS AND RECREATION AREAS

• **Athens Park** 🐾🐾 *See* ❶ *on page 118.*

This lakefront park juts out at a small point to provide a wonderful view of Lake Sidney Lanier and plenty of good water access. Leashes are required, and since it's less popular than some of the other parks, you and your pup may have it to yourselves. Most of the park is heavily shaded, so even longhaired dogs such as Laddie like it. And, of course, water dogs like Bandit will spend most of their time in the water. Keep your pooch away from the boat ramps.

Hours are daily from 7 A.M. to 10 P.M. United States Army Corps of Engineers system fees apply (see above). From Atlanta, take Highway 400 north to Highway 369 (Browns Bridge Road) and turn right.

Turn right on Vanns Tavern Road, then left onto Athens Park Road and follow it to where the road ends at the park. (770) 945-9531.

• Bennett Park 🐾🐾 🐕 *See ❷ on page 118.*

The fact that this large park is one of the few, the proud, the leash-free makes up for the lack of shade. Bandit is so overjoyed to be untethered that he thinks this place is heaven. Be sure to bring plenty of water for you and your dog, though even with a drink break, Bandit wilts in the sun here. Trails in the park wind around some of the baseball fields. Remember that you're required to have your dog under voice control at all times, and enjoy! The park also has picnic areas, tennis and basketball courts, and a playground.

Hours are daily from 7 A.M. to 11 P.M. From Atlanta, take Highway 400 north to exit 17 (Keith Bridge Road/Highway 306). Turn right, then right on Parks Road, then left on Burrus Mill Road to reach the park. (770) 781-2215.

• Bethel Park 🐾🐾🐾 *See ❸ on page 118.*

This park is generally not as crowded as some of the other lake access parks. Although there are no real trails, you'll find lots of places to walk your dog on the gravel and dirt roads. Leashes are mandatory as you and your pooch explore this large park. Large trees provide shade, but if your pup overheats, she can always cool off in the lake.

Hours are daily from 7 A.M. to 10 P.M. United States Army Corps of Engineers system fees apply (see page 119). From Atlanta, take Highway 400 north to Highway 369 and turn right, then right on Bethel Road. Turn left onto Swiss Air Road and follow it into the park. (770) 945-9531.

• Buford State Fish Hatchery 🔥 *See ❹ on page 118.*

Though the public is welcome at the Buford State Fish Hatchery, it's probably more interesting for you than your pooch. Don't bring a water dog here; since the ponds are off-limits to him, he'll just strain at his leash the whole time.

Hours are daily from 7 A.M. to 10 P.M. From Atlanta, take Highway 400 north to exit 14 (Buford Highway) and turn right. Turn left onto Pruitt Road, then right onto Trout Place Road and follow it into the park. (770) 945-9531.

• Charleston Park 🐾🐾🐾 🐾 *See ❺ on page 118.*

This lovely park has two trails winding through the woods and plenty of lake access for your leashed pup's enjoyment. He'll like sniffing out signs of the locals and splashing about in the water.

There's shade to keep a nonwater dog cool, and grassy fields for a game of Frisbee. Leashes are required. The park also has three boat ramps, a playground, and picnic areas.

Hours are daily from 7 A.M. to 10 P.M. United States Army Corps of Engineers system fees apply (see page 119). From Atlanta, take Highway 400 north to Highway 369 and turn right. Turn right on Charleston Park Road and follow it into the park. (770) 945-9531.

• Coal Mountain Park 🐾🐕 See ❻ on page 118.

This small park consists of three baseball fields, a basketball court, and a few picnic tables. While you and your dog could explore the entire park in less than 10 minutes, take your time and let your pup relish the off-leash novelty. As long as your pooch is under voice control, she can enjoy freedom from the tie that binds.

Hours are daily from dawn to dusk. From Atlanta, take Highway 400 north to the Browns Bridge Road exit and turn left. Turn right on Settingdown Road. The park is on your right. (770) 781-2215.

• Covered Bridge 🐾🐾🦴🐕 See ❼ on page 118.

Looking for a respite from city life? Few people in the Atlanta area know this covered bridge exists. Even better, it's off-leash bliss for your dog, as long as you can control him with your voice. The bridge is closed to traffic, so walk your pooch across and down to the creek. Water access is easy for dogs, and the sound of Settingdown Creek tumbling over the rocks drowns out the noise from civilization. It's a pleasant place to sit and eat your lunch while your pup splashes in the water. Too bad about all the trash that has been dumped on the other side of the bridge near the road. It's such a shame this historic structure isn't being protected.

Hours are daily from dawn to dusk. From Atlanta, take Highway 400 north to the Highway 20 exit and turn left. Turn right onto Heardsville Road, then take the first right after Pooles Mill Road to reach the bridge. (770) 781-2215.

• Cumming City Park 🐾🐾🐾🦴🐕 See ❽ on page 118.

Your pup can strut her stuff off leash at this delightful park, which has most of the best aspects of a dog park. A creek with good water access for your pooch cuts through the center of the park; a quarter-mile walking path gives her a chance to stretch her legs; and the trees around the perimeter are a great place to catch up on all the news from local canines. Remember to keep your leash-free wonder under voice control. The park also has picnic areas, baseball fields, basketball and tennis courts, a swimming pool, and a playground.

Park hours are daily from 8 A.M. to 10 P.M. From Atlanta, take Highway 400 north to Cumming. Turn left on exit 15 (Bald Ridge Road), then make a right turn on Pilgrim Mill Road. The park is on the right. (770) 781-2030.

• **Keith Bridge Park** 😺😺😺 🐾 *See* ❾ *on page 118.*

The paved trail through this park is approximately a mile long. With the good lake access, woods for sniffing, and an open field for sunning, your dog will be delighted with your choice for a day out. Pups aren't allowed on the beach and must be on leash at all times. You'll also find picnic areas and boat ramps here.

Hours are daily from 7 A.M. to 10 P.M. United States Army Corps of Engineers system fees apply (see page 119). From Atlanta, take Highway 400 north to exit 17 (Keith Bridge Road) and turn right. Stay on Keith Bridge Road into the park. If you hit Highway 53, you've missed a turn about 100 yards back. (770) 945-9531.

• **Long Hollow Access Point** 😺😺 🐾 *See* ❿ *on page 118.*

Highlights for your pooch at this lovely spot include paved trails that wind around the park and easy lake access, plus a grassy field right on the lake and a wooded area at the back where dogs like to nose around for signs of the locals. Amenities include picnic areas, a playground, and boat ramps. Pooches aren't allowed on the beach and must remain leashed.

Hours are daily from 7 A.M. to 10 P.M. United States Army Corps of Engineers system fees apply (see page 119). From Atlanta, take Highway 400 north to exit 17 (Keith Bridge Road). Turn right, then right again on Waldrip Road. Go left onto Bryant Road and follow it to the end. This park is right next to Lockheed Campground, a private campground for the use of company employees and their guests. (770) 945-9531.

• **Midway Park** 😺😺 🐾 🐕 *See* ⓫ *on page 118.*

Here's your chance to see if all those hours of obedience training really worked: dogs under voice control can explore this large park leash-free. A paved trail circles the baseball and soccer fields, but without much shade, your pooch will quickly heat up in the sun. Bring plenty of water. The park also has a football field, basketball and tennis courts, and picnic areas.

Hours are daily from 7 A.M. to 11 P.M. From Atlanta, take Highway 400 north to the Cumming/Bald Ridge Road exit and turn left. Turn right onto Highway 20/Canton Road, then left onto Post Road/Highway 371. Midway Park is on the left. (770) 781-2215.

• **Sharon Springs Park** 🐾🐾 🐕 *See ⑫ on page 118.*

Romp with your leash-free pooch on the 2.25-mile trail around the ball fields at this park. Bandit and Laddie take it at a snail's pace, finding a new scent to sniff every foot or so. Though part of the heavily used path dips through the woods, most of it isn't shaded, so be sure to bring water for your dog and a hat for yourself. I've come home with a sunburn even in the winter. (Where is my "woodswoman" hat when I need it!) The trail is paved, and a sign at the entrance states that only soft, rubber-soled shoes may be worn. It also says that no skating is allowed, though I've never seen this rule enforced. As always in Forsyth County, off-leash dogs must be under voice control. The park also has picnic tables with grills; soccer, baseball, and football fields; and tennis and basketball courts.

Hours are daily from daylight to 11 P.M., but the walking track closes at dusk. From Atlanta, take Highway 400 north to the Highway 141/Peachtree Parkway exit and turn right. Turn left onto Sharon Road, and then right into the park. (770) 781-2215.

• **Six Mile Creek Access Point** 🐾 *See ⑬ on page 118.*

While you and your pup won't find any trails at this park, there are plenty of places to walk on the gravel roads that lead to the boat ramps. Lake access is good and there are lots of trees for your dog to sniff while wearing the mandatory leash.

Hours are daily from 7 A.M. to 10 P.M. United States Army Corps of Engineers system fees apply (see page 119). From Atlanta, take Highway 400 north to Highway 369 and turn right, then turn right again into the park. (770) 945-9531.

• **Tidwell Park** 🐾🐾 *See ⑭ on page 118.*

If your dog likes water, she'll enjoy the lake at this park. A short path leads through a wooded area. Bring your lunch and relax on a blanket or one of the benches by the lake. There are no picnic tables. The park is used primarily as a boat launch, and leashes are required.

Hours are daily from 7 A.M. to 10 P.M. United States Army Corps of Engineers system fees apply (see page 119). From Atlanta, take Highway 400 north to exit 16 (Pilgrim Mill Road) and turn right. Follow Pilgrim Mill Road into the park. (770) 945-9531.

• **Two Mile Creek Access Point** 🐾🐾 *See ⑮ on page 118.*

Wonderful lakefront picnic sites are a highlight of this park. Two great sites are out on a point of land in the lake. A small island lies just offshore. When the lake is down, you can walk across a narrow spit of land to the island. If you have a water-loving dog like Bandit, this short jaunt will be the high point of the day. Even Laddie enjoys walking alongside me in the lake while I stick to the trail. Leashes are mandatory.

Hours are daily from 7 A.M. to 10 P.M. United States Army Corps of Engineers system fees apply (see page 119). From Atlanta, take Highway 400 north to Highway 369 and turn right. Turn right on Bethel Road and follow it into the park. (770) 945-9531.

• Vanns Tavern Access Point 🐾🐾 *See ⓰ on page 118.*

Water dogs love splashing around in the lake at this park. It helps keep them cool, too, since it can get sunny and hot here. I like to relax on a blanket and watch the boats on the lake while my dogs bark at the geese. Leashes are a must.

Hours are daily from 7 A.M. to 10 P.M. United States Army Corps of Engineers system fees apply (see page 119). From Atlanta, take Highway 400 north to the Highway 369 exit, and turn right. Turn right on Vanns Tavern Road and follow it into the park. (770) 945-9531.

• Veterans Memorial Park 🐾 🐕 *See ⓱ on page 118.*

Though this small park is little more than a square open field with no water, shade, or amenities, your dog can run around leash-free, as long as he responds to your commands.

Hours are daily from 7 A.M. to 11 P.M. From Atlanta, take Highway 400 north to exit 15 (Cumming) and turn left onto Bald Ridge Road, which becomes Main Street. Turn left onto Castleberry Road, then left into the park. (770) 781-2215.

• Young Deer Creek Access Point 🐾🐾 *See ⓲ on page 118.*

Your leashed pooch will find lots of places to get into the lake at this small park, though he's restricted from using the beach. Although there are no real trails here, the park does have a large squirrel population. You'll find some shade, but the park is mostly open.

Hours are daily from 7 A.M. to 10 P.M. United States Army Corps of Engineers system fees apply (see page 119). The park is located on Heard Road. Take Highway 400 north to the Highway 369 exit and turn right. Turn right on Shady Grove Road, right on Heard Road, and follow it into the park. (770) 945-9531.

PLACES TO STAY

Bald Ridge Creek Campground: This campground closes during the winter months. The 78 sites are fairly private, and many of them are right on the lake. Dogs must be leashed. Campsites run $15 per night, with a 14-day limit. Take Highway 400 north to exit 16 (Pilgrim Mill Road) and turn right. Turn right on Sinclair Shore Road. Turn left onto Bald Ridge Park Road and follow it into the campground. (770) 945-9531.

Sawnee Public Use Area: Many of the campsites here are on the lake. Though there are no trails, you'll find plenty of places to walk through the woods with your pooch. Campsite fees range from $10 to $15, depending on hookups. Leashes are required. The campground is closed during the winter months. Take Highway 400 north to exit 14 (Buford Highway) and turn left. Turn right on Atlanta Road, then right on Buford Dam Road, and watch for the signs to the campground on the left. (770) 945-9531.

Shady Grove Park: You'll find mostly private campsites separated by trees at this campground. Many of the campsites are right on the lake, with easy water access for your pooch. Paved trails lead through the campground and are a great chance for exercise. Campsite fees range from $8 to $15. Leashes are required. This campground closes during the winter months. Take Highway 400 north to Highway 369 and turn right. Turn right on Shady Grove Road, then left onto Shadburn Ferry Road and follow it into the park. (770) 945-9531.

GAINESVILLE

Although Gainesville is technically in Hall County, it's included here because it's just across the lake from Forsyth County and continues the cluster of parks around Lake Sidney Lanier.

PARKS AND RECREATION AREAS

• **Little Hall Park** 🐾🐾🐾 🐾 *See* ⑲ *on page 118.*

Step just across the border into Hall County to reach this park with paved trails that wind through the woods. Lake access is plentiful and easy, so your pooch should be able to get her paws wet, even though she must be leashed. This is one of the best access parks because it has several points that stick out into the water, giving nearly every spot a wonderful view.

On one of my visits here, I was taking a walk along the shore, camera in hand. I came up over a rock and looked down at the beach, startling a great blue heron. I fumbled to get the camera ready and snapped one picture as the bird took off, his feet trailing behind him. I ended up with a very strange shot that even I have trouble recognizing as two large feet, with the rest of the bird out of focus. I'm glad Bandit didn't see the bird: he's been known to cower at the site of ducks and geese, and a four-foot heron might make for some bad doggy dreams. You'll also find lots of picnic tables with grills, boat ramps, and rest rooms at this park.

Hours are daily from 7 A.M. to 10 P.M. United States Army Corps of Engineers system fees apply (see page 119). Take Highway 400 north to exit 17 (Keith Bridge Road), turning right. Turn right again on Highway 53, then right into the park. (770) 945-9531.

• Mountain View Park 🐾🐾 *See ⑳ on page 118.*

On my first visit to Mountain View Park, I walked up and down the lakefront looking for a mountain view across the lake to justify the name. This was no small feat, since the park is on steep terrain and heavily wooded. It wasn't until I gave up and turned to leave that I realized the view is of the park, from the lake, since the park is considerably higher than the rest of the land around the water. Although there are no real trails, there isn't much brush, so it's easy enough to wander through the woods. The boat ramp, which hasn't been in use on any of our visits, provides convenient access to the lake. Elsewhere you and your pooch will have to scramble down a four-foot drop to the water.

This park consists of the boat launch area, the "mountain," and a separate day-use and picnic area that may be permanently closed until there are budget funds to repair the rest rooms. Leashes are mandatory.

Hours are daily from 7 A.M. to 10 P.M. United States Army Corps of Engineers system fees apply (see page 119). Take Highway 400 north to the Browns Bridge Road exit and turn right. Turn right onto Old 141 Road and follow it into the park. (770) 945-9531.

• River Forks Park 🐾 *See ㉑ on page 118.*

This small park is next to a campground. The day-use fee structure here is a little different, because this is a Hall County park, not a United States Army Corps of Engineers park. The fee is $2 per day for up to six passengers in a car. Dogs aren't allowed on the beach and must be on leash throughout the park. Although you won't find any designated trails, your pooch can wander through the wooded area and splash about in the lake as long as he pleases. Most of the amenities are in the campground, but there are picnic tables and boat ramps in the day-use area.

Campsite fees range from $8 to $15, depending on the season and hookups. The campground is closed in January and February.

Hours are daily from 10 A.M. to 7 P.M. Take Highway 400 north to exit 17 (Keith Bridge Road), turning right. Keith Bridge Road ends at the park. (770) 531-3952.

PLACES TO STAY

Duckett Mill Park: This campground has 112 tent sites and 91 trailer sites with hookups, costing $8 to $15 per night. There are several boat ramps. United States Army Corps of Engineers system fees apply (see page 119), and leashes are mandatory. The campground is open from April through mid-September. Take Highway 400 north to exit 17 (Keith Bridge Road), turning right. Turn right on Highway 53, then right onto Duckett Mill Road, and follow it to the campground at the end. (770) 532-9802.

River Forks Park Campground: See River Forks Park on page 126.

LAKE LANIER ISLANDS

PLACES TO STAY

Lake Lanier Islands Campground: Although technically in Hall County, this campground is included because of its popularity and proximity to Forsyth County. It's near all of the attractions of Lake Lanier Islands, which are unfortunately off-limits to your pooch. The campground is conveniently located for trips to many lake parks, however. Dogs are welcome at no additional charge. Tent sites are about $15, and trailer sites with water and electrical hookups are $20. From Atlanta, take Interstate 85 north to Interstate 985 north. Take exit 1 and turn left, following the signs to the park and the campground. (770) 932-7270.

FULTON
COUNTY

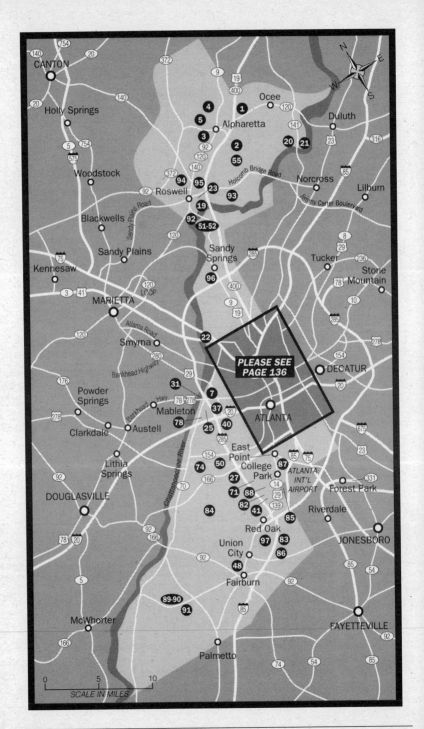

PLEASE SEE
PAGE 136

8
FULTON COUNTY

Like a big dog on your favorite chair, Atlanta sprawls over many counties, but the majority of the city lies within the confines of Fulton County. While most guidebooks to the Atlanta area spend a great deal of time debating how many Peachtree Roads, Streets, and Circles there are in the city, I've found that neither Laddie nor Bandit cares. Bandit might want to join the argument if he'd ever been able to shag a peach on one of our walks. He loves fruit, but we've never spotted a ripe peach (or even an unripe one) while wandering the streets. Actually, we don't spend much time wandering the streets, since Fulton County is blessed with an abundance of wonderful places to take your dog. If you live in the area, you've certainly been to Piedmont Park (see page 154), but there are many other parks available to pooches and their people. You're sure to find several in this chapter that you've never visited, and may be as surprised as I was to find a dog park near the Carter Presidential Center (see page 140) or just as amazed that you can walk your pooch at a different park in the county each weekend for almost five years.

Like most of the counties in the Atlanta metropolitan area, Fulton has a leash law. But surprisingly enough, there's no pooper-scooper law for the county, though there is for the city of Atlanta. Two cities outside of Fulton, Douglasville and Canton, have banned dogs from their parks due to complaints about dogs running loose and an abundance of dog mess. So despite the lack of a county law, do carry plastic grocery bags on your outings and use them to deposit your pup's mess in the nearest trash can.

ALPHARETTA
PARKS AND RECREATION AREAS

• **Alpharetta City Park** 🐾 🐾 *See* ❶ *on page 130.*

In-line skaters whiz by on the paved trail that runs along the road in this park, so keep a tight grip on your dog's leash. Even the mildest-mannered pup might overreact to children speeding by on wheels. Also be careful when you drive into the park. Even though there are several baseball and soccer fields, a game of street hockey is often taking place in one of the parking lots. Bandit is a sucker for the small pond with easy access to the water. Other amenities include picnic pavilions and tennis courts.

Hours are daily from 7 A.M. to 10 P.M. Take Highway 400 to the Haynes Bridge Road exit and turn left. Turn left at the dead end onto Duluth Street, then right onto Main Street. Turn left onto Cogburn Road, and the park is on your left. (770) 442-0105.

• **Autrey Mill Nature Preserve and Heritage Center**
🐾🐾🐾🐾 🐾 *See ❷ on page 130.*

This little-known park is a real gem. It not only has a wonderful trail that winds through the woods to a creek with good access to the water, but it's also both a nature preserve and a heritage center. Wildflowers along the trail make it particularly attractive in the spring and summer months. A special program on the wildflowers in the preserve is offered in May. You and your leashed pup will find plenty of shade as you wind through the woods to Sal's Creek, where dogs love to cool their pads. The trail is a mile and a half long, and the deep woods keep it cool even in the summer. You may also want to read the signs along the trail about forest succession, as this once heavily wooded area, stripped of its trees for farmland, is reclaimed by the forest. Because of the abundant wildlife, your pup should find plenty of interesting smells along the way. Mine are startled by the sounds of the frogs croaking in the wetlands.

The park takes a unique approach to education by incorporating the area's heritage into all of the nature programs. Call the number at the end of this write-up to get a current listing of park programs, which in 1996 included backyard habitat information, nature walks, animal identification from tracks, native tree and wildflower identification, and bird migration, among others.

I spoke with the program director, Michelle Sienkiewicz, about the buildings on the property, which date to the 1800s. My favorite is the deBray Chapel, a tiny stone chapel with rough-hewn wood doors that's frequently rented for weddings and special events. The blue and white Mediterranean-style floor tiles and the stained glass windows are beautiful. Other historic structures and rooms at the park can also be rented for group functions.

Michelle also told me a local legend about the Ghost Monkeys. As the story goes, sometime after the turn of the century, area residents were alarmed to find unusual animal prints in the woods. The locals formed a posse and followed the tracks to a small group of monkeys, who had apparently escaped when a circus train derailed in nearby Duluth. It's unfortunate that humans frequently destroy that which is strange to them or what they don't understand, but the monkeys were killed and eaten. One of the artists participating in the annual Arts Exhibition sculpted the Ghost Monkeys. They have been placed along the trail to add to your experience.

The Welcome Center—which, true to its name, welcomes dogs—is housed in an 1880s farmhouse and contains an exhibit of many of the types of animals found in the preserve, including red and gray foxes, flying squirrels, turtles, rat snakes, and hares. Other animals living in the park include beavers, raccoons, opossums, chipmunks, deer, wild turkeys, woodpeckers (including the yellow-shafted flicker, red-bellied, and red-headed), owls (barn, great horned, and screech), and red-tailed hawks. When a Fulton County sheriff moved into the upstairs at the Welcome Center to provide security, he spent several sleepless nights. The cry of a screech owl sounds just like a woman screaming, which is guaranteed to get a quick response from a sheriff.

The park is run by the Autrey Mill Nature Preserve Association, a nonprofit group that leases the land from Fulton County. They rely on donations and rental income to operate their many programs for the community. One way to help is to become a member of the association. Members receive a quarterly newsletter and special information and discounts on programs, and may volunteer to help on any of the association projects, from building restoration to trail management to general office work. If you have spare time, there's certain to be a project to fit your interests. You can pick up a membership application at the Welcome Center or write to the address below and one will be mailed to you.

My shopping radar went off as we entered the Welcome Center. Yes, they have some items for sale, including T-shirts and books.

If you're in the area, you're welcome to come out and eat your lunch at one of the picnic tables at this peaceful spot.

Hours are daily from dawn to dusk. From Atlanta, take Highway 400 north to the East Holcomb Bridge Road exit and turn right. Turn left at the fork onto Old Alabama Road, then left onto Autrey Mill Road and the park. Be forewarned that Autrey Mill Road is a gravel road and in poor repair, making for a bumpy ride. (770) 664-0660.

• **Hembree Road Park** 🐾🐾 *See ❸ on page 130.*
The one-mile graded loop trail at this lovely park drops below the road and along a creek, with shade most of the way. Your leashed

pooch will have a grand time splashing in the water and nosing around the wooded area. Tennis courts and baseball fields are among the amenities.

The park is open daily during daylight hours. Take Highway 400 north to Haynes Bridge Road and turn left. Turn left onto Morrison Parkway, which becomes Hembree Road. The park is on your right. (770) 442-0105.

• **Providence Park Outdoor Center** 😊 😊 😊 🐾
See ❹ on page 130.

With 13 short nature trails, a 28-acre lake, 42 acres of pine and hardwood trees, an old rock quarry, and a wetlands area, this park is sure to make any dog wag her tail. The land on the other side of the lake is not within the park, and you'll see cows wading in to cool off. The nature trails are all less than a third of a mile long and can be hiked in one larger loop. Dogs love to wander through the woods and along the trails, then cool off in the lake, which is inhabited by geese, ducks, and herons. Because of the topography of the land, rappelling, rock climbing, canoeing, map and compass reading, and backpacking are all taught at the park—for people, not pups, of course. Be sure to leash up here.

Hours are daily from 6 A.M. to midnight. Take Highway 400 to Haynes Bridge Road and turn left. Turn left at Duluth Street, then right onto Main Street. Turn left onto Mayfield Road, right onto Providence Road, and right into the park. (770) 740-2419.

• **Wills Park** 😊 😊 😊 🐾 *See ❺ on page 130.*

The city of Alpharetta took over maintenance of this park from the county in 1996, and a master plan was in the works when this book went to press. Overuse in the past has led to erosion problems. Even so, your leashed pooch will love it here. Horse shows are held in the equestrian center, and occasionally dog shows as well, so there are always interesting smells in that area. A creek with good access runs through the back. The park contains large open fields and heavily wooded areas, with trails crisscrossing throughout. Bring your lunch and plan to spend several hours. My dogs are never bored. Also here are baseball, football and soccer fields, tennis and basketball courts, a Frisbee golf course, a swimming pool, a game room, and picnic facilities.

Hours are daily from 6 A.M. to midnight. Take Highway 400 to Haynes Bridge Road and turn left. Turn left onto Morrison Parkway, which becomes Hembree Road. Turn right onto Wills Road. The park is on the right. (770) 410-5845.

SHOPPING IN ALPHARETTA

Petsmart: If you see someone in Petsmart who appears petless, check their shoulders. Not only is this a great place to parade your pooch, but on any visit you're likely to see an assortment of reptiles and birds accompanying their humans on a shopping excursion. And why not? Petsmart caters to pets of all persuasions. I like to think that it's particularly friendly to dogs, judging from the reactions my boys get from the staff and other customers. It's a great socialization experience for Bandit and other young dogs, and a fun place to shop for that new bandanna he's been wanting. 6370 North Point Parkway, Alpharetta, GA 30202; (770) 343-8511.

RESTAURANTS

Sonic Drive-In: Get a blast from the past at this old drive-in. You and your pooch can order by intercom from your car, and your food will be delivered by carhops on roller skates, just the way it used to be, while old rock and roll plays over the speakers. 1495 Highway 9, Alpharetta, GA 30202; (770) 751-8859.

PLACES TO STAY

Residence Inn by Marriott: This inn is a bit pricey at $59 to $162 for a one bedroom, and $152 to $162 for a two bedroom—and it gets worse. There's a nonrefundable pet fee of $100 per dog for a one bedroom, and $200 per dog for a two bedroom. You'll have much more room than at a standard hotel, though, plus a kitchenette. The rate includes breakfast and happy hour. 5465 Windward Parkway West, Alpharetta, GA 30201; (770) 664-0664.

ATLANTA

Atlanta has hundreds of city parks. All of them have a pooper-scooper ordinance, so be sure to bring plastic grocery bags or some other method of collecting your dog's waste. The parks run the gamut from tiny triangular stopovers that are good for a quick squat to hundreds of acres for a daylong outing. In between are the many parks with streams and creeks to splash in, such as South Bend Park (see page 156), and drier parks with large trees for shade and a good sniff, such as English Park (see page 145).

PARKS AND RECREATION AREAS

• **Adams Park** 🐾 *See* ❻ *on page 136.*

Adams Park has no trails, but there are many areas around the ball fields and picnic areas to walk your leashed pup. Human

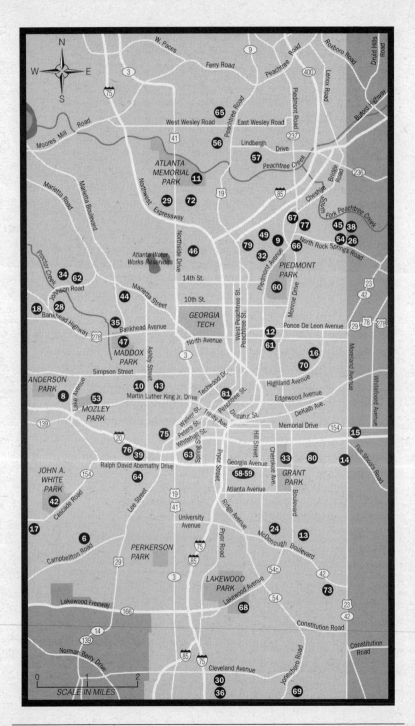

diversions include a pool, a gym, picnic areas with grills, and baseball fields.

Park hours are daily from 8 A.M. to 11 P.M. Take Interstate 285 south to Cascade Road, and then turn inside the Perimeter. Go right on Delowe Drive, which leads you straight into Adams Park. (404) 756-1827.

• **A. D. Williams Park** 🐾 *See ❼ on page 130.*

This large, heavily wooded park has been left undeveloped and has degenerated into a dumping ground for old tires and mattresses. If the community would only clean it up and put in some trails, it would have a lot of potential. There's a football field, a basketball court, and a playground, but I doubt they're in current use. You and your leashed canine companion won't want to stay any longer than nature requires.

A. D. Williams Park hours are daily from 6 A.M. to 11 P.M. Take the Bankhead Highway exit off of Interstate 285 and turn inside. Turn left onto James Jackson Parkway. The park is located at the corner of James Jackson Parkway Northwest and Northcrest Road. (404) 794-4690.

• **Anderson Park** 🐾🐾 👣 *See ❽ on page 136.*

Both you and your leashed pup will enjoy this park. The walking trail and the combination of open fields and heavily wooded areas make for a great place to spend an afternoon. Check the back of the tennis courts for stray balls. On one of our visits here, we found two balls and met two other dogs walking their best friends. Be sure to let your pooch spend time sniffing out the locals in the woods. You'll also find baseball fields, a swimming pool, a track, picnic pavilions, and a playground.

Park hours are daily from 6 A.M. to 11 P.M. Go north on Hightower Road from its exit off Interstate 20, then turn right onto Simpson Road. Turn right again onto Anderson Avenue Northwest. Anderson Park is located near the West Lake MARTA Station. (404) 794-1221.

• **Ansley Park** 🐾 *See ❾ on page 136.*

Bordered by Piedmont Avenue Northeast and Avery Drive Northeast, this tiny triangular spit of land is only worth a quick squat. Leashes are required. Parking is on street only.

Hours are daily from 6 A.M. to 11 P.M. Take Monroe Drive south from Interstate 85 and turn right onto Montgomery Ferry Road/Polo Drive. Turn left onto Beverly Terrace, and right onto Avery Drive. (404) 817-6766.

• **Ashby Garden Park/Mayson Turner Park/Washington Park**
🐾🐾 *See* ⑩ *on page 136.*

I couldn't stop laughing when the boys and I first visited this park. Normally, when you find what appears to be a single park with more than one name, there's some sort of natural division separating the parks, such as a cross street, creek, or ravine. But in the case of this park, each corner of the triangle simply has a sign with a different name. I can just picture a meeting to decide the name of the new park, with opinion split and no compromise in sight.

There are actually two areas to this park, one of which is either Ashby Garden Park, Mayson Turner Park, or Washington Park, depending on which sign you see, and the other, larger area which is labeled Washington Park also. The first triangular park is rather small, and its main attraction, a statue of Charles Lincoln Harper, doesn't do much for my dogs. But the rest of Washington Park is lovely and easily the best park within miles. Walking paths wind through fields, large trees provide shade, and the park itself is well maintained and clean. I suggest stopping at the triangle park to see the statue and chuckle over the multiple names, then walking your leashed pooch down Lena Street Northwest (one of the bordering streets) to the rest of Washington Park. The park also has tennis courts, baseball fields, a playground, and picnic pavilions.

Hours are daily from 6 A.M. to 11 P.M. Take the Martin Luther King Jr. Drive exit from Interstate 285 and turn east. Turn left onto Ashby Street. The triangular park is located between Ashby Street, Mayson Turner Road Northwest, and Lena Street Northwest. (404) 817-6766.

• **Atlanta Memorial Park** 🐾🐾 ◀● *See* ⑪ *on page 136.*

Your leashed pooch can wet his paws in the creek at this ravine park, then wander over to the tennis courts to hunt for a stray ball or two behind the fence. He'll also find plenty of trees to investigate. Several commemorative markers for Civil War battles dot the grounds.

Hours are daily from 6 A.M. to 11 P.M. Take the Moores Mill Road exit from Interstate 75 and turn east. Turn right onto U.S. 41/Northside Drive Northwest. The park is located next to the Bobby Jones Golf Course on Northside Drive Northwest near Norfleet Road. (404) 817-6766.

• **Bedford Pine Park** 🐾🐾 *See* ⑫ *on page 136.*

Since this park is situated next to an elementary school, you might want to come on a weekend if your pooch is easily distracted.

The park has several nice places to walk your leashed pup and large oak trees for shade. Take your pooch behind the tennis courts and check for stray balls, then spread out a blanket in the green grass and relax for a while. You'll also discover picnicking areas and baseball fields here.

Hours are daily from 6 A.M. to 11 P.M. Heading east along North Avenue from Interstates 75/85, turn right onto Bedford Place. The park is bordered by Angler Avenue Northeast, Lindon Avenue, Pine Street Northeast, and Bedford Place. (404) 874-1780.

• Beenteen Park 🐾 See ⓭ on page 136.

Beenteen Park is small but has lots of open areas for strolling with your leashed dog. If she gets hot, walk back to the woods behind the soccer field. There's no water, so be sure to bring your own. The park is next to an elementary school, which can be pretty distracting during the week.

Hours are daily from 6 A.M. to 11 P.M. The park is located on Casanova Street, just north of where Boulevard dead-ends into McDonough Boulevard. Turn east on Casanova Street from Boulevard. (404) 817-6766.

• Brownwood Park 🐾🐾🐾 🐾 See ⓮ on page 136.

Brownwood Park is a good choice for spending a day outdoors with your pup. It's well kept and peaceful, despite memorial markers to the battle of Atlanta. A small creek with easy water access for dogs flows down the back of the park, and there are plenty of trees along the pathways if your pooch is the nose-to-the-ground type like mine. Also here are tennis and basketball courts, a playground, and picnic areas.

Hours are daily from 6 A.M. to 11 P.M. Take the Moreland Avenue exit from Interstate 20 and turn south. Turn left onto Emerson Street Southeast. The park is located at the corner of Emerson Street Southeast and Brownwood Avenue Southeast. (404) 817-6766.

• Burgess-Walker Park 🐾 See ⓯ on page 136.

This park has a pleasant dog-walking area that offers some shade from the sun and feels cool except on the hottest days. With ball fields and a playground, though, Bandit is too distracted to enjoy it. Leashes are a must here. Parking is available on the street.

Hours are daily from 6 A.M. to 11 P.M. Take the Maynard Terrace exit from Interstate 20 and turn north. Turn left onto Memorial Drive, then left onto Memorial Terrace. The park is bordered by Memorial Terrace and Burgess Street. (404) 817-6766.

• **Carter Presidential Center** 🐾🐾🐾 🐕 *See* **16** *on page 136.*

In the most democratic of spirits, Jimmy and Rosalyn Carter have decreed that the wonderful lake and surrounding woods behind the library here are for the comfort of dogs and their human friends. To reach this oasis of freedom, follow the well-worn path from the parking lot at the library to the lake. On any given afternoon, you'll see dogs jumping and playing with each other and their people as they were meant to do, unfettered by the tie that binds. Some dogs jump into the lake and swim, while others play Frisbee or roll around in the grass.

Maybe one day Atlanta will have other parks where dogs are allowed to move about under voice control, but for now, you owe it to your pooch to check this one out. Please treat this park as the delicately balanced privilege that it is and clean up after your pup. Also, don't let your dog off leash if he isn't well enough trained, and be sure to immediately leash him if he causes any trouble. We could so easily lose this opportunity for our pets to have a wonderful time.

The park never closes, and is located off the Presidential Parkway at 1 Copenhill Avenue. (404) 331-3900.

• **Cascade Springs Nature Preserve** 🐾🐾 *See* **17** *on page 136.*

The trails at this park are generally level and wide, so even Laddie likes to walk me here. Bandit enjoys walking in and along Turkey Foot Creek. Part of the trail is wheelchair-accessible. Your dog must wear a leash.

Hours are daily from 8 A.M. to 11 P.M. Take Interstate 285 south to Cascade Road. Turn inside the Perimeter. The park is on the right after Childress Drive. (404) 306-3084.

• **Center Hill Park** 🐾 *See* **18** *on page 136.*

Dogs take to the field and the tiny creek at this small park where leashes are required, but even Bandit gets bored here after half an hour. You'll also find tennis and basketball courts, baseball fields, and a playground. The park is next to an Atlanta police precinct.

Hours are daily from 6 A.M. to 11 P.M. Take the Bankhead Highway exit off of Interstate 285 and turn inside. The park is on your left after you cross James Jackson Parkway. (404) 817-6766.

• **Chattahoochee River National Recreation Area**
   (see individual units for ratings)

The Chattahoochee River National Recreation Area consists of 14 separate land areas, called units, along a 48-mile stretch of the Chattahoochee River between Lake Lanier and Peachtree Creek. Each unit is described in the county chapter where it's located (see the index on page 263). For a complete description of the Chattahoochee River National Recreation Area, see page 57 in the Cobb County chapter. Keep in mind that our four-legged companions are in danger of losing access to these parks. To avoid more pooch-related complaints, please keep your dog leashed and scoop that poop.

Island Ford Unit 🐾🐾🐾🐾 🐾 *See ⓲ on page 130.*

Island Ford is one of my favorite parks. It's beautiful and the trail is just the right length for an afternoon hike with your leashed pup. If you don't stop, you can actually hike the loop in a little over an hour, but that's impossible with my curious canines, and probably yours as well. Be forewarned that this short hike can be fairly strenuous, with too many uphills for a dog like Laddie. Bandit loves it, since he gets to ford small streams along the way. To reach the trail, either come in on the dirt road (Island Ferry Road) and park by the gate, or turn in at the main entrance and wind back around to your left to reach the gate.

The Island Ford area is a shallow section of the Chattahoochee, and you can actually wade across the river on the large rocks and small islands. It's heavily wooded, which makes it almost comfortable in the summer, a big factor for my dogs. And when the boys get overheated, they can jump into the water and cool off.

The park is open daily from 7 A.M. to 9 P.M. From Interstate 285, go north on Roswell Road. Turn right on Roberts Drive, which is the last right turn before crossing the Chattahoochee River. The two entrances to the Island Ford Unit are on the left across from the Hunters Glen apartments. (770) 952-4419.

Jones Bridge Unit 🐾🐾🐾🐾 *See ⓴ on page 130.*

Trails through the heavily wooded Jones Bridge Unit offer easy access to the river and feeding creeks. You and your leashed pup can hike alongside the river, where water rushing over the rocks creates enough noise to drown out the sounds of civilization. (Homes are visible across the river, but at least they're beautiful, expensive, and well maintained.) Best of all, the trail is easy and Laddie-approved, and Bandit is in water-dog heaven. This park has rest rooms and picnic facilities, along with a boat ramp.

The park is open daily from 7 A.M. to 9 P.M. Take Highway 400 north from Interstate 285 and exit right onto Holcomb Bridge

Road. Turn left on Scott Road. Turn left on Nesbit Ferry Road, which becomes Old Alabama Road. Turn right on Jones Bridge Road, and left into the park. (770) 952-4419.

Medlock Bridge Unit 🐾🐾🐾 See ㉑ on page 130.

The only drawback to this park is that you're never completely out of earshot of Highway 141 (Medlock Bridge Road). Otherwise, it's an ideal place to spend the day hiking along the river with your leashed pooch. Bring your lunch and stop somewhere along the miles of trails for a relaxing picnic. Though you'll find several places along the river with good water access, I don't recommend allowing your dog to swim, even on a long leash. The river current is strong and a pup can quickly get into trouble.

The park is open daily from 7 A.M. to 9 P.M. Take Peachtree Industrial Boulevard north of Interstate 285 and turn left onto Medlock Bridge Road. Turn right into the park. (770) 952-4419.

Palisades Units (East and West) 🐾🐾🐾🐾 👞
See ㉒ on page 130.

The Palisades are granite cliffs on either side of the Chattahoochee. Both units offer superb hiking trails through woods, over rocks, and along the cliffs, the latter offering great views of the river. Be very careful on the cliffs and keep your dog close by your side away from loose rocks. Hiking boots are highly recommended.

The West Unit loop trail offers several ways into the river, and even one to a wide, sandy beach your dog will enjoy. Both units have trails through very scenic areas, with wildflowers in the spring and colorful hardwoods in the fall.

The park is open daily from 7 A.M. to 9 P.M. The Palisades Units are located on the east and west sides of Cobb Parkway, just south of Interstate 285. Small parking areas can be found on U.S. 41. For more parking, go south on Cobb Parkway from Interstate 285, and turn left onto Akers Mill Road. Turn right into the Woodmill Apartments at the waterwheel, and follow the signs. (404) 399-8070.

Vickery Creek Park 🐾🐾🐾 👞 See ㉓ on page 130.

Welcome to the infamous park where I found so many ticks on my dogs. Actually, the ticks were only a small part of what happened here that day, and I must admit that bad memories have kept me away ever since. The leash requirement probably saved Trixie's life.

On that unforgettable day, Trixie, Laddie, and I were hiking along the trail that winds along a cliff with my friend Betty, who was farther up the trail. I felt like the trail was getting more and more narrow, but Betty seemed fine ahead of us and never said anything about it. Since I'm slightly (well, more than slightly) afraid of heights, I just thought my phobia was affecting my senses.

I'm not sure exactly how it happened, but suddenly Trixie was over the edge of the cliff and hanging by her leash. I was horrified to think that my options were to let my dog die by hanging, or to let go of her leash and let her die by falling from the cliff. While Laddie made pitiful noises, I swung Trixie out a bit and then back against the cliff face. She was able to dig in with her nails while I pulled her up. I was really glad I hadn't brought the 25-foot retractable leash that day. Betty realized what had happened and came back to help, just as I grabbed Trixie and pulled her back onto the trail. We were all glad to retrace our steps to the car. Trixie kept me on the cliff side of her on the way out.

When we got back to the car, I happened to notice some ticks on Laddie. I started pulling them off and, after a few minutes, started to count. When I finished with the Lad, I found just as many on Trixie. Luckily I was wearing my woodswoman hat that day. Between the two dogs, I removed more than 100 ticks! I've since spoken with a ranger about the tick problem, and was assured that my experience was quite unusual. The whole day was quite unusual, as far as I was concerned.

I recommend keeping off the cliff trail and walking with your pooch on the northeast side of the river. You'll have a great view of the cliffs while staying closer to the ground. The trail is steep, but if your dog (and you) are in good condition, you can have a lot of fun. Regardless of what the ranger said, wear a hat and check your pup for ticks before getting back into your car.

The park is open daily from 7 A.M. to 9 P.M. Take Roswell Road north from Interstate 285 and cross the Chattahoochee River. Turn right onto Oxbo Drive and follow the signs. (770) 952-4419.

• **Chosewood Park** 🐾 🐾 *See ㉔ on page 136.*

Huge oak and pine trees provide shade at this lovely park, and if you make your way to the back, you'll find a small creek where your leashed pooch can have a splash. Also here are tennis courts, ball fields, and picnic tables.

Hours are daily from 6 A.M. to 11 P.M. This park is hard to get to since it seems to be surrounded by dead-end streets. Parking can be found on Nolan Street. Take Martin Luther King Jr. Drive south toward McDonough Boulevard, and turn left onto Nolan Street. (404) 817-6766.

• **Collier Drive Park** 🔥 *See ㉕ on page 130.*
Think of this park as a place for a quick pit stop and not much more as far as pooches are concerned, though people hang around for the tennis and basketball courts, playground, ball field, and picnic pavilions. Leashes are a must.

Hours are daily from 6 A.M. to 11 P.M. Take the Fulton Industrial Boulevard exit from Interstate 20 and turn northeast. Turn right onto Gordon Road and right again onto Collier Drive. (404) 691-4055.

• **Daniel Johnson Park/Herbert Taylor Park/Taylor-Johnson Nature Preserve** 🐾 *See ㉖ on page 136.*
These parks are actually one long, skinny ravine bisected by cross streets. Though there's water at the bottom of the ravine, it's difficult if not downright unpleasant to get to because of the wild, overgrown condition of the terrain. The parks are several blocks long, though, so if you stay along the road you and your leashed pooch can get in a good walk. You must park on the street.

Hours are daily from 6 A.M. to 11 P.M. Take Briarcliff Road north from Ponce De Leon Avenue (U.S. 78/278). Turn left onto Kay Lane. The parks are located along Helen Drive, Johnson Road, and Kay Lane. (404) 817-6766.

• **Deerwood Park** 🐾 *See ㉗ on page 130.*
While Deerwood Park doesn't have any real trails to walk along, it does have some large grassy areas where your leashed dog can romp. The best places are past the picnic pavilion and playground, around to the left.

Hours are daily from 6 A.M. to 11 P.M. From Hartsfield Atlanta International Airport, take Camp Creek Parkway to Fairburn Road and turn right. Turn right on Hogan Road. Turn right at the three-way stop onto Alexander Drive. The park is in a subdivision. There are actually three entrances to the park, but the Alexander Drive entrance has the only parking. (404) 306-3084.

• **Edwin Place Park** 🐾 *See ㉘ on page 136.*
Though this is a median park, it's actually quite large, starting off at approximately 100 feet across and fairly flat, then diving down deep into a ravine and becoming about 100 yards wide. Daffodils

have been planted along the top of the ravine, and it's very pretty in the spring. The ravine contains many large oak trees that provide shade and a creek with poor water access. If you walk your leashed dog down there, you're both going to get wet and muddy. A walkway encircles the ravine at the top, heading into thick woods at the far end where the creek flows underground. This far end is the best spot for water access, but it isn't very large. The park has on-street parking only.

Hours are daily from 6 A.M. to 11 P.M. From Interstate 285, turn inside on Bankhead Highway, then left onto Edwin Place Northwest. (404) 817-6766.

• Ellsworth Park/Norfleet Park/Springlake Park 🐾
See ㉙ on page 136.

These three adjacent deep ravine parks have no access to the creek and no easy walking except at the top. They're surrounded by lovely homes, and daffodils bloom around the ravine in the spring, which is sure to impress you more than your pooch. Leashes are a must.

Hours are daily from 6 A.M. to 11 P.M. Take the Northside Drive exit off of Interstate 75 and turn north. Turn left onto Norfleet Road Northwest. The parks are located between Springlake Drive Northwest and Norfleet Road Northwest. (404) 817-6766.

• Empire Park 🐾 See ㉚ on page 136.

The creek at this small park is hard for you and your dog to reach without getting good and muddy. Not even Bandit can convince me to slop around in that again! Empire Park does have a small patch of grass for a quick pit stop, alongside the tennis and basketball courts. In addition, you'll find a playground, picnic tables, and a baseball field. You must leash at this park.

Hours are daily from 6 A.M. to 11 P.M. Take the Crown Road/Old Dixie Highway exit off of Interstate 285 and turn north. Turn right onto Browns Mills Road, then left onto Oak Drive. (404) 817-6766.

• English Park 🐾 🐾 See ㉛ on page 130.

Lovely old shade trees are the main highlight of English Park. All of the other amenities at this small park, such as the football field and playground, won't interest your leashed pooch as much as nosing around the tree trunks.

Hours are daily from 6 A.M. to 11 P.M. Coming from downtown on Interstate 20, take the Fulton Industrial Boulevard exit and go right. The park is on your right at Bolton Road. (404) 817-6766.

• **Eubanks Park** 🐾 *See* **32** *on page 136.*

Just across the way from Winn Park (see page 159), this ravine park has not been cleaned up and is still full of brush, which makes walking around difficult. Your leashed pooch won't mind, though, since she can still get into the creek for a dip.

Hours are daily from 6 A.M. to 11 P.M. Go north on Piedmont Avenue from Ponce De Leon Avenue (U.S. 78/278), then left onto Maddox Road. The park is bordered by Parklane Road Northeast and Maddox Road. (404) 817-6766.

• **Grant Park** 🐾🐾🐾 *See* **33** *on page 136.*

If you like to run with your dog, you're going to love Grant Park. The park is huge even if you don't include Zoo Atlanta, the Cyclorama, or the pool, none of which allows dogs. Located in an older area of the city, the park contains many ancient oak trees to provide shade during the summer months. And it's large enough that it never seems overrun with other people. Pups must be leashed. Bring your lunch and eat either on one of the many picnic tables or on a blanket spread in the grass.

Bandit is fascinated by the large number of squirrels in the park, who seem to love to taunt any dog that shows an interest in them. The squirrels have learned that they are faster than the local pooch population, and they have the advantage of being able to sprint up one of the many trees for a quick getaway.

If you haven't seen the Cyclorama or been to Zoo Atlanta, plan a separate trip without your dog. You'll want to spend a full day. I remember going to what was then known as the Atlanta Zoo to see Willie B. This intelligent western lowland gorilla, named after William B. Hartsfield, the former mayor of Atlanta, was forced to spend 27 years in a small glassed-in room in the zoo. His only break from the incredible boredom was provided by a television set. I was initially frightened by his size, but the expression in his eyes changed that emotion to pity immediately. The entire city rejoiced when Willie B. was released into the new Ford African Rain Forest outdoor area of Zoo Atlanta, and again when he was introduced to other gorillas for the first time. Not only is Willie B. now living a more normal life, but he has formed a patriarchal clan with four adult gorillas and has a daughter, Kudzoo. Zoo Atlanta has duplicated their success with another gorilla named Ivan, who spent the first 27 years of his life in captivity in a shopping mall in the Pacific Northwest. Since being acclimated at the park, he has been introduced to other gorillas for the first time.

The Cyclorama is an immense diorama of the battle of Atlanta during the Civil War. Even if you aren't a history buff, you'll want to spend an hour here.

Hours for Grant Park are daily from 6 A.M. to 11 P.M. Take the Boulevard exit off of Interstate 20 and turn south. The park is on your right. (404) 622-3041.

• Grove Park 🐾 See ❸❹ on page 136.

Your leashed pooch will probably give this park a higher rating than you would. It does have a creek that's easy to reach and a large field for a nice romp. But the park's seedy appearance will certainly reduce your enjoyment of it. I wouldn't linger here. No one seems to use the playground, tennis courts, or picnic tables.

Hours are daily from 6 A.M. to 11 P.M. Take Bankhead Highway inside from Interstate 285, and turn left onto Hortense Place Northwest to reach the park. (404) 817-6766.

• Gun Club Park 🐾 See ❸❺ on page 136.

I felt so bad at this park that I wanted to cry. Gun Club Park is large; the terrain is hilly; the trees are huge; and you get the impression that you're up in north Georgia. With the wonderful creek and the heavy woods, this could be a four-paw park if cleaned up. Instead, it has been used as a dump by the locals and is completely trashed. I counted 15 tires in a 4-by-20-foot section along the road.

A civic organization should take this park on as a project. It would take a lot of work, but the neighborhood would end up with something truly beautiful. The park has all of the natural resources necessary to become one of the finest in the city. Park amenities include basketball, baseball, and a swimming pool. Leashes are required.

Hours are daily from 6 A.M. to 11 P.M. Take the Bankhead Highway exit off of Interstate 285 and turn inside. Turn left onto James Jackson Parkway, then right onto Hollywood Road. Turn right onto Gun Club Drive Northwest and follow it to the park. (404) 799-0314.

• Harper Park 🐾 See ❸❻ on page 136.

As you drive into Harper Park, you'll see a nice wooded area on your right. This is the best place to let your leashed pooch stretch his legs. It's shady, cool, and full of interesting smells. You'll have to walk across the sunny field from the parking lot to get there, but that doesn't take long with either Laddie or Bandit on the end of a leash. Despite obedience school for Bandit, he still pulls when taking me for a walk. Laddie was refused entry to school and picked up way too many street smarts before coming to live with me.

The park is next to a school, which makes it a poor choice during the week if your pup is easily distracted. There are lots of activities for your nondog friends, including basketball, baseball, and tennis, but not enough to occupy your pooch for more than a few minutes.

Hours are daily from 6 A.M. to 11 P.M. Take the Jonesboro Road exit off of Interstate 285 and turn inside. Turn left on Macedonia Road Southeast, and then make a hard left onto Gilbert Road Southeast. (404) 817-6766.

- **Harwell Heights Park** 🐾 *See* ❸❼ *on page 130.*
The trails at this small park merely wind around the baseball field, tennis courts (check for stray balls), and basketball courts—not worth more than a leg-lift or two for your leashed pooch.

Hours are daily from 6 A.M. to 11 P.M. Take the Hightower Road exit off of Interstate 20 and turn north. Turn left onto Collier Drive. The park is located next to Collier Heights Elementary School. (404) 817-6766.

- **Herbert Taylor Park:** See Daniel Johnson Park on page 144.

- **Homestead Park** 🐾 *See* ❸❽ *on page 136.*
This tiny park is a triangular-shaped plot of ground between Meadowdale Avenue and Homestead Avenue. Parking is on street only and pups must be leashed.

The park is open daily during daylight hours. Take Briarcliff Road north from Bankhead Highway (U.S. 78/278). Turn left onto Johnson Road, then right onto Meadowdale Avenue. (404) 817-6766.

- **Howell Park** 🐾 *See* ❸❾ *on page 136.*
The walking trail at this park will give your leashed pooch a chance to stretch his legs and explore the large oak trees. Also located in the park are basketball courts, a playground, and picnic tables and pavilions.

Hours are daily from 6 A.M. to 11 P.M. Take the Georgia Avenue exit from Interstate 75/85 and turn west. Turn right onto Pryor Street, then left onto Glenn Street, which becomes Ralph David Abernathy Boulevard. The park will be on your right, just past Ashby Street. (404) 817-6766.

- **Isabel Gates Webster Park** 🐾 *See* ❹❶ *on page 130.*
This small park has a jogging track around the football field, a convenient if boring way for your leashed pup to get some exercise. Peyton Forrest Elementary School is next door, so if your pooch is easily distracted, you might want to visit on the weekend. You'll also find tennis courts and a playground here.

Hours are daily from 6 A.M. to 11 P.M. Take the Martin Luther King Jr. Drive exit off of Interstate 285 and turn inside. Turn right onto Peyton Place. The park will be on your right. (404) 817-6766.

• **Jamestown Park** 🐾 *See* ❹ *on page 130.*
Stop by if your pooch must go, but the park's proximity to the airport makes it fairly loud, and if your leashed dog is skittish or easily distracted, you may be in for a long pit stop. The small park has tennis courts that don't appear to ever be in use and not much to offer your pet.

Hours are daily from 7 A.M. to 10:30 P.M. Take the Camp Creek Parkway exit off of Interstate 285 and turn toward Hartsfield Atlanta International Airport. Turn right onto Herschel Road. The park is on the corner of Herschel and Riverdale Roads. (404) 817-6766.

• **John A. White Park** 🐾 *See* ❷ *on page 136.*
You and your leashed pet won't find any real trails at this park, but it's large enough to offer a good choice of areas for walking. Amenities include a pool, golf course, ball fields, and picnic areas.

Hours are daily from 6 A.M. to 11 P.M. Take Interstate 285 south to Cascade Road. Turn inside the Perimeter, then turn left on Cascade Terrace, just past the cemetery, to reach the park. (404) 753-9842.

• **Kennedy Park** 🐾 *See* ❸ *on page 136.*
Though this small park does have a pleasant field for walking your leashed dog, there isn't quite enough space to really give her legs a good stretch. Amenities include a baseball field, a playground, a basketball court, and picnic pavilions.

Hours are daily from 6 A.M. to 11 P.M. From Bankhead Highway (U.S. 78/278) near Interstate 75/85, turn south on James P. Brawley Drive Northwest. The park will be on your left. (404) 524-7111.

• **Knight Park** 🐾🐾🐾 *See* ❹ *on page 136.*
Knight Park is almost perfect from a dog's perspective. The large fields aren't cluttered with baseball fields and other extraneous amenities that dogs don't care about. There are tennis and basketball courts, and a thorough check behind the tennis courts usually nets a stray ball or two. A footbridge crosses the small creek, which has good water access for your pooch, and the large trees are ripe for a whiff or two. I did say almost perfect—leashes are the law here.

Hours are daily from 6 A.M. to 11 P.M. Turn inside Interstate 285 onto Bankhead Highway. Turn left onto Ashby Street Northwest, left onto West Marietta Boulevard, and left onto Rice Street Northwest. The park is on the left. (404) 817-6766.

• **Lenox Wildwood Park/Sunken Garden Park/Sussex Park**
🐾🐾 *See ㊺ on page 136.*

These three parks feel more like one long, skinny park cut into pieces by crossroads. A shallow, easily reached creek flanked by heavy woods flows down the length of the parks, which makes Bandit's day. If your pooch isn't into water, you can always walk her in the surrounding woods or on the Morningside Nature Trail. You'll also find tennis courts, grills in the picnic area, and a playground for your noncanine pals. Sunken Garden Park is the best maintained of the three. Remember to leash your dog.

Hours are daily from 6 A.M. to 11 P.M. From downtown Atlanta, take Interstate 85 north to Buford Highway. Turn right at the Cheshire Bridge exit, then left onto Lenox Road Northeast. The parks are on the right. (404) 817-6766.

• **Loring Heights Park** 🐾🐾 *See ㊻ on page 136.*

The walking trail at this delightful park in a neighborhood filled with lovely homes winds around a lake, which is easy for your leashed pooch to reach. She'll also enjoy sniffing around the large shade trees and investigating messages left by the locals. Another wooded area with more trails can be found across from the lake.

Hours are daily from 6 A.M. to 11 P.M. Heading north on Northside Drive/U.S. 41/Highway 3 from 14th Street, turn right onto Deering Road. Turn left onto Loring Drive, then left onto Garden Lane to reach the park. (404) 817-6766.

• **Maddox Park** 🐾🐾 *See ㊼ on page 136.*

Open fields and huge shady oak trees make this park a worthy place to bring your leashed pup. Be sure to climb the hill to see the wonderful stone gazebo and the view of the surrounding area, with the added bonus of a welcoming breeze. The small lake keeps water-loving dogs happy, and sniffers won't find a shortage of trees. Your human pals can enjoy the swimming pool, tennis and basketball courts, gym, and picnic facilities.

Hours are daily from 6 A.M. to 11 P.M. Take the Bankhead Highway exit inside off of Interstate 285, then turn right onto Gary Avenue to reach the park. (404) 892-0119.

• **Mason Road Park** 🐾 *See ㊽ on page 130.*

I don't recommend Mason Road Park on Saturdays, when inmates from the nearby prison use the baseball field for exercise until 2:30 P.M. But on other days, if you walk your leashed dog in the back of the park, behind the tennis courts, she's almost certain to find a ball or two. The road becomes a rough gravel surface at the tennis courts, winding down and circling back. This is also a good spot to take your dog, though shade is in short supply.

Hours are daily from 6 A.M. to midnight. Traveling north on Roosevelt Highway/U.S. 29/Highway 14, turn left onto Mason Road just past the fork for Stonewall Tell Road. The park will be on your left. (404) 730-6200.

• **Mayson Turner Park:** See Ashby Garden Park on page 138.

• **McClatchey Park** *See 49 on page 136.*

Though this tiny park is very attractive, your leashed pooch will find little to do after visiting the large trees.

Hours are daily from 6 A.M. to 11 P.M. Go north on Piedmont Road from Ponce De Leon Avenue (U.S. 78/278), then left onto Maddox Road. Turn left onto Parklane Road Northeast. McClatchey Park is bordered by Westminster Drive Northeast and Parklane Road Northeast. (404) 817-6766.

• **Melvin Drive Park** *See 50 on page 130.*

Melvin Drive Park has plenty of grassy areas for walking your leashed dog, but with no trails and a generally unkempt appearance, it's only worth a quick squat. You'll also find tennis and basketball courts and a large picnic pavilion.

Hours are daily from 8 A.M. to 11 P.M. Take Interstate 285 south to Cascade Road. Turn outside the Perimeter. Turn left on Fairburn Road, then right on Melvin Drive, and the park will be on your right. (770) 306-3084.

• **Morgan Falls Park** *See 51 on page 130.*

This popular park is just down the road from the Morgan Falls Reservoir put-in spot for rafting on the Chattahoochee River. Take your leashed pup up the trail that leads off from the back of the parking area and winds through deep woods. Amenities include baseball fields, a playground, and picnic facilities.

Park hours are daily from 6 A.M. to midnight. Go north on Roswell Road from Interstate 285, and turn left onto Morgan Falls Road, just north of Abernathy Road. Turn left into Morgan Falls Park. (404) 730-6200.

• **Morgan Falls Reservoir** *See 52 on page 130.*

Georgia Power operates the dam on the Chattahoochee River and releases water as needed to generate electricity for the metropolitan area. Your leashed pup won't care about the dam, but will enjoy exploring the woods in this park. You can also walk her down the boat ramp for a safe place to get into the river. Although the ramp drops off fairly quickly, the biggest danger is getting bumped by rafters as they swarm down the ramp.

This park would be rated higher if it wasn't so congested. It's one of the most popular put-in sites on the river, and parking can be a real problem. If the lot is full, you may have to park along Morgan Falls Road.

The park is open daily from 7 A.M. to 6 P.M. Go north on Roswell Road from Interstate 285, and turn left onto Morgan Falls Road, just north of Abernathy Road. The park is at the river at the end of the road. (404) 329-1455.

• **Mozley Park** 🐾🐾🐾 *See* ❸ *on page 136.*

An enjoyable afternoon can be had at this park with a large open field bordered by huge oak trees for shade. Your leashed pooch can lead the way on the walking and bicycle paths that wind through the grounds, and if he's like my boys, he'll stop at every tree. If only the park had water, it would be close to perfect. You're required to scoop here. Noncanine types will enjoy the swimming pool, picnic facilities (including a large grill that could handle a crowd), baseball fields, tennis and handball courts, playground, and sandpile. Frank L. Stanton Elementary School is located next door.

Hours are daily from 6 A.M. to 11 P.M. The park is located on the north side of Martin Luther King Jr. Drive Southwest near West Lake Avenue. (404) 758-1903.

• **Noble Park** 🐾 *See* ❺ *on page 136.*

Though this tiny park is well maintained, it's only worth a quick stop on your way to somewhere else. Leashes are required. The only human amenities are a playground and benches.

Hours are daily from 6 A.M. to 11 P.M. Take Briarcliff Road north from Ponce De Leon Avenue (U.S. 78/278). Turn left onto Johnson Road, then right onto Meadowdale Avenue. The park is located on the corner of Noble Drive and Meadowdale Avenue. (404) 730-6200.

• **Norfleet Park:** See Ellsworth Park on page 145.

• **Ocee Park** 🐾🐾 *See* ❺ *on page 130.*

You won't find much shade on the quarter-mile trail around the ball fields here, but the trees in the woods offer a welcome respite for you and your leashed dog. Laddie usually conducts a tree-by-tree inspection, while Bandit searches in vain for someplace to wet his paws.

Hours are daily from 6 A.M. to midnight. From Atlanta, take Highway 400 north to the east Holcolm Bridge Road exit and turn right. Turn left at the fork onto Old Alabama Road, which becomes Jones Bridge Road. Turn left onto Buice Road. The park is located on Buice Road, just off of Old Alabama Road. (404) 730-6200.

• **Peachtree Battle Park** 🐾 *See* 56 *on page 136.*

This median park offers both a level area for sniffing around large magnolia trees and a ravine with good access to the creek. Sit on one of the benches and lust after the dignified old homes while your pooch investigates signs from the locals. Leashes are mandatory.

The park is open daily from 6 A.M. to 11 P.M. Traveling north from downtown on Peachtree Road/U.S. 19/Highway 9, turn left onto Peachtree Battle Avenue Northwest. The park will be on your right. (404) 817-6766.

• **Peachtree Hills Park** 🐾 *See* 57 *on page 136.*

Small Peachtree Hills Park has a creek, but with no access you'll only frustrate your leashed dog if you point it out to her. There's always the opportunity to pick up a stray tennis ball behind the courts. Also here are basketball courts, picnicking areas with grills, and a playground.

Hours are daily from 6 A.M. to 11 P.M. From Atlanta, go north on Peachtree Road Northeast to Lindbergh Drive and turn right. Turn right on Peachtree Hills Avenue, and the park is on your right. (404) 817-6766.

• **Phoenix Park II** 🐾🐾 *See* 58 *on page 136.*

Atlanta is nicknamed the Phoenix City because it rose from the ashes of the Civil War. This park is located next to King Middle School, but it's large enough that you can get your easily distracted pooch far away from the children. You and your leashed pooch can romp or picnic in the large open fields, then rest under the ancient oak trees when you're ready for some shade. The park also has a paved trail for stretching those furry legs. Laddie, of course, is content just wandering from tree to tree. Tennis courts, playgrounds, a ball field, and picnic tables can also be found here.

Hours are daily from 6 A.M. to 11 P.M. Take the Georgia Avenue exit from Interstate 75/85 and turn east. The park is on your right at the corner of Martin Street and Georgia Avenue. (404) 817-6766.

• **Phoenix Park III** 🐾 *See* 59 *on page 136.*

Home to the Martin Luther King Jr. South Recreation Center and a playground, this park provides little for the pooch population. The park isn't large enough to get much exercise, though there are large trees for shade during the summer months and benches to rest on.

Park hours are daily from 6 A.M. to 11 P.M. Take the Georgia Avenue exit from Interstate 75/85 and turn east. The park is located on your left at the corner of Connally Street and Georgia Avenue. (404) 817-6766.

• **Piedmont Park** 🐾🐾🐾 🐾 *See ❻ on page 136.*
Piedmont Park is the most famous park within the city limits. Atlantans have been walking their dogs here for more than a century. While pooches aren't permitted in the Atlanta Botanical Gardens next door, Laddie and Bandit are welcome in Piedmont Park except during certain special events, such as the Arts Festival of Atlanta, held each September.

The four-mile loop trail through the park crosses lovely rolling green lawns, circles Lake Clara Meer, and runs in front of the tennis center. Most people, though, just spread out a blanket or start a game of Frisbee in the grass. This is one of the best places in Atlanta for meeting other dog lovers, since the pup population rivals that of the humans on any weekend afternoon.

If your dog gets too warm, seek refuge under one of the huge oak trees for shade. There are ducks to gawk and bark at in the lake and plenty of grass to roll in. Although many of the dogs you'll see in the park are joyously leaping and running leash-free, a leash law is in effect. And the police are never far away, since the stables for the police horses are in the park by the tennis center.

Hours are daily from 6 A.M. to 11 P.M. The entrance for Piedmont Park is located downtown at the intersection of 12th Street and Piedmont Avenue. (404) 658-6016.

• **Renaissance Park** 🐾 *See ❻ on page 136.*
You might love this large park with a walking trail through manicured gardens, but your leashed pooch will soon be bored. Parking is on the street only, which seems to limit the park's use.

Hours are daily from 6 A.M. to 11 P.M. The park is on the corner of Piedmont Avenue and Pine Street, south of Ponce De Leon Avenue. (404) 817-6766.

• **Rockdale Park** 🐾 *See ❻ on page 136.*
Here's another park that would be very nice if it hadn't become a dumping ground for old tires and trash. Parking is on street only, and you won't want to wander too far from your car. Leashes are required.

Hours are daily from 6 A.M. to 11 P.M. Take Hollywood Road north from Bankhead Highway (U.S. 78/278). Turn right onto Johnson Road. The park is at the intersection of Johnson Road and Habershal Drive. (404) 817-6766.

• **Rosa L. Burney Park** 🐾 *See* ❻❸ *on page 136.*
This small park is only worth a quick stop for your leashed dog. There's a large field and lots of shade from old oak trees, but the neighborhood is generally rundown and unkempt. Amenities include a playground and tennis courts.

Hours are daily from 6 A.M. to 11 P.M. Take Ralph David Abernathy Avenue east from the Wren's Nest. Turn left on Windsor Street Southwest to reach the park. (404) 817-6766.

• **Rose Circle Park** 🐾 *See* ❻❹ *on page 136.*
Rose Circle Park is very long and as wide as a football field. The walking trails wind around the basketball courts, playground, and large swings. You and your leashed pal are never far from one of the spreading oak trees that not only give shade but serve as message boards for the local canine population.

Hours are daily from 6 A.M. to 11 P.M. Take Lee Street north from the Lakewood Freeway and turn left onto White Street Southwest. The park is bordered by Ashby Street Southwest, White Street Southwest, and Rose Circle Southwest. (404) 817-6766.

• **Sibley Park** 🐾 *See* ❻❺ *on page 136.*
This ravine park has water at the bottom, but no good way to reach it. You and your leashed pooch are better off just wandering around the top.

Hours are daily from 6 A.M. to 11 P.M. Take Peachtree Road/U.S. 19/Highway 9 north from downtown and turn left onto West Wesley Road. The park is located at the corner of West Wesley Road and Habersham Road Northwest. (404) 817-6766.

• **Sidney Marcus Park** 🐾 *See* ❻❻ *on page 136.*
Your leashed pooch will enjoy nosing around the shady hardwood trees—beacons of the local male dog population—at this small, well-maintained park. There are several benches and a playground, but Sidney Marcus Park isn't large enough to warrant lingering for too long.

Hours are daily from 6 A.M. to 11 P.M. Heading north on Piedmont Avenue, turn right onto Morningside Drive, right onto Cumberland Place, and left onto Sherwood Road Northeast. The park is on your right. (404) 817-6766.

• **Smith Park** 🐾 *See ⑥⑦ on page 136.*

This tiny park, a triangular spit of land bordered by Piedmont Avenue and Monroe Drive, is only worth a quick stop for your leashed pooch. Parking is on street only.

Hours are daily from 6 A.M. to 11 P.M. Take Piedmont Avenue south from Interstate 85. The park will be on your left at Monroe Drive. (404) 817-6766.

• **South Bend Park** 🐾🐾🐾 *See ⑥⑧ on page 136.*

Wander with your leashed pooch through heavy woods, across well-manicured fields, and into and alongside a creek at this large park with somewhat hilly terrain. Take the walking path or strike out on your own; your pup will enjoy it either way. The park also offers diversions aplenty for human visitors, with several playgrounds, ball fields, a gym, and picnic pavilions. Plan your next company picnic at South Bend Park, and bring your dog along for the fun.

Hours are daily from 6 A.M. to 11 P.M. The park is located across from the Lakewood Fairgrounds on Compton Drive Southeast. (404) 622-4115.

• **Southside Park** 🐾 *See ⑥⑨ on page 136.*

Most of the land in this large park is taken up by ball fields. Unfortunately, dogs aren't allowed to set paw inside the softball complex, meaning they're restricted to two small unshaded fields and a creek. The creek is small, even by Bandit's standards, and there are precious few trees for sniffing and doing leg-lifts. To top it off, leashes are required. Also here are tennis and basketball courts. Picnic tables are available, but there's too much concrete and steel for them to be a relaxing place to eat your lunch.

Hours are daily from 6 A.M. to 11 P.M. Take the Jonesboro Road exit off of Interstate 285 and turn inside. The park will be on your right, about half a mile down the road. (404) 730-6200.

• **Springlake Park:** See Ellsworth Park on page 145.

• **Springvale Park** 🐾 *See ⑦⓪ on page 136.*

You may have trouble finding this park, since it drops down from the road. Once you do, you'll discover a paved walkway around a small lake. Large trees along one side offer some shade. Leashes are mandatory.

Hours are daily from 6 A.M. to 11 P.M. Take Euclid Avenue Southwest from Findley Plaza in Little Five Points and turn right onto Park Lane to reach the park. (404) 730-6200.

• **Stone Hogan Park** 🐾 *See ❼ on page 130.*

Although I personally wouldn't call a paved walkway a nature trail, Laddie appreciates pavement for its even terrain and gentle grade. The trails at this park (some with streetlights!) lead from the parking areas to basketball courts, picnic pavilions, and playgrounds. There's also one that leads to a barbed wire fence separating the park from an abandoned apartment complex. Leashes are required wear at this park.

Park hours are daily from 6 A.M. to 11 P.M. From Hartsfield Atlanta International Airport, take Camp Creek Parkway until you reach Welcome All Road. Turn right, then right again at the dead end onto Fairburn Road. Turn right onto Hogan Road, right onto the Hogan-Stone Connector, and continue to the park, which will be on your left at Stone Road. (404) 306-3084.

• **Sussex Park:** See Lenox Wildwood Park on page 150.

• **Tanyard Creek Park** 🐾🐾🐾 🦴 *See ❼❷ on page 136.*

Your leashed pooch can easily get into the creek at this sizable ravine park. Just head over to the footbridge from the parking lot and your dog will take it from there. Most of the underbrush has been removed, leaving the tall trees and a multitude of wonderful smells behind.

Tanyard Creek is a tributary of Peachtree Creek, and there are several commemorative markers here for the battle of Peachtree Creek, waged during the Civil War. You'll also find a playground and a baseball field.

Hours are daily from 6 A.M. to 11 P.M. Take the Northside Drive/U.S. 41 exit from Interstate 75 and head north. Turn right onto Collier Drive Northwest, then right onto Walthall Drive Northwest. The park will be on your left. (404) 817-6766.

• **Taylor-Johnson Nature Preserve:** See Daniel Johnson Park on page 144.

• **Thomasville Park and Recreation Center** 🔥
See ❼❸ on page 136.

A shadeless walking track is about all you and your leashed pup will find at this park. It's also located in a rundown area next to low-income housing.

Park hours are daily from 8 A.M. to 1 A.M. Take Moreland Avenue north to McDonough Boulevard and turn left. Turn left onto Henry Thomas Drive Southeast. The park is located at the corner of Thomasville Drive Southeast. (404) 622-3045.

• **Trammell Crow Park** 🐾 *See ❼❹ on page 130.*

Take your leashed pup on a leisurely stroll on the nature trail at this small park. Amenities include tennis courts, picnic pavilions, and a children's playground.

Hours are daily from 6 A.M. to 11 P.M. Take Interstate 285 south to Cascade Road. Turn outside the Perimeter. The park will be on your left after New Hope Road. (770) 306-3084.

• **University Park** 🐾 *See ❼❺ on page 136.*

This park is next to the Atlanta University Complex, and students outnumber dogs by far. Laddie has sniffed in vain around the large shade trees, but never found evidence of local canines. Leashes are required. You'll also find basketball courts and a playground.

Hours are daily from 6 A.M. to 11 P.M. Take the McDaniel Street exit off of Interstate 20 and turn north. Turn left onto Lee Road/U.S. 29, then right onto Northside Drive/Stewart Avenue/U.S. 41/Highway 19. The park is located at the corner of Fair Street Southwest and Northside Drive. (404) 817-6766.

• **Washington Park:** See Ashby Garden Park on page 138.

• **West End Park** 🐾 *See ❼❻ on page 136.*

Dogs like soaking up the rays on the grassy fields and exploring the large shady oak trees at this park. People can use the tennis and basketball courts, playground, and baseball fields. Remember to leash your pup.

Hours are daily from 6 A.M. to 11 P.M. Take the Ashby Street exit off of Interstate 20 and turn south. Turn left onto Ralph David Abernathy Boulevard, then right onto Lawton Street Southwest. The park is bordered by Lawton Street Southwest, Oak Street Southwest, and Dargan Place Southwest, near Ralph David Abernathy Boulevard Southwest. (404) 817-6766.

• **Wildwood Park** 🐾 *See ❼❼ on page 136.*

Even Bandit gave up on getting to the creek at the bottom of this park, basically a heavily wooded, steep ravine. Leashes are required. You must park on the street.

Hours are daily from 6 A.M. to 11 P.M. Take Piedmont Avenue south from Interstate 85, and turn left onto North Rock Springs Road. Turn left onto Wildwood Road. The park is located on Wildwood Road at Wildwood Place. (404) 817-6766.

• **Wilson Mill Park** 🐾🐾 *See ❼❽ on page 130.*

Depending on the weather, you may want to spread a blanket in the sun or stick to the shade of the ancient trees in this large park with plenty of places for you and your leashed pup to walk. Wilson Mill Park has the largest population of squirrels that I have ever seen. Once while waiting for Laddie to thoroughly investigate a tree, I counted 20 squirrels dashing across the field and scampering up and down trees. Bandit didn't know where to look or what to do. The squirrel overload kept him rooted to the spot. Also here are tennis and basketball courts, a playground, and baseball fields. Benches, but no picnic tables, can be found throughout the park.

Hours are daily from 6 A.M. to 11 P.M. Take Interstate 20 west from downtown Atlanta to Fulton Industrial Boulevard and turn right. Turn right onto Martin Luther King Jr. Drive (Highway 139), right on Bakers Ferry Road, and left onto Wilson Mill Road Southwest. The park is on the left. (404) 817-6766.

• Winn Park 🐾🐾 See ❼❾ on page 136.

After seeing so many roughly cut and unkempt ravine parks, Winn Park is a true delight. The park has the same long, lean shape as so many of the other city parks, but this one is manicured, with usable space and trails through to the water in the middle. The underbrush has been cut out and the large oak and pine trees remain. The creek actually disappears underground and isn't accessible, but that's a small price to pay for the lovely space your leashed pooch can walk and run in. Winn Park is popular with pups and their people, so you're sure to see many joyous dogs inspecting the trees. Laddie is in tree-sniffing heaven here, and Bandit is fascinated by the number of birds.

You'll find on-street parking only along both sides of the ravine. The park is bordered by lovely, well-maintained homes. Also here are a baseball field and a playground.

Park hours are daily from 6 A.M. to 11 P.M. Take Peachtree Street north from Ponce De Leon Avenue and then turn right onto 15th Street. Turn left onto Peachtree Circle. The park is bordered by Peachtree Circle Northeast, Lafayette Drive Northeast, and Westminster Drive. (404) 817-6766.

• Woodland Garden Park 🐾 See ❽⓪ on page 136.

Since this small park is adjacent to Southside High School, you may find conditions to be too distracting for your pet. There's a trail with exercise equipment, but my boys have never gotten into doing chin-ups; with no shade, you won't want to, either. Your canine companion is required to wear her leash.

Park hours are daily from 6 A.M. to 11 P.M. Take the Glenwood Avenue/Highway 260 exit from Interstate 20 and head southeast.

Turn right onto Chester Avenue Southeast. The park will be on your right. (404) 817-6766.

• **Woodruff Park** 🐾 *See* **❽❶** *on page 136.*

You have to stop at this park at least once if you live in Atlanta. Located at Five Points in downtown, this is the park with the famous Phoenix statue, representing Atlanta rising from the flames of the Civil War. The park is used primarily by downtown office workers seeking a place to eat their lunch in the sunshine. There's a small amount of on-street parking available. Your leashed pup will probably just want to do his business and move on.

Hours are daily from 6 A.M. to 11 P.M. The park is located at Five Points, where Auburn Avenue Northeast, Luckie Street, and Peachtree Street converge. (404) 817-6766.

SHOPPING IN ATLANTA

abbadabba's: This eclectic shoe and clothing shop carries Rockports, Birkenstocks, and other trendy footwear. Best of all, your pooch is as welcome as you are. Be sure to take your pup with you if you go into one of the dressing areas. 322 East Paces Ferry Road Northeast, Atlanta, GA 30305; (404) 262-3356.

Cheshire Pets: Your pet—and everyone else's—is welcome to come on in with you and peruse the full assortment of dog, cat, bird, and small animal supplies. 6518 Roswell Road Northwest, Atlanta, GA 30328; (770) 256-9166.

Petsmart: If you haven't yet discovered Petsmart, you're missing a real treat, both for you and your pooch. Petsmart was one of two chain pet stores in the Atlanta area that elevated shopping with your pet to an art form. Petsmart is located all over the city, including branches at 3221 Peachtree Road Northeast, Atlanta, GA 30308, (404) 266-0402; and 129 Perimeter Center West, Atlanta, GA 30346, (770) 481-0043.

PLACES TO STAY

Ansley Inn: You and your pal will find this lovely inn right off of Peachtree Street. Room rates range from $115 to $250, and there's no charge for your pooch. 253 15th Street Northeast, Atlanta, GA 30309; (404) 872-9000.

Atlanta Airport Marriott: Your small pooch (that means those who weigh 25 pounds or less) is welcome to stay with you for free at this hotel. Rates range from $114 to $120. 4711 Best Road, Atlanta, GA 30337; (404) 766-7900.

Cheshire Motor Inn: Rates are $42 to $57, with no additional fee for your pooch. 1865 Cheshire Bridge Road, Atlanta, GA 30324; (770) 872-9628.

Doubletree Hotel at the Concourse: Room rates range from $79 to $180, in addition to a $75 pet deposit, $25 of which is refundable. 7 Concourse Parkway Northeast, Atlanta, GA 30328; (770) 395-3900.

Peachtree Plaza Hotel: This luxury hotel will cater to your small (under 20 pounds) pooch. Standard rates for a double range from $225 to $295 per night, but you can get a discounted rate of as little as $95 when they have a special. 210 Peachtree Street Northwest, Atlanta, GA 30303; (404) 659-1400.

Radisson Hotel Airport: There's a nonrefundable $25 fee for your pet. Room rates are $89 to $170. 165 Courtland Street, Atlanta, GA 30303; (404) 659-6500.

Renaissance Hotel: Your pooch must be kept on leash when walking about the hotel and in his carrier if you leave him in the room unattended. Rates are $79 to $160, which includes a complimentary breakfast and afternoon hors d'oeuvres. 590 West Peachtree Street Northwest, Atlanta, GA 30308; (404) 881-6000.

FESTIVALS

Flea Fair: Your pooch isn't invited, but would you really want to take your dog to a *flea* fair? For humans, though, it's a lot of fun and a good cause. Held each May during Be Kind to Animals Week, the Flea Fair is a great place to donate or pick up articles that will benefit the Atlanta Humane Society. Call the Society at (404) 875-5331 for more information.

DIVERSIONS

Who's that doggy in the picture?: Each October, the Atlanta Humane Society sponsors a photo session with Santa for you and your pet—and we're not just talking dogs here. Besides canines and cats, Santa's lap has held guinea pigs, boa constrictors, iguanas, turtles, and even monkeys. It's a great chance to have some fun with your pet and benefit a good cause at the same time. Call (404) 875-5331 for more information.

Meet you at the Animal Scramble: Although pets aren't allowed, the annual Animal Scramble in March, sponsored by the Atlanta Humane Society, involves a one-mile fun run and a 5k race, with all proceeds benefitting the Atlanta Humane Society. Even though your pooch has to stay home, go anyway. It's for a good cause. For more information, call (404) 875-5331.

COLLEGE PARK
PARKS AND RECREATION AREAS

• **Brannon Memorial Park** 🐾 *See ❽❷ on page 130.*

My boys and I would rate this park much higher if it were in a better location. It's in the rear part of an apartment complex, and since the entrance gate is always closed, you must park and walk into the park. Because it's so difficult to reach, the park isn't used much, so you and your leashed pooch might have the large, grassy fields all to yourselves. I just don't like leaving my car in a slightly seedy apartment complex for long.

Hours are daily from 6 A.M. to 11 P.M. From the airport, take Camp Creek Parkway to Herschel Road and turn left. Turn right onto Charleston Drive, into the Charleston Apartments. The park is near the back on the left. (404) 669-3767.

• **Burdette Park** 🐾🐾 *See ❽❸ on page 130.*

The trails at this large park lead through the woods and end up at a creek, a popular spot for the leashed doggy crowd. Bring your lunch and spread a blanket near the creek or use one of the picnic tables. Burdette Gym is off-limits to your pup, as are the tennis courts and the football and baseball fields, but the shady woods and creek more than make up for this.

Hours are daily from 6 A.M. to midnight. Take the Old National Highway/Highway 279 exit off of Interstate 285 and turn outside. Turn right onto Burdette Road. The park is located on Burdette Road just off of Old National Highway. (404) 996-9145.

• **Cliftondale Park** 🐾 *See ❽❹ on page 130.*

While there are no trails at Cliftondale Park, there's plenty of shade for walking your leashed pooch on a warm day. This attractive, well-kept little park also has ball fields, picnic pavilions, and a playground, but little to keep the doggy set happy for long.

Hours are daily from 6 A.M. to midnight. From the airport, take Camp Creek Parkway to Butner Road and turn left. The park is on your right after Tell Road. (404) 306-3061.

• **College Park** 🐾 *See ❽❺ on page 130.*

Located in a subdivision, College Park has no walking trails, and since my boys aren't into tennis, it's only worth a quick stop. Leashes are required.

Park hours are daily from 6 A.M. to 11 P.M. From the airport, take Camp Creek Parkway to U.S. 29, just at the intersection of Interstate 85. U.S. 29 becomes Main Street in College Park. Turn right onto

Hawthorn Avenue. The park is located at the corner of Adams Street and Hawthorn Avenue. (404) 306-3061.

• **Sherwin Tucker Park** 🐾 *See* 🚒 *on page 130.*

If you're new to the South and don't know what kudzu looks like, this park has excellent examples strangling all of the trees and reaching across the grass toward the road. Kudzu is said to grow more than a foot per day. Let's just say it grows rampantly and will climb anything it touches.

Several years ago, before the Chattahoochee Raft Race was canceled after it got too big to manage, one of the local TV stations sent a camera crew to film part of the race. When the crew was preparing to leave in the afternoon, they found that kudzu had started to climb the legs of the camera tripods.

I used to work in an office building across from the Varsity Drive-In. Each spring I would watch the kudzu grow across an empty lot and completely cover an abandoned car. By summer, you'd never know a car was under there.

Some people make baskets from the strong vines after they die back in the winter. But since I know they come back to life each spring, I wouldn't trust a kudzu basket in my house.

Regardless of the ample kudzu crop, there's nothing special for your pooch to do at this park. Much of it is taken up by baseball and football fields. But if she's in need of a pit stop, she'll find plenty of room to squat between the athletic fields. Leashes are a must.

Hours are daily from 6 A.M. to midnight. Take the Old National Highway/Highway 279 exit off of Interstate 285 and turn outside. Turn left onto Pleasant Hill Road. The park will be on your right. (404) 817-6766.

SHOPPING IN COLLEGE PARK

Mu-Mae Antiques: This delightful shop welcomes both you and your pooch. Do keep a sharp eye on her as you wander through the antiques and collectibles. 3383 North Main Street, College Park, GA 30337; (404) 768-6121.

Royal Touch Antiques: The kind folks here sell, refinish, and restore antique furniture, all in a dog-friendly atmosphere. 3395 North Main Street, College Park, GA 30337; (404) 669-9525.

PLACES TO STAY

Atlanta Renaissance Hotel—International Airport: A double room is $85, and your pup stays free. 4736 Best Road, College Park, GA 30337; (404) 762-7676.

Budgetel Inn—Atlanta Airport: A double at this inn is $41 to $62, with no extra charge for your pooch. 2480 Old National Parkway, College Park, GA 30349; (404) 766-0000.

La Quinta Inn Airport: All La Quinta Inns allow pets, and the courteous staff won't make you feel like a second-class citizen for bringing along your best friend. Room rates range from $64 to $72 per night. 4874 Old National Parkway, College Park, GA 30337; (404) 768-1241.

Marriott Atlanta Airport: Rates are $114 to $142. Only small dogs (under 20 pounds) are allowed. 4711 Best Road, College Park, GA 30337; (404) 766-7900.

Ramada Hotel Atlanta Airport South: Your pooch can stay with you in some of the rooms here, so be sure to reserve a special pet room in advance. Rates are $84. 1551 Phoenix Boulevard, College Park, GA 30349; (770) 996-4321.

Red Roof Inn Airport: You and your four-footed companion can stay at this Red Roof Inn for $60 per night, with no extra fee for your pet. 2471 Old National Parkway, College Park, GA 30349; (404) 761-9701.

EAST POINT
PARKS AND RECREATION AREAS

• **South Park** 🐾 *See* **87** *on page 130.*

This small park is only worth a quick stop for your leashed pet. There's no water and no shade.

Park hours are daily from 6 A.M. to 11 P.M. Take Camp Creek Parkway from Interstate 285 and turn inside. Proceed left onto Main Street/U.S. 29/Highway 14. Turn right at Woodward Academy onto Cambridge Avenue. South Park is located behind the academy. (404) 765-1082.

• **Sykes Park** 🐾 *See* **88** *on page 130.*

Though this little park is fine for a picnic or game of tennis, dogs won't find much to do. With no trails, the only place to walk your leashed pup is along the many little roads coming into the park, which isn't much fun for either of you.

Hours are daily from 8 A.M. to 11 P.M. From Hartsfield Atlanta International Airport, take Camp Creek Parkway. Turn right on Herschel Road, then right on Dodson Drive. The park is on your right. (404) 306-3061.

FAIRBURN
PARKS AND RECREATION AREAS

• **Cedar Grove Park** 🐾 *See ❽❾ on page 130.*

If your leashed pooch is in need of a shady pit stop, this small park will do. Otherwise, it's mainly composed of tennis courts and baseball fields.

Hours are daily from dawn to dusk. From Atlanta, take Interstate 85 south to the Fairburn Road exit (Highway 74) and turn right. Turn right onto Roosevelt Highway, and left onto Highway 92. Take the left fork onto Rivertown Road. Turn right on Bishop Road, which leads into the park. You can also take Interstate 20 west to exit 92 (Fairburn Road). Turn left, then turn right on Highway 70 (Cochran Mill Road). Stay on Cochran Mill Road as it turns right at a four-way stop, and turn left onto Rivertown Road. Turn left on Bishop Road, which leads into the park. (404) 730-6200.

• **Clarence Duncan Park** 🐾 *See ❾❿ on page 130.*

Although this large park has no trails, there are plenty of places to walk your leashed pooch by the lake and under the large shade trees. The park also has baseball and soccer fields, a swimming pool, basketball courts, a playground, and a recreation center.

The park is open daily from 6 A.M. to midnight. From Atlanta, take Interstate 85 south to the Fairburn exit (Highway 74) and turn right. Turn right onto Roosevelt Highway, and left onto Highway 92. Take the left fork onto Rivertown Road, and the park is on your left. (770) 306-3136.

• **Cochran Mill Park** 🐾🐾🐾🐾 *See ❾❶ on page 130.*

A wonderful variety of trails makes this park an enjoyable destination for a day of hiking with your leashed pup. None of the trails are very long, so even couch-potato pooches can manage them.

I always head for the Cochran Mill waterfalls first, which I think are the best falls in the Atlanta area. Spread out a blanket and have a picnic in the grassy field opposite them. This is also the way to the loop trails, so your pet won't know whether to watch for falling sandwich bits or guard your spot from hikers.

Each of the trails is labeled and short, varying from about a third of a mile to about a mile in length. On some of them, you must ford the creek. Although Bandit and Laddie don't even break their stride when they come to a fallen log crossing over water, I avoid such makeshift bridges whenever possible, since I prefer something more substantial beneath my feet.

There's a great viewpoint a short scramble up behind the waterfalls. You can also walk to the Cochran Shoals Nature Center from the park, but I wouldn't recommend it. Your pooch won't be allowed inside, and the Nature Center keeps large animals, including a mountain lion, in small pens. It's depressing watching them pace back and forth in their enclosures. It's also a bit disconcerting to see the interest they show in Bandit and Laddie.

Hours at the park are daily from dawn to dusk. From Atlanta, take Interstate 85 south to the Fairburn Road exit (Highway 74) and turn right. Turn right onto Roosevelt Highway, and left onto Highway 92. Take the left fork onto Rivertown Road. Turn left onto Cochran Mill Road. The park is on your right. Turn left into the parking area and walk across the road to reach the trailhead. An alternate route is to take Interstate 20 west to exit 92 (Fairburn Road). Turn left, then turn right on Highway 70 (Cochran Mill Road). Stay on Cochran Mill Road as it turns right at a four-way stop and goes straight at the next four-way stop. The park is on your left, with parking on the right. (770) 463-6304.

ROSWELL

Roswell encompasses a wonderful series of city parks. Some are purely people places, but if you're in the mood for more than a quick walk, several of these parks will provide many hours of fun for you and your pet.

PARKS AND RECREATION AREAS

• **Chattahoochee River Park** *See (92) on page 130.*

Not to be confused with the Chattahoochee River National Recreation Areas, Chattahoochee River Park is a beautiful stretch of land along the river south of Roswell. The park is heavily used, thanks to its location in a congested residential area. During the work week, office workers eat their lunch along the river. On the weekends, the park is overrun with joggers, bicyclists, and dog lovers. You can rent canoes and rafts, though your pooch isn't allowed on board. Leashed dogs will find plenty to do on land here, whether it be sniffing for evidence of fellow canines, watching the waterbirds that frequent the park, or barking at the horses grazing on the other side of the river. The park is long but narrow, so although you can get in a good bit of walking, you're never out of sight or earshot of Azalea Drive, a busy local thoroughfare. The park also has a children's play area and plentiful places to sit and just watch the flowing river.

Hours are daily from 6 A.M. to midnight. From Interstate 285, go north on Roswell Road. Turn left onto Azalea Drive at the Chattahoochee River. The park is on the left at the first traffic light. (770) 640-3055.

• **East Roswell Park** 🐾🐾🐾 🦴 *See* ㊳ *on page 130.*
The two-mile trail at this park, which winds through the woods and by the baseball fields and tennis courts and offers some shade along the way, is a real treat for you and your leashed pup. As the sign on the trail says, your pooch must be on a nonretractable leash, and you must pick up after her. Other amenities include a children's playground and a recreation center that offers numerous classes and activities for adults and children.

Park hours are daily from 7 A.M. to 11 P.M. From Atlanta, take Interstate 400 north to Holcomb Bridge Road and turn right. Turn right on Fouts Road, then right into the park on A. C. Lavender Drive. (770) 594-6134.

• **Roswell Area Park** 🐾🐾🐾 🦴 *See* ㊴ *on page 130.*
The four trails at this attractive park range in length from 1.25 to 3.1 miles and can be walked as one longer loop if desired. One of the graded trails leads around the small lake, and another leads to a creek. (Dogs aren't allowed in the lake, but can splash around in the creek.) Nature lovers may bemoan the fact that they're never out of sight of some sign of civilization, whether it's a picnic table, one of the baseball, football, or soccer fields, a tennis or basketball court, or one of the park buildings, such as the gym, the visual arts building, the community activity building, the physical activity center, or the swimming pool. But the dogs who frequent the park—and there are many—enjoy it all the same. Leashes are mandatory here.

A host of outdoors-oriented programs are taught at this park, including map and compass reading and backpacking, but you'll have to leave your pup at home if you're taking a class.

Hours are daily from 7 A.M. to 11 P.M. Take Highway 400 north to the West Holcomb Bridge Road exit. Turn left onto Alpharetta Highway, then right onto Woodstock Road. The park is on the right. (770) 641-3760.

• **Waller Park I/Waller Park Extension** 🐾🐾 *See* ㊵ *on page 130.*
This delightful park, really two parks joined by a wonderful trail, could become one of your favorites. The trail is part of the Historic Roswell Trail System. It hugs a very noisy creek, which once powered a clothing factory, for part of its length. If you sit by this creek,

you can't hear anything but the water. Your dog may not appreciate the implications of this, but you will. Lean out over the footbridge and close your eyes, and you can easily imagine you're in north Georgia, next to a waterfall such as Amicalola Falls. Leashes are mandatory.

Hours are daily from 7 A.M. to midnight. Take Highway 400 north to the west Holcomb Bridge Road exit. Turn left onto Warsaw Road, which becomes Norcross Street. Turn left on Myrtle Street, and left onto Oak Street to reach the park. (770) 641-3997.

SHOPPING IN ROSWELL

abbadabba's: Stop at this shoe and clothing shop for Rockports, Birkenstocks, and trendy footwear. Your pooch can come in, too. 1580 Holcomb Bridge Road #18, Roswell, GA 30076; (770) 998-2222.

PLACES TO STAY

Budgetel Inn: A double room at this inn is $60, and your dog can stay free. 575 Old Holcomb Bridge Road, Roswell, GA 30076; (770) 552-0200.

DIVERSIONS

Count your blessings: Saint David's Episcopal Church in Roswell holds a Blessing of the Animals each year around the fourth of October, the Feast Day of Saint Francis. Since Saint Francis was the patron saint of all animals, pet owners bring their dogs, cats, turtles, goldfish, hamsters, guinea pigs, and even horses to a special service. The Episcopal Church teaches that animals are a blessing in our lives, and the priest blesses each animal and its owner individually. The church is located at 1015 Old Roswell Road, Roswell, GA 30076; (770) 993-6084.

Go on a Volksmarch: If you and your pooch love to walk, consider joining the Roswell Striders, who participate in Volksmarchs all over the city and beyond. Volksmarching, which started in Germany and is now international, is a noncompetitive, family-oriented sport in which members participate in organized walks. In this country, standard Volksmarchs are 10k in length (6.2 miles), while European Volksmarchs are typically 11k to 12k. Each member keeps track of their walks in a special book, which is stamped at the end of each Volksmarch. The Roswell Striders meet at the Community Activity Building at Roswell Area Park (see page 167) the third Monday of the month at 7 P.M. Many of the members bring their dogs to the marches, and one of the dues-paying members is a dog. Beau, a basset hound, has his own book (although he gets a little help filling it out). He wears a scarf to the walks, adorned with the patches he has earned. The Volkswalk club in Helen sponsors two marches a year that the Roswell Striders attend, one during the Octoberfest celebration. The group in Madison holds a march in April each year that the local group attends. Contact Linda Nichols at (770) 594-6127 for more information.

SANDY SPRINGS
PARKS AND RECREATION AREAS

• **Allen Road Park** 🐾🐾 *See* 96 *on page 130.*

Allen Road Park may be small, but if your dog is like either of mine, she'll love it. She probably won't be impressed by the tennis courts or playground, but there's plenty of shade provided by black walnut, sweet gum, and oak trees, and wild violets pop up each spring. Best of all for Bandit, the park has two creeks, his idea of dog heaven.

The park is heavily used by lunching office workers during the week and families on weekends. And since it's a popular rendezvous spot, parking may be limited. Leashes are required.

Hours are daily from 6 A.M. to midnight. From Interstate 285, turn north on Roswell Road. Make the first left onto Allen Road. The park is at the corner of Allen Road and Lake Forest Drive. (770) 306-3061.

UNION CITY
PARKS AND RECREATION AREAS

• **Ronald W. Bridges Park** 🐾🐾 *See* 97 *on page 130.*

With a nice mix of open and wooded areas, you and your leashed pooch could spend a fine afternoon at this large park. A nature trail winds through heavy woods, and there's a small creek at the back, just deep enough for wading. Also here are tennis courts, baseball fields, a playground, and picnicking areas.

Hours are daily from 8 A.M. to 11 P.M. on Monday through Saturday, and noon to 11 P.M. on Sunday. Take the Jonesboro Road exit off of Interstate 85 and turn north. Turn right onto Roosevelt Highway/ U.S. 29/Highway 14. Turn left onto Dixie Lake Road and the park. The park is also bordered by Longino and Alexander Streets. (770) 306-6852.

GWINNETT COUNTY

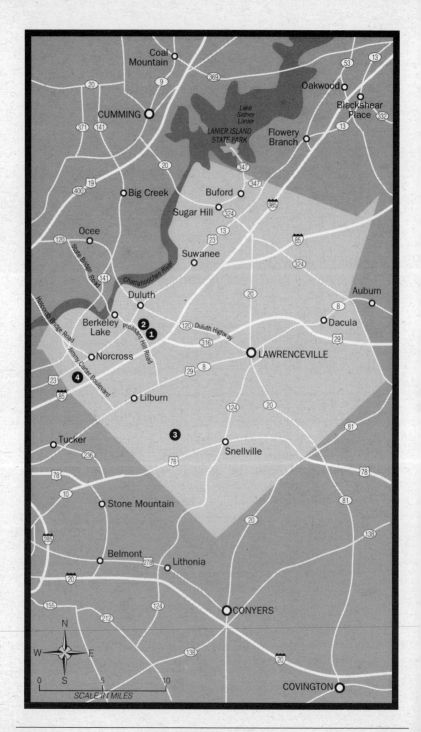

GWINNETT COUNTY

9
GWINNETT COUNTY

According to the county slogan, Gwinnett is great! Your dog may agree when the two of you visit some of the great parks featured in this chapter. And from a hotel standpoint, this is one of the doggone dog-friendliest places in the Atlanta area. Remember to keep your pooch leashed and wearing her rabies tag at all times as proof of vaccination.

For a northern suburb, Gwinnett is remarkably well situated with the Atlanta expressway system. Several years ago a friend bought a house up by Gwinnett Place Mall. I was surprised that anyone would want to live that far out and work where she did, in mid-town. As it turned out, Interstate 85 was widened about that time and she was able to get into work in under half an hour, while it always takes me an hour coming from Marietta.

DULUTH

• **Shorty Howell Park** 🐾🐾🐾🐾 🐾 🐕 *See* **1** *on page 172.*

My dogs have loads of fun at this delightful park, even though leashes are required. Bandit, my hunter, enjoys spying on the ducks on the lake. Laddie, my dog-foodaholic, hasn't figured out the caloric potential in these animals and ignores them. Both of them like the two-mile walk around the park, which winds behind the ball fields, parking areas, and the lake, meandering through cool woods and open fields.

Shorty Howell Park is such a relaxing place to spend the day that you'll certainly want to bring a lunch to enjoy at one of the picnic tables or on a blanket spread near the lake. You won't need to use the fitness stops if you do the trail once or twice with your pooch. There are always plenty of other people and their dogs at this park, but it's large enough that you don't have to socialize if your pet isn't too friendly. Even the trail is wide enough to allow dogs to pass each other without getting too close for comfort.

The park is open daily from 7 A.M. to midnight. From Interstate 85 heading north, exit left on Pleasant Hill Road. The park is on the right. (770) 623-2784.

• **W. P. Jones Memorial Park** 🐾🐾🐾 👟 *See* ❷ *on page 172.*

You and your leashed pooch are going to love this park. First, there's the caboose that both of you can wander through (very popular with younger humans). You and your dog may find the steep, narrow steps leading into the caboose easier to navigate going up than down. Back on the ground, you'll be facing the playground, and beyond that, the creek.

With such easy access to the water, it may take a while to get your dog out of the creek. When you do, you can both walk the one-mile nature trail that winds through the 17 acres of woods behind the circa 1940s train depot. The dense shade and streams you'll cross keep the temperature low, but if your dog gets hot, there's always the creek to cool him off.

The only drawback to the park is its popularity. With tennis and volleyball courts and picnicking areas in addition to the playground, there are always lots of families here. You'll also see lots of other dogs and their best friends, especially on the walk through the woods and by the creek.

Hours are daily from 7 A.M. to midnight. From Atlanta, take Interstate 85 north to the Pleasant Hill Road exit and turn left. The park will be on your right, about two miles down. (770) 623-2781.

SHOPPING IN DULUTH

Petsmart: When you need dog supplies, Petsmart is your best bet. It carries a wide variety of treats guaranteed to please even the pickiest of pooches. Best of all, the store doesn't sell cats and dogs. With more than 10 million dogs being put to sleep every year in this country, I appreciate their efforts to help by sponsoring adoptions on their premises through the local humane societies. Petsmart is located all over the Atlanta area. 3823 Venture Drive Northwest, Duluth, GA 30144; (770) 813-8400.

PLACES TO STAY

Amerisuites: There is a 25-pound limit for dogs, and they cost an extra $10 a day. Rates are $65 to $105, plus the $10 fee. 3390 Venture Parkway Northwest, Duluth, GA; (770) 623-6800.

Atlanta Marriott Gwinnett Place: A refundable damage deposit of $100 is required for your pooch. Double rooms go for $129. 1775 Pleasant Hill Road, Duluth, GA 30136; (770) 923-1775.

Days Inn—Gwinnett Place: The rate for a double room (including the $5 per day charge for your canine companion) is $74. 1948 Day Drive, Duluth, GA 30136; (770) 416-1211.

DIVERSIONS

Show Rover the iron horse: All aboard, furry train-buffs! The dog-friendly Southeastern Railway Museum, run by the Atlanta chapter of the National Railway Historical Society, has ancient railcars to explore, a miniature train for the kids to ride, and a gift shop. Dogs are welcome, as long as you leash and pick up any deposits made by your pet. Bandit wasn't terribly impressed by the 1930 Pullman lounge and 1928 dining car. My favorite was the 1911 private car that, according to the sign, was used in 1923 by President Warren Harding on a whistle-stop tour from Washington, D.C., to Tacoma. His speeches from the platform were the first presidential addresses to be broadcast coast to coast. After Harding died, the car carried his body back to Washington for the funeral, and then on to Marion, Ohio, for burial. The gift shop carries train memorabilia and displays mementos from the nineteenth century. Brochures trace Atlanta's development from the city of Terminus, through the fiery period of the Civil War, to its rise from the ashes to begin again. The railroad was not just important in Atlanta's development but was the reason for Atlanta itself. The Southeastern Railway Museum is a fun and different place to bring visitors from out of town. Pack a lunch and eat at one of the picnic tables.

The grounds are open every Saturday from 9 A.M. to 5 P.M. Children can ride the miniature train the third weekend of each month from April through November. On those weekends, the park is also open on Sunday. The museum is located on Buford Highway. From Interstate 85 heading north, exit left on Pleasant Hill Road. Turn left on May Road, just before Buford Highway. 3966 Buford Highway, Duluth, GA 30136; (770) 476-2013.

LAWRENCEVILLE
SHOPPING IN LAWRENCEVILLE

Petsmart: Taking your pooch to Petsmart is like taking your kid to the mall. You'll find grooming supplies, toys of every description, basic clothing needs, and special seasonal costumes, plus a huge selection of dog food. In addition, the store offers special services, such as grooming and dog training. There's even a full-service veterinary hospital on site during extended hours, seven days a week, ready to care for the medical needs of your pooch from vaccination through surgery. 875 Lawrenceville Suwanee Road, Lawrenceville, GA 30243; (770) 995-2449.

PLACES TO STAY

Days Inn—Lawrenceville: A $25 refundable deposit is charged for your pooch. Your room will run $53 per night. 731 West Pike Street, Lawrenceville, GA 30245; (770) 995-7782.

DIVERSIONS

Smart dogs, stupid tricks: The Atlanta Pet Fest is the place to take your talented pooch if you want to make him a star. Winning entries in the Stupid Pet Tricks contest are featured on the *David Letterman Show*. Other activities include demonstrations of sheepdog herding, Frisbee catching, pet grooming, and basic health care, including the prevention of fleas and ticks. The objective is to promote responsible pet ownership. At the petting zoo, you'll be able to admire everything from miniature ponies and potbellied pigs to ferrets and fish. Pooches must be leashed, and you should be sure to bring proof of your pup's rabies vaccination. This all-day event is held in April and is sure to be lots of fun for you and your pup. The cost is $3, with children under six free. It all takes place at the Gwinnett County Fairgrounds, just off Highway 316 on the corner of Johnson and Davis Roads. For more information, contact Richard Wooley at (770) 263-3939 or (770) 434-6002.

LILBURN

SHOPPING IN LILBURN

Petsmart: Petsmart has great pooch treats and toys, in addition to a wide range of services such as grooming and training. It's harder to get Laddie out of this store than to get me out of a bookstore. Best of all, Petsmart has a very "green" concept about the pet population problem and sells no dogs or cats. Instead, they work with area humane societies to sponsor adoptions on their premises. Petsmart is located all over the city. 2150 Paxton Drive, Lilburn, GA 30247; (770) 985-0469.

MOUNTAIN PARK

PARKS AND RECREATION AREAS

• **Mountain Park Park** 🐾🐾 *See* ❸ *on page 172.*

After you do a double take at the name of Mountain Park Park, you're leashed pooch is sure to bark bark with glee while splashing through the creek and exploring the woods in this large park. Laddie spends hours sniffing every tree, which is fine with me since this is a delightful place to bring a picnic lunch and while away the afternoon. If your dog still needs more exercise when you've finished checking out the woods, walk around the baseball fields. You can also hunt for stray tennis balls behind the tennis courts.

Hours are daily from 7 A.M. to midnight. From Atlanta, take U.S. 78 east past Stone Mountain and turn left onto Rock Bridge Road. Turn right onto Five Forks Trickum Road. The park will be on your right. (770) 993-4231.

NORCROSS
PARKS AND RECREATION AREAS

• **Best Friend Park** 🐾🐾 *See* **4** *on page 172.*

If this wonderful park had any trails, it would be hard to beat. As it is, there's so much to do here and so much space to do it in that you and your leashed pup will have a great time. The wooded area is full of dog-approved trails, or you can forge new paths behind the ball fields. Trees provide plenty of shade and keep the park relatively cool even in August. Your two-legged friends may want to tag along, since the park also has basketball courts, baseball fields, a swimming pool, a children's play area, picnic tables, and tennis courts.

The park is open daily from 7 A.M. to midnight. Take Interstate 85 north from Atlanta, exit on Jimmy Carter Boulevard, and turn left. The park is on the left just past Best Friend Road. (770) 417-2200.

PLACES TO STAY

Amberley Suites Hotel: You and your pooch can stay here for $65 to $85 per night. There's a refundable $50 deposit against damages. 5885 Oakbrook Parkway, Norcross, GA 30093; (770) 263-0515.

Budgetel Inn: A double room at the inn is $57 per night, and your dog stays free. 5395 Peachtree Industrial Boulevard, Norcross, GA 30092; (770) 446-2882.

Clubhouse Inn: Room rates are $60 to $79, and dogs are $10 extra per day. 5945 Oakbrook Parkway Northwest, Norcross, GA 30093; (770) 368-9400.

Comfort Inn—Norcross: This hotel was formerly the Heritage Inn. Rates are $69, and pooches stay free. 5990 Western Hills Drive Northwest, Norcross, GA 30071; (770) 368-0218.

Hilton Atlanta Northeast: This hotel has all of the amenities you would expect at a Hilton. Rates are $75 to $124, with a $50 refundable deposit per pet. 5993 Peachtree Industrial Boulevard, Norcross, GA 30092; (770) 447-4747.

Homewood Suites: Your suite at the hotel will cost $69 to $99 per night, plus a nonrefundable $25 cleaning fee for your dog. 450 Technology Parkway, Norcross, GA 30092; (770) 448-4663.

La Quinta Inn—Jimmy Carter: All La Quinta Inns allow pets, and they don't make you feel like a second-class citizen when you bring in your dog. A double room will cost $50 per night. Your pooch stays with you for free. 6187 Dawson Boulevard, Norcross, GA 30093; (770) 448-8686.

La Quinta Inn—Peachtree: This pooch-friendly La Quinta Inn frequently has dog biscuits at the front desk. A double room runs $48 per night, with no charge for your pup. 5375 Peachtree Industrial Boulevard, Norcross, GA 30092; (770) 449-5144.

Red Roof Inn—Indian Trail: Dogs are welcome at this inn. A double room costs $50 per night, and there is no extra charge for your pooch. 5171 Brook Hollow Parkway, Norcross, GA 30071; (770) 448-8944.

SNELLVILLE
SHOPPING IN SNELLVILLE

Petsmart: Not only is your pet welcome at any of the Petsmart stores throughout the Atlanta area, but you'll likely be in the minority if you don't have your pooch in tow. Keep a sharp eye on your dog as you navigate the aisles of pet treats and toys. It's a lot like taking a child through a toy store, with exciting "grab me" items at floor level. I find that putting Laddie in my shopping cart is the safest way to get him in and out without discovering unplanned purchases in his mouth when we reach the checkout counter. Petsmart is located at 2150 Paxton Drive Southwest, Snellville, GA 30247; (770) 985-0469.

HENRY COUNTY

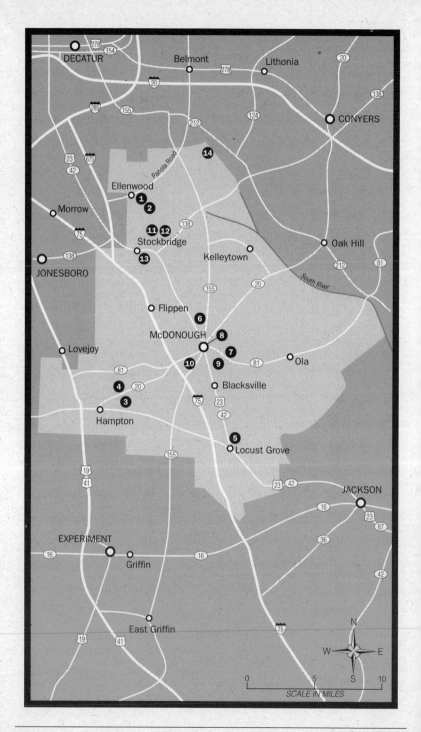

10
HENRY COUNTY

Your pooch will certainly find the drive to Henry County worth her time as she explores the many parks here. Laddie likes the fact that the county is more flat than those to the north, and Bandit enjoys all the lakes and streams. As elsewhere, a leash law is in effect, and your dog must wear her rabies tag at all times.

ELLENWOOD
PARKS AND RECREATION AREAS

• **Fairview Civic Center** 🐾 *See* ❶ *on page 180.*

You and your leashed pal can choose sun or shade at this pleasant park with a large manicured area on one side and woods on the other. A paved path circles the woods. The park also has a lighted baseball field, a playground, and picnic areas.

Hours are daily from 8 A.M. to 11 P.M. From Interstate 675, take the Ellenwood/Panola Road exit and turn east. The park is located on Panola Road. (770) 954-2031.

• **Hidden Valley Park** 🐾🐾🐾 👣 *See* ❷ *on page 180.*

The quarter-mile paved loop trail at this park is worth a visit. Although the trail is short, it's heavily wooded, giving you and your leashed pooch ample shade. It also offers a more natural feel than is typical for such a short trail, since the woods block off any views of the parking lots and ball fields. We've met some of the local dogs on this trail, out to stretch their legs with their companions. One woman pointed out a gravel road that leads off the picnic pavilion and winds down to a pretty creek with good access, allowing your pup to cool off in the water. A dirt road continues out the other side from a bridge over the creek, but it doesn't look as if it has been used in some time. If you drive down to the creek, there's a turnaround on the far side of the bridge.

I recommend taking the loop trail in a counterclockwise direction and then walking down to the creek. You probably won't see anyone in either place without a dog in tow, and your pooch will enjoy sniffing out the scents left by the locals. The park also has baseball and softball fields and basketball courts.

Hours are daily from 8 A.M. to 11 P.M. From Atlanta, take Interstate 285 to Interstate 675 and head south. Exit at Panola Road/Fairview Road. Hidden Valley Park is located on Fairview Road in Ellenwood. (770) 954-2031.

HAMPTON
PARKS AND RECREATION AREAS

• **Claude T. Fortson Memorial Gardens** 🐾 *See* ❸ *on page 180.*
Set next to the library, this lovely park—also known locally as Miss Claude's Garden—has attractive walking paths, with a nice canopy of trees providing shade. Your leashed pooch should enjoy sniffing out traces of the local canines.

Hours are daily from 9 A.M. to 9 P.M. From Atlanta, take Interstate 75 south of Interstate 285. Take the Highway 20 exit at McDonough and turn right. Stay on Highway 20 until you reach Hampton and turn left onto Old Griffin Road. The park is located next to the Fortson Public Library at Old Griffin Road and Fortson Drive. (770) 946-4306.

• **Wiley Evans Park** 🐾 *See* ❹ *on page 180.*
Though this small park is located next to an elementary school (much too distracting for Bandit), the walking trail around the playground and two baseball fields is pleasant enough for stretching your leashed pup's legs. Lucky pooches might find a tennis ball behind the courts. There's a small ditch with water in the spring and the summer, but even Bandit isn't impressed by it.

Hours are daily from 8 A.M. to 11 P.M. Coming into Hampton on Highway 20 from McDonough, turn right on Main Street, right on Oak Street, and right on College Street to reach Wiley Evans Park. (770) 954-2031.

LOCUST GROVE
If you haven't been to Locust Grove, you're in for a treat. The town is full of stately old homes dripping with gingerbread, turrets, gables, and wraparound porches.

PARKS AND RECREATION AREAS
• **Warren Holder Park** 🐾🐾 *See* ❺ *on page 180.*
The two creeks that flow through this park are sure to mean a paw-stomping good time for your leashed pooch. Park your car where the pavement ends and walk down the gravel road. This mostly sunny trail leads to a water treatment plant, which is a tiny

structure inside a fence, then circles back to the parking area. A large field by the parking area is also good for walking your pup. You'll find both open fields and wooded areas here, so your pooch can head for a sunny or shady spot. Amenities include football and baseball fields and picnicking areas.

Hours are daily from 8 A.M. to midnight. From Atlanta, take Interstate 75 south to the Locust Grove exit and turn left. Turn right onto U.S. 23/Highway 42, then left onto Peeksville Road. The park is located on Peeksville Road. (770) 954-2031.

SHOPPING IN LOCUST GROVE

McLemore Antique Gallery: I love antique shops and I love having my dogs with me, so I love this dog-friendly shop. Just one mile east of Interstate 75 at exit 68, it carries beautiful furniture and glassware. 3833 Highway 42, Locust Grove, GA 30248; (770) 957-8822.

PLACES TO STAY

Super 8 Motel: The rate for a double room is $40, plus a $3 per day charge for your pooch. 4605 Hampton Road, Locust Grove, GA 30248; (770) 957-2936.

McDONOUGH

Here's another delightful town full of antebellum homes with huge, wraparound porches and architectural interest. Every time I drive through I debate stopping at a real estate office, just to check it out. With the boys along, though, it's not a good time to house hunt.

PARKS AND RECREATION AREAS

• **Big Spring Park** 🐾🐾 *See* **6** *on page 180.*

Your leashed pooch will enjoy wetting his whiskers while you read the plaque stating the "City of McDonough was founded at this site in 1825 due to the abundant water flowing from this natural spring." There's also a four-mile paved walking track so you can both stretch your legs, plus tennis and basketball courts, picnic areas, a playground, and a football field.

Hours are daily from 8 A.M. to 11 P.M. From Atlanta, take Interstate 75 south to the Highway 20/Highway 81/McDonough exit and turn left. In downtown McDonough, turn left onto Lawrenceville Street, then left onto Spring Street and into the park. (770) 954-2031.

• **Franklin Rape Field** 🐾 *See* **7** *on page 180.*

As you might guess from the sign that greets you at this park—a giant baseball bat and ball—baseball is the name of the only game here. Unless your pooch is a big fan of the sport, he'll find little more to do than lift his leg. Leashes are a must.

Hours are daily from 7 A.M. to 10 P.M. From Atlanta, take Interstate 75 south to the Highway 20/Highway 81/McDonough exit and turn left. Stay on Highway 81 through downtown McDonough. The park is located next to J. B. Henderson Elementary School on Highway 81. (770) 954-2031.

• **Public Park** 🐾 *See ❽ on page 180.*

Set on McDonough's town square, this small park is home to a commemorative statue dedicated to "Our Confederate Dead," erected by the Daughters of the Confederacy in 1910. It's a convenient place for a quick squat if you and your leashed pooch are out investigating the eclectic shops in the area (see Shopping in McDonough on page 185).

The park is open 24 hours a day, seven days a week. From Atlanta, take Interstate 75 south to the Highway 20/Highway 81/ McDonough exit and turn left. Stay on Highway 81 through downtown McDonough. The park is located on the square in front of the courthouse. (770) 954-2031.

• **Sandy Ridge Park** 🐾🐾 *See ❾ on page 180.*

The paved walking track around the basketball courts in this park won't keep your pooch amused for long, but the horsey smells at the Lindsey A. Maddox equestrian arena just might. You and your leashed pup can also explore several large fields in the park, but don't be surprised if he tries to pull you back to the arena. Be sure to bring lots of water. Though the park is surrounded by tall trees, you won't find much shade on the walking path, at the arena, or out in the fields. The park also has a baseball field and a playground.

Hours are daily from 8 A.M. to 11 P.M. From Atlanta, take Interstate 75 south to the Highway 20/Highway 81/McDonough exit and turn left. Stay on Highway 81 through downtown McDonough. Turn right onto Keys Ferry Road to reach the park. (770) 954-2031.

• **Windy Hill Park** 🐾 *See ❿ on page 180.*

Don't be alarmed when you see the "NO PETS" sign as you drive into this park. In small letters it adds "allowed during activities," and refers to pets in the fenced baseball fields, a rule you would have followed regardless. The paved walking trail is half a mile long. There's also a small creek, but with no easy way to get to the water, you might end up taking an unplanned bath if your pooch likes water as much as mine do. Amenities include soccer and softball in addition to the baseball fields, a horseshoe court, and a 260-foot-long "Women's Field," where the women's softball league games are held.

Hours are daily from 8 A.M. to 11 P.M. From Atlanta, take Interstate 75 south to the Highway 20/Highway 81/McDonough exit and turn left. Turn right on Phillips Drive. Turn right on Windy Hill Road, the second road to the right. (770) 954-2031.

SHOPPING IN McDONOUGH

All of these shops are within walking distance of parking on McDonough's town square. Laddie is probably not the best emissary to take on a shopping trip, but I've only noticed a few sideways glances from the folks in McDonough.

The Country Mouse: This antiques, giftware, and country collectibles shop also sells my favorite treat, Jelly Belly jelly beans. Best of all, your pup is welcome to come in while you browse. 10 Macon Street, McDonough, GA 30253; (770) 957-0278.

For You, Only: An eclectic range of antiques and gifts are sold here, including jewelry, furniture, Egyptian perfume bottles, old metal toys, glassware, and prints. You and your pooch are welcome to browse through the shop. 15 Keys Ferry Road, McDonough, GA 30253; (770) 957-8850.

Front Row Center, Inc.: Only Georgia-made goods are sold in this shop, such as food, T-shirts, and kudzu baskets. (Does anyone actually buy something made from kudzu? I'd be afraid it would wake up and take over my house!) As far as I know, kudzu has never attacked a pup in his owner's presence, so you should both be safe here. 2 Macon Street, Suite H, McDonough, GA 30253; (770) 914-1248.

McDonough Hardware: As the name implies, this dog-friendly shop on the square sells hardware and also seeds, wind chimes, afghans, weather vanes, gardening supplies, and gifts. We met a golden retriever in one of the aisles on our last visit. 8 Macon Street, McDonough, GA 30253; (770) 957-2814.

Moye's Pharmacy: If you have a choice, wouldn't you rather stop at a shop that welcomes your pooch as well as you? 735 Airline Road, McDonough, GA 30253; (770) 957-9155.

Off the Square Antiques and Gifts: Please carry your pooch when you visit this store. The aisles are very narrow and there isn't room to walk your dog at your side. Keys Ferry Street, McDonough, GA 30253; (770) 954-1060.

Peachtree Music: You're far from Peachtree Street in this shop, but sure to have a good time anyway with your tune-loving pooch. Peachtree Music has a wide assortment of musical instruments and sheet music of every genre. 47 Macon Street, McDonough, GA 30253; (770) 914-2524.

Peddler's Porch: I love antiques, but I'm always a little uneasy about taking one of the boys into an antiques shop. The one and only time I visited this store with Laddie, he plunked himself down in the middle of the main aisle and spread out, just as the owner was telling me how well-trained dogs were more than welcome. I called Laddie and tugged and shook on the leash, but he refused to budge. Several customers were forced to step over him. All the while, the owner looked at me steadily and repeated that only well-trained dogs could come in. Finally, I picked him up and carried him out. Stop in and browse—if your pooch is more civilized than mine. 35 Macon Street, McDonough, GA 30253; (770) 914-5600.

The Right Touch: Your small dog is welcome in this boutique as long as you carry her, though Laddie's long hair tends to cling to the clothes. 2 Macon Street, Suite D, McDonough, GA 30253; (770) 914-9277.

Ward Drug: This drugstore with an old-fashioned feel carries a little bit of everything. Located right on the square, your pooch is welcome to join you as you shop. 13 Keys Ferry Road, McDonough, GA 30253; (770) 957-3911.

PLACES TO STAY

Atlanta South KOA: Rates at this campground are $16 to $25, with no charge for your pup. 281 Mount Olive Road, McDonough, GA 30253; (770) 952-2610.

Brittany Motor Inn: Rates are $34 per night. Be sure to reserve your room in advance. The inn only allows dogs to stay in one group of rooms, but they stay for free. State Route 20, McDonough, GA 30253; (707) 957-5821.

Holiday Inn McDonough: Your small pooch (under 30 pounds) is welcome to stay with you. Rates are $74 per day, plus an additional charge of $5 a day for your dog. 930 Highway 155 South, McDonough, GA 30253; (770) 957-5291.

Masters Economy Inn: Rates are $31 per night, with an additional $5 fee per night for your pooch. All sizes are welcome. 1311 Hampton Road, McDonough, GA 30253; (770) 957-5818.

FESTIVALS

Geranium Festival: Each spring on the third Saturday in May, McDonough's courthouse square is abloom with geraniums during the annual Geranium Festival. Your well-behaved (aren't they all?) pooch is welcome to attend this outdoor arts festival sponsored by the McDonough Lion's Club. More than 325 artists offer a variety of one-of-a-kind handmade items for sale. You won't go away hungry, either. You'll find typical festival fare to sample, including barbecue, sausage biscuits, peanuts, popcorn, homemade ice cream, fudge, and baked goods, all while enjoying live entertainment provided by local school groups. For more information, write to the Geranium Festival, P.O. Box 224, McDonough, GA 30253.

STOCKBRIDGE
PARKS AND RECREATION AREAS

• **Cochran Park** 🐾 *See* ⓫ *on page 180.*

This small park has a grassy area around one of the baseball fields for your leashed pup to explore. But the best place to walk your dog is in the woods between Cochran Park and Garner Park (see below). Stay away from the creek no matter how much your pooch whimpers and pulls on his leash—signs say to watch for poisonous snakes.

Hours are daily from 8 A.M. to 11 P.M. From Atlanta, take Interstate 75 south to the Highway 42/Stockbridge exit and turn left. Turn left onto Atlanta Road, then left onto East Atlanta Road and proceed to the park. (770) 954-2031.

• **Garner Park** 🔥 *See* ⓬ *on page 180.*

The best place to walk your leashed pooch here is the nice walking trail between Cochran Park (see above) and Garner Park. You can also wander around by the tennis courts and look for stray balls. During ball games, your pup isn't allowed near the fields.

Hours are daily from 8 A.M. to 11 P.M. From Atlanta, take Interstate 75 south to the Highway 42/Stockbridge exit and turn left. Turn left onto Atlanta Road, then left onto East Atlanta Road. (770) 954-2031.

• **Mickie D. Cochran Park** 🐾🐾 *See* ⓭ *on page 180.*

This park has one of those heart-stopping signs that starts out with "NO PETS," but it goes on to explain that this only applies to the athletic fields during games. Your leashed pooch is welcome on the paved walking track and in the woods. Basketball and tennis courts (check for stray balls behind the fence), a football field, a horseshoe court, and a playground can also be found at the park.

Hours are daily from 8 A.M. to 11 P.M. From Atlanta, take Interstate 75 south to the Stockbridge/Hudson Bridge Road exit and turn left. Turn left onto Rock Quarry Road, then left on Banks Road to reach the park. (770) 954-2031.

- **Panola Mountain State Park** 😼 *See* ⓮ *on page 180.*

Panola Mountain is a granite outcropping similar to Stone Mountain, but it isn't as commercialized. As a result, the many miles of trails would be perfect to explore with your pooch. Would be, that is, if dogs were allowed on the trails. Unfortunately, they aren't allowed out of the day-use area, thanks to an incident between a dog and a doe protecting her fawn. Due to the large amount of wildlife in the park, especially deer, pets have been restricted from the trails. This is as much for their protection as for the deer. Although deer seem mild-mannered and gentle, people and dogs are killed by these wild animals every year. (I'll never forget the signs in Yosemite National Park showing the three ways deer can kill you.)

The day-use area is quite large, though, so if you're in the vicinity, it's worth a stop. You'll have to keep a tight grip on the tie that binds near the picnic tables, since we always find chicken bones on the ground in this park. But Laddie does love checking out all of the trees, and Bandit loves the fuss the children make over him. The day-use area is always full of kids, something to keep in mind if your pup isn't too social.

The boys are allowed in with me at the visitors center, where you can pick up information about the park. Inside, an interesting display on why an area such as Panola Mountain should be protected shows the rare plants and animals found on this type of granitic outcrop that aren't found in other ecosystems.

Like all other state parks in Georgia, a parking pass is required. You can purchase a day-use pass for $2 from one of the rangers or buy an annual pass for $25. Unlike other taxes we pay, the day and annual pass revenue goes directly into park services, and not into the general fund.

Hours are daily from 7 A.M. to dusk. From Atlanta, take Interstate 20 east to exit 36 (Westley Chapel Road). Go straight across the exit onto Snapfinger Road. Turn right onto Highway 155 (Flat Shoals Road), and the park will be on your left. (770) 389-7801.

SHOPPING IN STOCKBRIDGE

Peachtree Music: Your pup is welcome in this shop where there's usually someone trying out a new guitar or keyboard from the assortment of instruments. All of my dogs have definite preferences in musical styles and performers, and it's fun to watch them experience live music. Trixie always liked to listen to Diana Ross and the Supremes. Laddie prefers Santana. Bandit is happy with anything except country music. 5013 North Henry Boulevard, Stockbridge, GA 30281; (770) 474-9177.

PLACES TO STAY

Best Western Atlanta South: Your medium-sized or smaller dog is welcome here at no fee. You, however, will have to pay $50 for a room. 3509 Highway 138, Stockbridge, GA 30281; (770) 474-8771.

Super 8 Motel Atlanta South: Pups are charged a $5 per day fee, or $51 per day for a double room for both of you. 1451 Hudson Bridge Road, Stockbridge, GA 30281; (770) 474-5758.

ATLANTA GETAWAYS

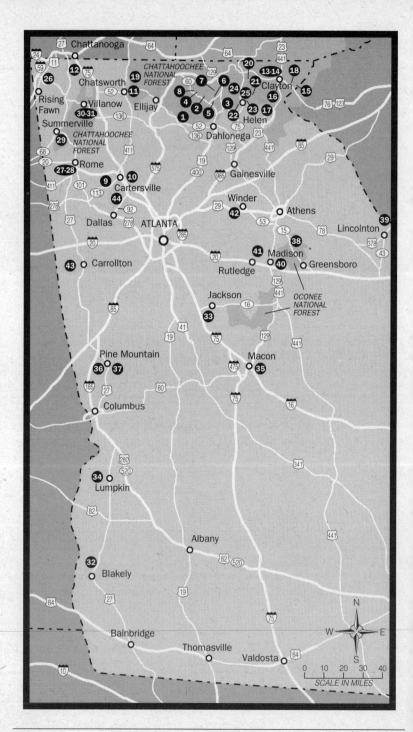

11
ATLANTA GETAWAYS

One of the great things about living in Atlanta is how accessible the city is to many outstanding parks throughout Georgia. Before moving to Atlanta, I'd lived on an island in Florida and had never gone hiking in my life. Upon relocating here, I was horrified to discover just how far I was from a beach. Luckily for me, I met my friend Betty, who introduced me to hiking. I was also lucky to have a dog who enjoyed taking to the trails as much as I did.

Most Atlantans prefer to travel north on the weekend to escape the heat, and they're rewarded with waterfalls, mountain lakes and streams, and shady hikes up the Appalachian Trail. But for a change of pace, try a day trip to the south of the city, where you and your pooch can take in the incredible beauty of Callaway Gardens (see page 228) during the Azalea Festival (see page 229) or gawk at the formations in Providence Canyon (see page 226). To the east, you'll find state parks aplenty, plus a delightful little antebellum community that welcomes all visitors, human and canine alike. And west of the metropolitan area are more state parks you'll want to explore.

I haven't included Savannah, a fabulous place to visit. At six hours one way, it's out of the realm of a day trip. I've also left out the Okefenokee Swamp. The gators are plentiful, and, while they won't generally approach someone of adult size, they tend to show a great deal of interest in dogs and young children. Anywhere one of my boys is featured as a menu item is not popular with me.

What follows is my opinion of the best getaways for you and your pooch outside of metropolitan Atlanta. I've indicated where a trail in a particular park shouldn't be attempted without hiking boots that are high enough to support your ankles and thick-soled enough to keep you from feeling every rock along the way. Mountain trails in Georgia are littered with small rocks and stones that make it easy to sprain an ankle or bruise the bottoms of your feet. While you can get plenty of blisters at the back of the ankle, hiking downhill creates blisters on your toes in ill-fitting shoes as well. I frequently see hikers limping along a trail wearing completely inappropriate shoes, such as sneakers or even sandals. Women's street shoes in particular are generally thin-soled. If you wear the wrong shoes, you're going to suffer for it. Proper boots will increase your enjoyment on most of the hikes.

Your pooch relies on her pads to protect her from the small rocks on the trails. If your pup isn't used to this type of hiking, work her up gradually, especially in the mountains. Even if she's in good physical condition, her paws may need toughening up before she's comfortable. You certainly don't want to end up carrying her back to the car on one of your jaunts!

NORTH GETAWAYS
BLAIRSVILLE/DAHLONEGA
PARKS AND RECREATION AREAS

• **Amicalola Falls State Park** 🐾🐾🐾🐾 🐕 *See ❶ on page 192.*

Amicalola Falls, at 729 feet, is the highest waterfall east of the Mississippi River, and its proximity to Atlanta makes it a popular destination year-round. In the spring, mountain laurel, rhododendron, and other wildflowers bloom in profusion. In the summer, the deep shade and mist from the falls keep hikers and their leashed dogs cool. In the fall, maples, sourwoods, and other hardwoods turn brilliant shades of red and gold. In the winter, the falls are covered with ice and snow.

Several trails wind through the park. The most popular is the Falls Trail, an easy, paved trail leading from the reflection pool of Amicalola Creek to the base of the falls. Wildflowers abound along the trail in the spring, including spotted touch-me-nots and violets. There are two observation platforms near the base of the falls that allow for great photo opportunities. Trixie was four months old the first time we took this hike. We were hiking up the trail toward the waterfalls when I felt a tug on the leash, and then it slipped out of my hand. Trixie had never seen water deeper than a bathtub before, and either slipped or jumped into the rolling white water. I felt as if my heart stopped as she disappeared beneath the water. But there must be something to the "throw them in the deep end" school of swimming lessons; she recovered almost instantly and was able to swim against the strong current back to the bank. She didn't seem the least bit concerned as she shook herself off and I scooped her up.

Another trail that starts behind the visitors center leads to the Falls Overlook area. It continues on to Springer Mountain on the Appalachian Trail, but at 7.5 miles each way, you would need to either start early or bring a tent. Otherwise, continue from the Falls

Overlook down the other side to the visitors center. The entire loop (without the Springer Mountain piece) is about 2.5 miles long, and is moderate in places. There are opportunities to walk through shallow water, if desired, which, combined with the deep shade, will keep you and your pooch comfortable even in the height of the summer.

Be sure you're wearing sturdy, thick lug-soled boots and carrying enough water for you and your pooch, before attempting the hike. Like all other state parks in Georgia, a parking pass is required. You can purchase a day-use pass for $2 from one of the rangers or buy an annual pass for $25.

The campground in the park has 18 tent or trailer sites for $15 per night. All sites have water and electrical hookups. To reserve a campsite, call (770) 389-7275.

The park is open 24 hours a day, and is about 65 miles, or an hour and a half by car, from Atlanta. Take Highway 400 north toward Dahlonega. Turn left on Highway 52 and follow the signs to the park. (706) 265-8888.

• **Cooper Creek Recreation Area and Wildlife Management Area**
🐾🐾🐾🐾 🦴 *See* ❷ *on page 192.*

The Cooper Creek area is where I first discovered camping as an adult. At the age of 20, I thought nothing of sleeping on a blanket on the ground and digging a hole for a toilet. Now, I prefer a bit more comfort. I consider a self-inflating foam mattress and a sleeping bag roughing it, and I only camp at campgrounds with flush toilets and hot showers. If you enjoy primitive camping, though, it's hard to beat the Cooper Creek area. There's a beautiful waterfall in the campground. Unfortunately, foolish humans try to climb the rocks, which are slick with wet moss, and a fatal accident occurs here nearly every year.

There are also several wonderful trails through the Wildlife Management Area for you and your leashed dog to enjoy. Other than a few short treks that are rather steep, the trails are rated moderate. The area is open for hunting during the season (from September to January), so if you plan to hike during that time, which I don't recommend, be sure you're wearing bright orange. Hunters react to movement and sometimes shoot before they fully realize what they're aiming at. A few years ago, a woman was shot and killed in her own backyard. She wasn't wearing orange, and the hunter wasn't convicted. I've always believed the act of picking up a gun has a negative impact on a person's intelligence, and I've seen nothing to change that opinion.

The Yellow Mountain Trail starts at the campground at the recreation area and leads to the top of Yellow Mountain, with ample opportunities along the way for your pooch to wade in the creeks that feed into Cooper Creek. You can stay on the Yellow Mountain Trail as it winds around and returns to the campground for a total of 3.6 miles, or you can pick up one of the other trails along the way.

The Cooper Creek Trail is a short connector between the Yellow Mountain Trail and is a little less than half a mile long. Rhododendron and mountain laurel are thick throughout this region and beautiful in the spring.

The 2.5-mile Millshoal Creek Trail has some steeper sections but crosses more water than the Yellow Mountain Trail. It can also be a little confusing since the blaze marks change colors three times.

You'll need your thickest-soled boots for hiking in this rocky area. Also carry water for both you and your pooch.

The campground at Cooper Creek is rather primitive, but does have pit toilets. It's closed from September to March. Sites on the water are $8, and sites farther from the water are $6.

The park is open 24 hours a day, and is located about 100 miles, or a two-hour drive, from Atlanta. To reach the park, take Highway 400 north to U.S. 19 and Highway 60. Stay on Highway 60 for 26 miles. You'll go through Dahlonega and Suches. Turn right on Forest Service Road 4. The recreation area is six miles down. (706) 632-3031.

• DeSoto Falls Recreation Area 🐾🐾🐾🐾 🐾

See ❸ on page 192.

Three spectacular waterfalls await you and your dog in DeSoto Falls, so named because a piece of armor found here was rumored to belong to someone in Hernando de Soto's party. Three short trails lead to the falls. The lower and middle falls are easy to reach; the trail to the upper falls is a more strenuous hike, but the high vantage point offers a fabulous view.

Have lots of towels ready at the car, since your pup will have plenty of opportunity to get into the water at side creeks along the trail. This may or may not be an advantage from your perspective, but he's certain to enjoy it, even wearing his leash. The trail is heavily used in the summer months. In the spring, rhododendron and mountain laurel bloom along with a variety of wildflowers.

Don't hike in this area without sturdy boots to protect your ankles, and be sure to bring along water.

Camping in the park is $7 a night. The campground is open from Memorial Day through Labor Day.

The day-use area is open year-round, 24 hours a day. The park is about 90 miles, or a two-hour drive, from Atlanta. To reach it, take Highway 400 north to U.S. 19. Stay on U.S. 19 about four miles after it joins with U.S. 129. The park is on your left. (706) 745-6928.

• **Dockery Lake** 🐾 🐾 🐾 See ④ on page 192.

The Dockery Lake Trail to the Appalachian Trail is more strenuous than my dogs and I enjoy, but I've included it in case it appeals to you and your more athletic dog. Laddie absolutely refuses to do this trail, and Bandit had to be carried part of the way when I took him on it.

If you and your leashed pooch are up to the challenge, the hike is spectacular. In late spring, flame azalea is in bloom along part of the trail. You'll also see a profusion of wildflowers from early spring to midsummer. A friend of mine and his Labrador do this hike regularly and don't understand why my boys and I want to hang out around the lake. We can do the half-mile Lake Loop Trail several times while they hike the seven-mile Dockery Lake Trail. Like all lake loop trails, this one is flat and Laddie-approved. There are numerous side trails that lead to concrete fishing piers on the lake, also useful for just sitting and relaxing after a long work week.

Be sure you're wearing sturdy, thick lug-soled boots and are carrying water for you and your pooch, before attempting the hike.

The area is open year-round, 24 hours a day. It's about 90 miles, or a two-hour drive, from Atlanta. To reach the park, take Highway 400 north to U.S. 19 and Highway 60. Stay on Highway 60 as you go through Dahlonega and Stonepile Gap. A little more than 3.5 miles past the gap, turn right on Forest Service Road 654 and follow the signs to the picnic area. (706) 745-6928.

• **Lake Winfield Scott** 🐾 🐾 🐾 🐾 See ⑤ on page 192.

Lake Winfield Scott is an 18-acre lake with beautiful hardwood trees all around it. One of the best times to see the lake is in the fall, when the leaves are red and gold. On a calm day, the trees reflected in the lake are worthy of a postcard. Be sure to bring a camera.

As pretty as the picture is, what interests my boys more is the trail around the lake. Laddie likes the fact that it's level, while Bandit likes it because most of it is in the shade and the lake is easily accessible for wading in and blowing bubbles. The trail is short, a little less than half a mile, and it's a great warm-up for the other trails here. Leashes are mandatory.

Two trails lead from Lake Winfield Scott to the Appalachian Trail. Both are moderate, so it takes proper incentives (in the form of food, of course) to convince Laddie to make the climbs. Both trails start off from the lake loop trail near the footbridge where Slaughter Creek flows into the lake. A wide path moves off away from the lake, plainly marked with a blue blaze. The trail sign mentions both the Jarrard Gap Trail (about a mile one way) and the Slaughter Creek Trail (2.7 miles one way). After walking along the creek for a short distance, you'll have to cross over the creek on a log to get to a gravel road. Turn right on the gravel road and follow the blue blazes to the trail signs. First the Slaughter Creek Trail will leave the road and cut off into the woods, with the Jarrard Gap Trail doing the same a few yards farther down.

Of the two climbs, the Jarrard Gap Trail is easier, but the Slaughter Creek Trail has the most spectacular wildflowers in the spring, including lady's slippers, dwarf crested iris, foamflower, trillium, and bloodroot. Since both trails lead to the Appalachian Trail, you can hike up the Jarrard Gap Trail to the Appalachian Trail, continue over to Slaughter Gap, and come back down using the Slaughter Creek Trail. Bring your lunch and have a picnic in one of the gaps as you gaze out over the mountains.

Another trail leads up Blood Mountain from Slaughter Gap, but I'm convinced that the blood the name refers to is from hikers trying to make the climb. It's more strenuous than a beginner should tackle, and there's no inducement that will get Laddie up that trail. At 4,458 feet, it's the highest point on the Appalachian Trail in Georgia, and the view from Blood Mountain is spectacular if you have a pooch more energetic than mine.

You'll want rugged, thick-soled boots with high tops to protect your ankles on this hike. Carry water for both you and your dog.

The campground has tent sites with no hookups. The cost is $10 per night.

The park is open 24 hours a day, all year, and it's located about 100 miles, or two hours by car, from Atlanta. Take Highway 400 north to U.S. 19 and Highway 60. Stay on Highway 60 as you go through Dahlonega, then turn right onto Highway 180 at Suches. Lake Winfield Scott is about four miles up Highway 180 on the right. (706) 745-6928.

• **Sosebee Cove** 🐾 🐾 🐾 🐾 *See ❻ on page 192.*

Getting to Sosebee Cove can be a bit of a challenge. You'll only see one sign from each direction warning you of your approach, and because the mountain road twists and turns, you won't see the limited parking area until you go shooting by it. You won't be able to turn around for several miles either, so I recommend slowing way down when you see the sign and crawling down the snaking road until you're able to edge over to a parking spot. There's only room for three or four cars, but that is seldom a problem.

The main draw for people at Sosebee Cove is the incredible variety of flowers, but your leashed pooch will probably show about as much interest in them as mine do (none). She will enjoy Sosebee Cove, however, if you continue down the old forest road when the main path turns. There are several signs pointing off to the left, and, since everyone else stays on the official trail, you and your dog will have the forest road to yourselves. The road winds down by a creek and goes on for several miles, so your pup can stretch her legs or splash in the water as long as she wants, but do remember that it's all uphill on the way out. This road isn't maintained and can be very muddy after a rain, so your pooch may enjoy this far more than you do. Make sure you and your dog are in good condition before hiking too far in, or you may both feel the climb the next day.

Once back on the official trail, take the time to wander the half-mile loop to see wildflowers as lovely as any cultivated in a garden, including my favorites—showy orchis, many varieties of trillium, and dwarf crested iris. Also here are trout lily, foamflower, bloodroot, several types of violets, star chickweed, and yellow lady's slipper orchid. This would be the best place to try out a wildflower hike if you aren't already an enthusiast. Your pooch will enjoy the short walk, since springs flow across the trail in several places.

Be sure to wear sturdy, thick lug-soled boots and carry water for you and your pooch.

The park is open 24 hours a day, all year. It's located about 95 miles, or two hours by car, from Atlanta. Take Highway 400 north to U.S. 19 and Highway 60. Stay on Highway 60 as you go through Dahlonega, then turn right onto Highway 180 at Suches. The Cove is on your left about halfway to Vogel State Park. (770) 745-6928.

• Vogel State Park 🐾🐾🐾🐾 🐾 *See* **7** *on page 192.*

This wonderful park is located near Sosebee Cove and Lake Winfield Scott, and since I frequently can't decide between them, I tend to visit at least two of the three whenever I'm in the area. I could easily spend all day feeding the ducks here. The trading post by the lake sells duck food by the bag, and the ducks congregate near the post and wait for willing visitors like me. Although they won't let you get close enough to touch them, they'll come within a few feet of you while they gobble up the cracked corn.

Laddie, who has never shown any interest in wildlife, lies on the bank of the lake and looks bored, while the ducks keep a watchful eye on him. Since his main motivation in life is food, I'm always surprised that he hasn't made the connection between the ducks and dinner. Bandit, on the other hand, sees himself as a major hunter. In the backyard he goes after the squirrels, who can easily leap away from him to safety. He watches the birds at the feeder and drools. I know better than to go near the ducks when my predator Bandit is with me.

I eventually pull myself away from the ducks and head for the trails in the park. (Leashes are a must on all trails and in the campground.) The Byron Reese Nature Trail is less than half a mile long and easy. Signs along the way point out almost two dozen varieties of trailside trees.

If you and your pooch want a longer, more challenging hike, the Bear Hair Gap Trail is a moderate, 3.6-mile hike through shady woods, along streams, and on the ridge. Your dog will love the water access on this trail. It crosses Wolf Creek twice and Burnett Branch several times, once on a footbridge and the rest via the rocks in the creek. The hike can be walked in either direction, but you and your dog will enjoy it more hiking counterclockwise.

The Coosa Backcountry Trail is a strenuous, 12.5-mile loop, and the park service recommends that this hike be done over a two-day period. Free permits for camping along the trail must be obtained from the visitors center.

Vogel State Park is a wonderful park for camping. In the spring, wildflowers blanket the ground, even in the campground, and include showy orchis, trillium, jack-in-the-pulpit, both Solomon's seal and false Solomon's seal, star chickweed, and foamflower. My usual campsite backs out over the creek. Campground sites rent for $14 per night. All sites have water and electrical hookups. To reserve a campsite, call (770) 389-7275.

Be sure to wear sturdy, thick lug-soled boots and carry water for you and your pooch. As in other state parks in Georgia, a parking pass is required. You can purchase a day-use pass for $2 from one of the rangers or buy an annual pass for $25.

The park is open 24 hours a day, all year, and is located about 100 miles, or two hours by car, from Atlanta. Take Highway 400 north to U.S. 19 and Highway 60. Stay on Highway 60 as you go through Dahlonega, then turn right onto Highway 180 at Suches. Turn right on U.S. 19/129. The park will be on your right. (706) 745-2628.

• **Woody Gap** 🐾🐾🐾🐾 🐾 *See* **8** *on page 192.*

If you want to hike part of the Appalachian Trail with your pooch, you won't find a better spot than Woody Gap. My dogs and I prefer to hike just part of the distance for a day trek, but with Neels Gap just 11.5 miles away and both gaps on the highway, you can go with a friend, leave one car at each end, and hike between them. If you and your dog are in good condition, there's no reason you couldn't do this hike. There's only one long, steady climb if you take the trail from Woody Gap to Neels Gap, so it's not as hard as it sounds. The view from either end is spectacular. Dogs are required to wear their leashes at all times here.

My couch potato dogs and I prefer to hike around at Woody Gap, picnicking on the large rocks and admiring the view. The trail from the gap to Big Cedar Mountain and back is only two miles, and not too strenuous. Whichever approach you take, drop a long-sleeved shirt in your day pack, even in the summer. The wind in the gaps can feel pretty cool after you've worked up a sweat. Also be sure to wear sturdy, high-topped boots to protect your ankles when hiking any part of the Appalachian Trail. Always carry water, both for you and your pooch.

The park is open 24 hours a day, all year, and is located about 90 miles, or two hours by car, from Atlanta. Take Highway 400 north to U.S. 19 and Highway 60. Stay on Highway 60 as you go through Dahlonega and Stonepile Gap. Woody Gap is about 5.5 miles farther on Highway 60. (706) 532-6366.

PLACES TO STAY

Amicalola Falls State Park Campground: See Amicalola Falls State Park on page 194.

Cooper Creek Recreation Area and Wildlife Management Area Campground: See Cooper Creek Recreation Area and Wildlife Management Area on page 195.

DeSoto Falls Recreation Area Campground: See DeSoto Falls Recreation Area on page 196.

Holiday Inn—Sky Top Center: While in the Dahlonega area, stay here for $65 to $75 per night. Your pooch is free. 20 U.S. 411 East, Dahlonega, GA 30161; (706) 295-1100.

Lake Winfield Scott Campground: See Lake Winfield Scott on page 197.

Vogel State Park Campground: See Vogel State Park on page 199.

FESTIVALS

Gold Rush Festival: The third weekend in October marks the date for the annual Gold Rush Festival in Dahlonega, held on the square. Arts, crafts, food, and fun are open to both you and your leashed pooch. At each festival, the TLC Humane Society in Dahlonega has a booth to sell popcorn, soft drinks, and cotton candy. TLC stands for Talonega Lumpkin County, as well as Tender Loving Care. (Talonega was the Indian word for Dahlonega and means "yellow metal.") Have a fun day with your pup and support a good cause. For more information, contact the TLC Humane Society of Dahlonega at P.O. Box 535, Dahlonega, GA 30533; (706) 864-2817.

Celebrate the Fourth: Toucans, turtles, and tarantulas, as well as dogs and cats, are welcome to enter the annual Fourth of July Pet Show sponsored by the TLC Humane Society of Dahlonega. For more information, contact the TLC Humane Society of Dahlonega at P.O. Box 535, Dahlonega, GA 30533; (706) 864-2817.

DIVERSIONS

Pan for gold with your pooch: Dahlonega, while not the first place gold was discovered in Georgia, is nevertheless Georgia's gold capitol since it was the site of the first major gold rush in North America in 1828. As a matter of fact, the gold leaf that covers the capitol dome in downtown Atlanta came from Dahlonega. It has to be repainted every 15 years or so, since acid rain washes the gold away. Two of the gold mines in Dahlonega allow you to bring your pup with you as you try your hand at panning. Consolidated Gold Mines offers underground mine tours, a rock shop, and, of course, gold panning. Unless you can take turns walking the dog with a friend, you'll have to skip the underground mine tour, since pooches aren't permitted. If you do go, the 45-minute tour takes you 200 feet below the surface and is highlighted by actual equipment used at the mine, shut down in 1906. Back on the surface, your pup can provide moral support as you try to separate gold nuggets from the gravel and river rock. 125 Consolidated Gold Mine Road, Dahlonega, GA 30533; (706) 864-8473.

The Crisson Gold Mine also invites you to bring your canine companion along while you try your luck panning for gold or screening for gemstones, including rubies, emeralds, garnets, and sapphires. The mine was opened in 1847, and some of the original mining equipment is on display. Route 5, Box 807, Dahlonega, GA 30533; (706) 864-6363.

CARTERSVILLE
PARKS AND RECREATION AREAS

• Dellinger Park 🐾🐾🐾🐾 *See* ❾ *on page 192.*

My leashed dogs could spend an entire day at this delightful park in Cartersville without getting bored. Bandit enjoys walking around the lake and getting his feet wet, though he's somewhat intimidated by the size of the ducks and geese. The two-mile walking trail, which you can pick up anywhere but officially starts at the swings, takes you in and out of the woods, crossing a creek along the way. The woods surround the park and separate you from the road, while the interior of the park is mostly cleared.

Amenities for people include baseball and soccer fields, playgrounds, picnicking areas, basketball and tennis courts, and a clubhouse. The park, donated by the Dellinger family, gets a lot of use by the pups and people of Cartersville.

Hours are daily from 6:30 A.M. to 11 P.M. except in the winter, when the park closes at 10 P.M. It's located about 40 miles, or 45 minutes by car, from Atlanta. Take Interstate 75 north to exit 124 and turn left onto Main Street. Turn left onto Etowah Drive, then right onto Pine Grove Road. The park is half a mile down on the left. (770) 387-5626.

• Red Top Mountain State Park 🐾🐾🐾🐾 👣
See ❿ *on page 192.*

Red Top Mountain State Park is one of my favorites, thanks to its close proximity to Atlanta and its nice hiking trails. The park is in a beautiful part of Georgia, and hiking here in the summer is a cool break from the heat of the city. This is also one of the only places where I've seen deer when I had my dogs in tow. Unfortunately, the deer were being chased by off-leash dogs at the time. A group of dog owners from Atlanta meets frequently at the park with their pooches to hike together. Even though leashes are mandatory, as soon as they get out of the immediate area of the visitors center, many of them take the leashes off and let their pets run free in the woods. Allowing a dog to chase wildlife in a state park is totally unconscionable and is likely to get all of us banned from using it. All of the national and state park rangers I spoke with while researching this book mentioned the problem at Red Top Mountain State Park, even those as far away as Panola Mountain State Park. Please obey the leash law so we can continue to enjoy this park.

Pick up a trail map at the visitors center to help you find the five trails at this 1,950-acre park, which range from handicapped-accessible to moderately strenuous. The half-mile trail that leads off the breezeway of the lodge is less traveled than the trails at the visitors center, so it's generally quieter. All of the trails offer dense woods, stream crossings, and abundant wildflowers in the spring. Deer are often spotted around dusk. My dogs have shown great interest in the smells along the trail by the visitors center, probably because of the dog hiking group that frequents the park. Whatever the reason, you won't get any argument from your pooch about a day spent at this park. Wear your sturdy, thick-soled boots and bring along water for you and your pup.

As in other state parks in Georgia, a parking pass is required. You can purchase a day-use pass for $2 from one of the rangers or buy an annual pass for $25.

The campground's wooded sites rent for $12 to $14 per night. All sites have water and electrical hookups. To reserve a campsite, call (770) 389-7275.

Hours are daily from 7 A.M. to 10 P.M. The park is located about 40 miles, or 45 minutes by car, from Atlanta. Take Interstate 75 north to exit 123 (Red Top Mountain Road) and follow the signs to the park. (770) 975-4203.

SHOPPING IN CARTERSVILLE

Apple Cart Gifts: Your pooch will enjoy sniffing out the many gifts and collectibles in this shop. If you have a rambunctious pup, you may want to carry him around the antiques and glassware sections. 19 East Main Street, Cartersville, GA 30120; (770) 606-1856.

Sallie B's Collectibles: Though the shop is filled with unusual items, I'm partial to the stone dog sculptures. Your well-behaved pup is welcome to join you while you do your shopping. 26 East Main Street, Cartersville, GA 30120; (770) 386-4106.

PLACES TO STAY

Allatoona Landing Marine Resort: This resort located near Red Top Mountain State Park (see page 203) has campsites with water and electricity for $15.75 per night. Pets must be leashed. 24 Allatoona Landing Road, Cartersville, GA 30120; (770) 974-6089.

Family Leisure Resorts: This campground near Red Top Mountain State Park (see page 203) is in the Camp Coast to Coast membership group. If you're not a member, your stay will be limited to one night. Dogs must be kept on a leash and picked up after. Rates are $15 for full hookups. 1001 Poplar Springs Road, Adairsville, GA 30103; (770) 773-7320.

Red Top Mountain State Park Campground: See Red Top Mountain State Park on page 203.

CHATSWORTH
PARKS AND RECREATION AREAS

• **Fort Mountain State Park** 🐾🐾🐾🐾🐾 ◀━● *See ⑪ on page 192.*

Fort Mountain State Park gets its name from the prehistoric stone wall found here. Though many archaeologists and geologists have speculated about who built the wall and why—for protection, for sun worship—no one really knows. It stretches from a cliff on the east side of the mountain to another cliff on the west, and varies in height from seven feet down to about two feet. There are more than two dozen pits at fairly regular intervals along the wall. No one even knows if it was all the same height at one time.

These mysteries make hiking here more interesting, at least for you and your human companions. My dogs have never shown a lot of interest in the wall, but they do like some of the trails in the park, which vary in length and intensity. Spring is the best time to hike all of the trails. In May, the rhododendron is in bloom all over the park, along with mountain laurel and wildflowers.

The Big Rock Nature Trail, at .7 miles, is a delight in the spring. Look for the sign at the trailhead on the road in back of the dam on Gold Mine Creek. Bandit has a hard time deciding what to do on this trail, as it winds between a stream on one side and another stream with a cascading waterfall on the other. If your dog likes water, she'll love this trail. For the most part, it's flat enough to be Laddie-approved. There's only one steep section, and it's at the end, where the promise of a car snack can motivate even Laddie to keep moving. Stop to enjoy the view of Chatsworth and the surrounding mountains while on the trail. On a clear day, you can see Lookout Mountain in Chattanooga, Tennessee.

The Lake Loop Trail is an easy mile-long circle around the lake. Both of my dogs like this trail, for different reasons. Laddie likes the fact that it's level and fairly short, while Bandit likes the fact that the trail goes through a wetlands area and he gets to wander through the water. Where the going gets muddy, the park service has installed boardwalks. Otherwise, you can wander over the rocks.

The Gold Mine Creek Trail is longer at a little more than two miles, but it's also fairly level. This trail follows the creek, with plenty of opportunities for your dog to get in and get wet. You'll actually be fording the creek at one point.

Both you and your pooch will enjoy the popular trail leading you to the stone wall. The easy loop trail is about a mile and a half long and contains several signs describing the different theories of the wall's origin and purpose.

The longest trail at the park is the Gahuti Backcountry Trail, which goes on for slightly more than eight miles, varying in length from moderate to strenuous.

Pick up a brochure with maps of the trails at the park office. Since this is a state park, you'll need a day-use parking pass, which costs $2 and is available from the rangers as you enter the park. An annual pass, allowing entry to all state parks for $25, is also available.

Before hiking in this rocky and root-strewn terrain, invest in a good pair of boots to protect your ankles. Always bring water for you and your dog, and remember to keep your pup leashed.

The campground has lovely wooded sites, which rent for $14 per night. All sites have water and electrical hookups. To reserve a campsite, call (770) 389-7275.

The park is open daily from 7 A.M. to 8 P.M. It's 85 miles, or two hours by car, from Atlanta. To reach the park, take Interstate 75 north to the Chatsworth exit (Highway 52) and turn east. The park is just past Chatsworth on Highway 52. (706) 695-2621.

PLACES TO STAY

Fort Mountain State Park Campground: See Fort Mountain State Park on page 205.

CHATTANOOGA, TN
PARKS AND RECREATION AREAS

• **Chickamauga and Chattanooga National Military Park**
🐾🐾🐾🐾 🦴 *See ⓬ on page 192.*

If you and your pooch enjoy the distance but not the intensity of long hikes, come to this park on the Georgia-Tennessee border. Seven trails through the park cross rolling hills, dense woods, and small streams, but they demand none of the more vigorous climbing required on most mountain hikes.

The main draw of the park is its historical significance, but if your dog is like mine, she won't care that this was the sight of one of the bloodiest battles in the Civil War. Your dog must wear a leash, but she'll be too busy enjoying herself to notice if you stop to read a plaque or two.

Some of the trails are simply too long for either of my dogs, especially during the summer. The Perimeter Trail, at 20 miles, is too far for them, as are the Historical and Cannon Trails, at 14 miles each. Even the Memorial Trail, at 12 miles, is more than they can handle.

But happily, the park has three trails that are short enough for the average dog (and dog lover) to trek, and long enough to provide a pleasurable day hike. The General Bragg Trail, at seven miles, the Confederate Line Trail, at six miles, and the Nature Trail, at five miles, are all within the stride of my dogs and me. The Nature Trail is periodically closed due to water damage caused by the large population of overambitious beavers.

I have three recommendations for walking these trails. Carry plenty of water, both for you and your dog. Also carry insect repellent. I don't know if the mosquitoes and flies are Yankees or Confederates, but they definitely won out on my first hike here. And be sure to wear boots, since the park is frequently muddy.

I prefer the mountains for hiking, but this park is a good alternative when your favorite trails are icy or just too cold. Although you'll be hiking through woods here, you're frequently out in the open, and you and your dog will warm up quickly.

Hours are 8 A.M. to 4:45 P.M. The park is 120 miles, or two hours by car, from Atlanta. Take Interstate 75 north to Highway 2. Follow Highway 2 to Fort Oglethorpe, and turn left on U.S. 27. The park is south of Fort Oglethorpe, on the left. (706) 866-9241.

CLAYTON
PARKS AND RECREATION AREAS

• **Black Rock Mountain State Park** 🐾🐾🐾🐾 👣
  See ⑬ on page 192.

Black Rock Mountain State Park has a lot to offer people and leashed pups, and it's one of my favorite places to camp. At 3,640 feet, it's the highest state park in Georgia and is in the remote northeast corner. If you ever want to photograph star trails at night with no light pollution, come to this park.

Because of the park's high vantage point, the views of the surrounding mountains are exceptional, and even the North Carolina Smoky Mountains are visible on a clear day. Fall is especially pretty, with the reds and golds, and of course spring offers the added allure of wildflowers.

If your dog prefers flat hikes, as Laddie does, she'll refuse to do the nature trail from the campground trading post down to Ada-Hi Falls. The sign says the trail is only .2 miles long, but with a change in elevation of 220 feet, both of you will be sure to feel it climbing out. The falls are especially pretty in the spring when the rhododendron is in bloom.

My dogs prefer the Tennessee Rock Nature Trail, which is easier though longer at 2.2 miles. It's rated moderate, but, after the Ada-Hi Falls Trail, will seem pretty tame. Maybe that's because there are more than two dozen markers along this self-guided trail that refer to numbered entries in the park booklet, and you have a good excuse to stop frequently. The wildflowers along the trail include the spectacular flame azalea, along with showy orchis, mountain laurel, and trillium.

If you're camping here, you may want to spend a day hiking the longer James E. Edmonds Backcountry Trail. Be sure both you and your dog are in good condition for the 7.2-mile hike—it's rated moderate to strenuous. The campground here has 52 tent or trailer sites for $14 per night. All sites have water and electrical hookups. To reserve a campsite, call (770) 389-7275.

As in all other state parks in Georgia, a parking pass is required. You can purchase a day-use pass for $2 from one of the rangers or buy an annual pass for $25.

You'll need your sturdy, thick lug-soled boots for this park. Plan to carry water for you and your pooch.

Hours are 8 A.M. to 5 P.M. The park is located about 120 miles, or two and a half hours by car, from Atlanta. Take Interstate 85 north to U.S. 441. Stay on U.S. 441. The park is three miles north of Clayton. (706) 746-2141.

• **Coleman River Scenic Area** 🐾 🐾 🐾 🐾 👣
  See ⓮ *on page 192.*
Little-used Coleman River Scenic Area is a great place to spend a relaxing day when you and your pooch don't feel like breaking any speed or endurance records. At about two miles round-trip, the trail along the river is easy and short, but quickly takes you into deep woods of huge white pines and hemlocks, with a feeling of peaceful isolation from civilization. Your dog will find plenty of opportunities to splash in small streams feeding into the river. Even with his leash on, he should be able to get his paws good and wet.

As is usual along mountain streams, you'll find a wide variety of wildflowers in the spring, including rhododendron, showy orchis, and Vasey's trillium. The maidenhair ferns growing along the trail remind me of the many that have died at my hands, despite (or perhaps because of) my pampering.

For hiking in this remote area, you should wear high-top hiking boots that will provide support for your ankles. Bring plenty of water for both you and your pooch.

The park is open 24 hours a day, all year. It's located 110 miles, or two and a half hours by car, from Atlanta. Take Interstate 85 north to U.S. 441. Stay on U.S. 441 until you pick up U.S. 23 North. At Clayton, turn left onto U.S. 76 West and follow the signs to the Coleman River Wildlife Management Area. Park at the camping area. (The park's primitive campground, with no toilet facilities, is free.) The trail starts at the bridge. (706) 782-3320.

• Holcomb Creek Falls 🐾🐾🐾🐾 🐾 See ⓯ on page 192.

My longhaired dogs appreciate the thick shade from the rhododendron and mountain laurel that line the trail to the two waterfalls here, Holcomb Creek Falls and Ammons Creek Falls. Even in the heat of the summer, the approach to the falls stays cool. The one-mile round-trip trail is as pretty as any you'll find in the mountains and is not as heavily used as the more well known waterfall trails. Wildflowers, including several varieties of trillium and violets, make the hike all the better in the spring. Leashes are required.

While you can see the falls through the trees at several places along the trail, when you get to the base of Holcomb Creek Falls, you may not be able to see all of it as it cascades 120 feet over several drops. Your dogs have easy access to the stream at the base of the falls. Continue on the trail past Holcomb Creek Falls to reach Ammons Creek Falls. Though these are not as impressive as the earlier falls, there's a good view from an observation deck.

The terrain is rocky, so be sure to protect your ankles by wearing thick-soled, high-top boots. You'll also want to bring water for both you and your pup.

The park is open 24 hours a day, all year, and is located about 105 miles, or a two-and-a-half-hour drive, from Atlanta. Take Interstate 85 north to U.S. 441. Stay on U.S. 441 until you pick up U.S. 23 North. At Clayton, turn right onto Warwoman Road. Turn left onto Forest Service Road 86, immediately after crossing the Chattooga River. Seven miles down Forest Service Road 86, you can park along the pull-out on the right, near a sign for the Holcomb Creek Falls. (706) 782-3320.

• Minnehaha Falls 🐾🐾 🐾 See ⓰ on page 192.

If you're looking for a waterfall that isn't overrun with other people, try the very short (less than half a mile) hike to Minnehaha Falls. Even Laddie can handle the slow, gradual climb of the trail, so you and your leashed pooch of any age and condition are sure to enjoy the walk and the sights, including splashing in the stream. This is another hike where sturdy, thick lug-soled boots are a must. Also be sure to bring water for you and your pooch.

The park is open 24 hours a day, all year. It's located about 90 miles, or two hours by car, from Atlanta. Take Interstate 85 north to U.S. 441. Stay on U.S. 441 past Tallulah Falls, and turn left on Lake Rabun Road. Follow the road about seven miles, then turn left on the first dirt road after Seed Lake Dam. About two miles down the road, park by a Forest Service sign pointing at the trail on the right. (706) 638-1085.

• Panther Creek Falls 🐾🐾🐾🐾 🐾 *See ⑰ on page 192.*

At eight miles round-trip, this trail is a bit longer than most, but the grade is easy, so all but very old or very young pups should be able to handle it if they're used to hiking. Bandit and I first took this hike when he was just four months old. He wore out after racing around at the falls for half an hour, so I got to sit on a rock and daydream while he dozed. When we started back, he wanted to be carried about half the way, and actually fell asleep while I was holding him. Packing an extra 15 pounds increases the intensity of this hike substantially!

If your dog is up to the challenge, though, this is a beautiful place to eat lunch and listen to the water. You'll pass small waterfalls on the way, but Panther Creek Falls is actually three cascades into separate pools. Water dogs love crossing the small streams on rocks and splashing in the rock pools. Leash up for this park.

As you would expect, the wildflowers are spectacular in the spring. And wildflower lovers are in for two special treats: three different varieties of trillium and large patches of gay wing, a pretty orchid-colored flower that blooms profusely in April.

The creekside trail to the falls is rugged, so wear lug-soled, high-top boots to protect your ankles. Also be sure to carry water for you and for your pooch.

Hours are daily from 9 A.M. to 9 P.M. The park is located about 80 miles, or less than two hours by car, from Atlanta. Take Interstate 85 north to U.S. 441. Stay on U.S. 441 until you see the sign for the Panther Creek Recreation Area, between Hollywood and Tallulah Falls. (706) 754-6221.

• Warwoman Dell 🐾🐾🐾🐾 🐾 *See ⑱ on page 192.*

If you or your dog aren't up to a long or strenuous hike but still want to get up to the mountains, drive to the Warwoman Dell near

Clayton. Both of the trails here are less than half a mile and mostly easy. The unusual name of this area has sparked a controversy, but the most likely theory relates to the Cherokee practice of having women decide the fate of prisoners in times of war.

The Warwoman Dell Trail loops around the picnic area to a waterfall and back. Along the way, you'll find wildflowers such as Vasey's trillium, violets, and bloodroot.

The Becky Branch Falls Trail has a steep section, but is so short that your dog shouldn't have any trouble. In spring, the mountain laurel and rhododendron bloom profusely. The falls tumble 25 feet between rhododendron hedges and make a beautiful picture in May when the flowers are blooming.

You'll need sturdy, thick lug-soled boots on these primitive trails. As always, carry water for you and your pooch. Leashes are required.

The park is open 24 hours a day, all year, and is located about 100 miles, or two hours by car, from Atlanta. Take Interstate 85 north to U.S. 441. Stay on U.S. 441 until you pick up U.S. 23 North. At Clayton, turn right onto County Road 5 East. Warwoman Dell is on the right, three miles from U.S. 23. (706) 782-3320.

ELLIJAY
PARKS AND RECREATION AREAS

• **Lake Conasauga Recreation Area** 🐾 🐾 🐾 🐾 ◄●
See ⑲ *on page 192.*

Most lake trails are Laddie-approved, since they're generally flat and allow him ample opportunities to cool his pads on a hot day. The Lake Conasauga Recreation Area offers three trails of varying difficulty, so you and your pooch are sure to find at least one path you both like. One of them is the garden variety lake loop trail, which Laddie likes. Another is slightly more strenuous, climbing a hill and traveling around beaver ponds. The last trail climbs to a lookout tower and is even more intense. The nice thing about this recreation area is that you have a chance to do all three trails on the same day. Your dog must wear a leash.

Start with the Loop Trail as it winds its way around the lake. Your pooch can wander into the water in lots of places along this milelong path. Be sure to watch for snakes.

The Songbird Trail starts at the overflow camping area and continues for .6 miles to a culvert. Along the way you'll pass a beaver pond and several wet, muddy stretches. Though the presence of your pooch will most likely keep any wildlife away, look for animal and bird tracks in the mud. Beavers, deer, bears, and raccoons frequent the area.

The Grassy Mountain Tower Trail is two miles one way to the lookout tower. You'll cross over the culvert that marks the end of the Songbird Trail before climbing to the top of the mountain. The trail is well graded and rated moderate. Though you won't be able to climb all of the way up the lookout tower, you can climb up to the first landing for a spectacular view of the mountains. Laddie can make it to the top of the mountain but refuses to climb the tower for the view. If you bring a buddy with you, one of you can stay with the dogs while you take turns checking out the view. It's superb.

Bring water for both you and your dog. The campground has rest rooms but no showers. Sites are $5 a night.

The park is open daily from 6 A.M. to 10 P.M., and is located about 100 miles, or two and a half hours by car, from Atlanta. Take Interstate 75 to Interstate 575. Take Interstate 575 to where it becomes Highway 5, and continue north to Ellijay. Turn left on Highway 52. Turn right on Forest Service Road 18 at the Lake Conasauga Recreation Area sign, about 9.5 miles down Highway 52. Follow the signs to the camping area. (706) 695-6736.

PLACES TO STAY

Lake Conasauga Recreation Area Campground: See Lake Conasauga Recreation Area on page 211.

HELEN

PARKS AND RECREATION AREAS

• **Andrews Cove Recreation Area** 🐾 🐾 🐾 🐾 👣
See ⓴ on page 192.

The Andrews Cove Recreation Area is a campground and a hiking trail. Since the campground is only open from Memorial Day through Labor Day, the hiking trail is nearly empty the rest of the year. Although this trail is not very long, about four miles round-trip, it can get fairly strenuous in parts as it climbs to the Appalachian Trail through dogwood, oak, and hickory trees. While I may fantasize about through-hiking the Appalachian Trail, neither my dogs nor I are up to the challenge. I do like hiking parts of the trail, though, and the Andrews Cove hike is one of the easiest ways to reach it.

The views at the top are sensational. Be sure to bring your camera. This is a good trail for wildflower photography in the spring when the blooms are thick.

Laddie likes to sniff out the spring as it flows from underneath a large boulder on the trail, while Bandit is happy just to put his nose under water and blow bubbles. When Trixie and I did this hike together, she spent a long time checking out all of the ground around the spring. I like to think that this was because the spring is visited by a variety of wildlife, but it may have just been due to other dogs who passed that way.

The trail ends at Indian Grave Gap on the Appalachian Trail. You can continue your hike toward Tray Mountain to the right, or toward Unicoi Gap to the left. My dogs and I usually poke around the gap and stretch out on some of the large rocks to enjoy a picnic lunch together.

As always in the mountains, you'll want your thick-soled hiking boots in this rocky park. Also, carry water for you and your pooch. Leashes are a must.

The campground has no hookups. Sites are $7 per day. It's open from Memorial Day through Labor Day.

The gate into the campground is open from Memorial Day through Labor Day. Other times of the year, park outside the gate and walk through the campground to get to the trailhead. The park is located about 80 miles, or two hours by car, from Atlanta. Take Interstate 85 to Interstate 985 to Gainesville. At Gainesville, take U.S. 129 to Cleveland, and turn right on Highway 75. Take Highway 75 through the village of Helen. About 6.5 miles after the bridge over the Chattahoochee River in Helen, turn right into the Andrews Cove Recreation Area and follow the signs to the camping area. Turn right opposite campsite number five. Park at the sign for the trailhead. (706) 754-6221.

• Anna Ruby Falls 🐾 🐾 🐾 🐾 🦴 *See ㉑ on page 192.*

Although the falls are beautiful any time of year, in the spring a profusion of wildflowers are in bloom, including showy orchis, squaw root, dwarf crested iris, and violets. Spring runoff can also increase the volume of water as it cascades from the York and Curtis Creeks. The twin falls, which meet and form Smith Creek, can be seen and photographed from the observation platforms at the end of the .4-mile paved trail.

As beautiful as the falls are, this is a heavily visited park, a factor that can reduce the enjoyment for you and your pooch. One way to please both of you is to continue on the trail past the falls. The Smith Creek Trail leads you to a campground at Unicoi State Park, about 4.5 miles away. If you have two vehicles, you can leave one at the campground for an afternoon hike. Otherwise, keep in mind that the round-trip distance back to your car at the Anna Ruby Falls parking lot will be about 10 miles, so make an early start. Although the trail doesn't stay near Smith Creek for long, it crosses several other streams along the way, providing lots of splashing opportunities for water-loving pooches such as Bandit.

Even if you don't have time to make the entire hike, go on past the falls onto the Smith Creek Trail far enough to get out of the crush of humanity. About midway on the trail you'll find huge boulders, a convenient landmark for turning around. It's also a good spot to relax for an hour or so while your dog noses around or while you eat lunch.

The purplish-pink rhododendron along the trail is in bloom in May. Starting in early April, as many as 30 varieties of wildflowers will be in bloom at any time during the spring.

The trails in this park can be rocky, so wear sturdy, thick lug-soled boots. Carry enough water for both you and your canine companion. Leashes are a must.

The park is open 24 hours a day all year and is located about 70 miles, or an hour and a half by car, from Atlanta. Take Interstate 85 to Interstate 985 to Gainesville. At Gainesville, take U.S. 129 to Cleveland and turn right on Highway 75. Take Highway 75 through the town of Helen to Robertstown and then turn right on County Road 56. Turn left into Unicoi State Park and follow the signs to the park. (706) 878-2201.

• **Dukes Creek Falls** 🐾🐾🐾🐾 🐾 *See* ㉒ *on page 192.*
This waterfall is one of the best in Georgia, not just because of its natural beauty but because of the recreational possibilities. If you like public attractions such as White Water Park, you're going to love Dukes Creek Falls. A slick rock at the base is used by kids (and adults) as a waterslide. I wouldn't recommend it for your leashed pooch, but you'll enjoy it. What your dogs will like about this place is splashing about in the water and stretching out on one of the rocks for a nap in the sun.

The hike down to the falls is short, although it seems a lot longer on the climb back up to your car. After viewing the falls, if you feel like a more strenuous walk, take a side trail to the left just before the rock staircase. It leads down to Dukes Creek at a more private spot, where your pup can cool her feet in the cold mountain water. Bring a picnic lunch and take off your shoes, and you'll both have a good time.

During the spring, this is an excellent trail for wildflowers, including rhododendron, mountain laurel, violets, dwarf crested iris, spring beauty, and foamflower. In the fall, the hardwoods are gorgeous.

One of the best vantage points for photographing the falls is at the wooden observation deck at the end of the wheelchair-accessible portion of the trail.

Throw an extra pair of boot socks in your pack if you plan to play in the falls. You'll also want to bring water on this hike, for both you and your pooch.

The area is open 24 hours a day, all year, and is located about 90 miles, or two hours by car, from Atlanta. To reach it, take Interstate 85 to Interstate 985 to Gainesville. At Gainesville, take U.S. 129 to Cleveland, and turn right on Highway 75. Take Highway 75 through Helen and turn left onto Highway Alternate 75 South. After a little more than two miles, turn right onto the Richard B. Russell Scenic Highway/Highway 348 North. The sign for the trail will be on your left after 1.7 miles. (706) 754-6221.

• **High Shoals Falls** 🐾 🐾 🐾 *See* ㉓ *on page 192.*

There are actually five waterfalls here, although you'll only be able to reach two of them easily. They're very dependent on rainfall, so try to visit this park in the spring after a day or two of rain. The hike is rated moderate, so plan to take the return climb slowly, particularly if your pup isn't used to strenuous climbing. Laddie doesn't like this trail and frequently sits down in front of me to prevent us from going farther. If you have a senior or overweight dog, you may want to choose another hike.

You're also in for a small adventure just getting here, since your car will have to ford a usually shallow stream across Forest Service Road 283. If your car is low to the ground, you may want to talk a friend into driving.

The hike itself is about two miles each way. Dogs must wear a leash. There are observation decks set up to view the falls and keep people and pups off the slick rocks.

All of the falls are pretty, but the last one, High Shoals Falls, is the most spectacular, with the water dropping more than 100 feet. Wildflowers line the trail in the spring, which gives you an excuse to stop on the way up and catch your breath.

Be sure you're wearing sturdy, thick lug-soled boots and are carrying water for you and your pooch, before attempting the hike.

The area is always open. It's located about 100 miles, or a two-hour drive, from Atlanta. Take Interstate 85 to Interstate 985 to

Gainesville. At Gainesville, take U.S. 129 to Cleveland and turn right on Highway 75. Take Highway 75 through Helen and turn right onto Forest Service Road 283/Indian Grave Gap Road, which is the first right turn after Unicoi Gap. After fording the stream on Forest Service Road 283, park where the road widens, about a mile and a half from Highway 75. (706) 745-6928.

• **Raven Cliff Falls** 🐾 🐾 🐾 🐾 🔹 *See ㉔ on page 192.*
I don't know a pooch who wouldn't enjoy this delightful trail. The grade is generally easy, so Laddie likes it, and Bandit loves the numerous fords of small springs and streams, which make it easy to get into the water to splash and blow bubbles. This is a great place to go for a picnic and spend the day, since there are lots of places for your pooch to explore at the end of the trail. It's heavily used, however, and you'll generally encounter several other dogs out for a day hike. Leashes are required.

The five-mile round-trip trail to the falls is abloom with wildflowers in the spring, including Vasey's trillium, trout lilies, dwarf crested iris, jack-in-the-pulpit, and foamflowers. The trail passes through a thick stand of mountain laurel and rhododendron, which forms a canopy above you. In the summer, the deep shade and proximity to water keep even longhaired dogs comfortable.

Your feet will appreciate thick-soled boots on this rocky terrain. Carry water for you and your pooch.

The park is open 24 hours a day, all year. It's located about 100 miles, or a little over two hours by car, from Atlanta. Take Interstate 85 to Interstate 985 to Gainesville. At Gainesville, take U.S. 129 to Cleveland, and turn right on Highway 75. Take Highway 75 through Helen and turn left onto Highway Alternate 75 south. After a little more than two miles, turn right onto the Richard B. Russell Scenic Highway/Highway 348 north. Go past the sign for Dukes Creek Falls and continue on Highway 348 until the road crosses over Dukes Creek. The parking lot will be on your left. (706) 754-6221.

• **Unicoi State Park** 🐾 🐾 🐾 🐾 🔹 *See ㉕ on page 192.*
Georgia is full of fine state parks, and Unicoi is one of the best. That usually means you'll run into a crush of people here, but if my dogs and I visit during the week, we have the park practically to ourselves. You can take your pick from several trails, none more than three miles long. Be sure to leash up.

The 2.5-mile Unicoi Lake Trail is rated easy. Unlike most lake trails, which tend to be short, flat, and kind of dull, this one offers a floating bridge across a creek and a variety of trail surfaces. The lake was drained to repair the dam and is scheduled to be refilled by December of 1996.

Wildflower enthusiasts shouldn't miss the Bottoms Loop Trail, which is only a little more than two miles long. In late April and early May, the trail comes alive with the rare pink lady's slipper orchid, jack-in-the-pulpit, several varieties of trillium, dwarf crested iris, and mayapple. Your dog will enjoy the good stream access from this trail.

If you and your pooch are up for something longer, the Helen Trail winds through the woods for three miles to the alpine village of Helen. The trail follows along a stream for much of the way, giving your pooch a chance to splash around and cool off. Helen is a very popular tourist town with lots of dog-friendly shops. Just remember that if you buy anything, you'll have to carry it all the way back!

As in other state parks in Georgia, a parking pass is required. You can purchase a day-use pass for $2 from one of the rangers or buy an annual pass for $25.

You'll need sturdy hiking boots to protect your ankles on this type of rocky terrain. Bring water for yourself and your pooch.

Unicoi State Park has two camping areas. The sites range from $14 to $16 per night, all with water and electrical hookups. To reserve a campsite, call (770) 389-7275.

The park is open 24 hours a day, all year, and is located about 90 miles, or an hour and a half by car, from Atlanta. Take Interstate 85 to Interstate 985 and Gainesville. At Gainesville, take U.S. 129 to Cleveland, and turn right on Highway 75. Take Highway 75 through Helen to Robertstown and turn right on County Road 56. Turn left into Unicoi State Park. (706) 878-2201.

PLACES TO STAY

Andrews Cove Recreation Area Campground: See Andrews Cove Recreation Area on page 212.

Unicoi State Park Campground: See Unicoi State Park on page 216.

RISING FAWN
PARKS AND RECREATION AREAS

• **Cloudland Canyon State Park** 🐾🐾🐾🐾 🦴
See ㉖ on page 192.

Cloudland Canyon State Park is my favorite park in Georgia. The canyon rim trail is long enough for a good walk; the waterfalls are beautiful and loud, easily drowning out all sounds of civilization;

and there are several places with water access so Bandit can get in and blow bubbles. Except for a few spots, the trail is level enough even for Laddie. Leashes are mandatory.

The West Rim Loop Trail is lined with mountain laurel and rhododendron, both of which burst into bloom near the middle of May. Numerous other wildflowers can be found along the trail, including dwarf crested iris, spring beauty, and wild geranium.

Trails from the campgrounds connect to the rim trail near the cabins. If you're not camping, park at the overlook parking lot and pick up the trail from there. If you leave Atlanta early, you can get to Cloudland Canyon State Park (about two and a half hours), hike the West Rim Loop Trail, and get back in time for a late dinner.

There are three main trails in the park, and you'll want to explore at least two of them. The Waterfall Trail is the shortest, so my dogs and I always do it first. This trail comes off the main trail by the cabins, where a sign points to the right for the waterfalls, to the left for the West Rim Loop Trail. Continue on the trail toward the falls. After a third of a mile, the trail forks; take the left fork a tenth of a mile to the upper falls. Here, Daniel Creek dives over a rock wall 50 feet into a pool. As beautiful as the upper falls are, the lower falls are even better—and well worth the short but more strenuous hike. After retracing your way back to the fork, take the right path a third of a mile to where Daniel Creek plunges 100 feet down to a green basin. On the hike back from the lower falls, I always wish I'd spent more time doing step aerobics. The trail is so steep that steps had to be installed. I haven't counted the number, but there are built-in benches along the way; give yourself a break and use them coming out. Laddie's sled-dog heritage comes in handy here as he helps haul me back up the steps.

The West Rim Loop Trail is about five miles long. Most of it is Laddie-approved, and even the few steeper areas aren't too bad. Before starting the trail at the parking lot, look out over the canyon at any of the overlooks to the opposite canyon wall. You'll frequently see hikers waving at you from across the canyon. A few hours later, you'll be doing the same thing. This yellow-blazed trail winds down along the rim and crosses Daniel Creek. The view from the bridge is spectacular in May when the rhododendron is blooming. Your dogs can get to the creek on either side of the bridge. I always stop here to listen to the water and let Bandit blow bubbles. The trail continues over to the opposite rim of the canyon, where many times the trail goes across bare rock near the cliff's edge. The rocks tilt slightly into the canyon. If you're brave enough to look over the edge, you'll see rocks that used to be where you're standing but have fallen to the canyon floor. If your pooch is unused to hiking, keep a tight grip on her leash. It's a long way down. (The only thing I've dropped into the canyon is a lens cap off my camera. I started down the bare rock after it and realized just how precarious my position was. I fell to my knees and crawled back up the rock. My dogs have always been more surefooted than I!) The overlooks along the trail offer spectacular views. Bring a picnic lunch so you can sit out on the rocks and enjoy them.

My friend Vickie and her adorable Pomeranian, What, hiked the rim trail with Laddie and me prior to the arrival of Bandit. What is so small, at just five pounds, that she couldn't just step over roots and small rocks in the trail. She had to gather herself over her hind legs and leap mightily into the air, touch down briefly, and hurl herself toward the trail below. Although she needed to be carried for brief periods, she hiked and leaped the majority of the trail on her own little paws. What a trouper!

Laddie, on the other hand, could step over most roots and rocks. When he came to a log, he leapt over it like a deer. When I lagged behind, huffing and puffing on an incline, Laddie pulled against his leash and tried to haul me up the trail. What, who likes to think of herself as a big dog, also strained against her leash when Laddie was exhibiting his sled-dog tendencies.

Before leaving Cloudland Canyon, drive past the main day-use parking lot and watch for deer near the swimming pool. Even if there aren't any, the picnic shelter there is a beautiful place to view the sunset.

You should wear hiking boots that support your ankles and carry water for both you and your pooch.

Like all other state parks in Georgia, a day-use pass is required here. You can purchase a day-use pass for $2 from one of the rangers or buy an annual pass for $25.

The wooded campground in the park has 75 tent or trailer sites for $13 per night. All sites have water and electrical hookups. To reserve a campsite, call (770) 389-7275.

Hours are 7 A.M. to 10 P.M. Cloudland Canyon is in the extreme northwestern corner of the state, about 110 miles, or two and a half hours by car, from Atlanta. Drive north on Interstate 75 to the Resaca exit (Highway 136). Stay on Highway 136 through LaFayette and to Cloudland Canyon. (706) 657-4050.

PLACES TO STAY

Cloudland Canyon State Park Campground: See Cloudland Canyon State Park on page 217.

Days Inn: Your small (under 30 pounds) pooch will cost $2 per day in addition to the room rate of $45. Route 12, Box 12920, Ringgold, GA 30736; (706) 965-5730.

ROME

Like its more famous sister city in Italy, the town of Rome is built on seven hills. The Etowah and Oostanaula Rivers converge downtown and become the Coosa, and though there are lovely parks and trails throughout the scenic area, my favorites are the paved pathways along the three rivers. Rome reminds me of countless other small towns in Georgia. The shops are small, the shopkeepers friendly, and they all seem to like dogs. Laddie and I have spent many an afternoon exploring this town, especially the paths along the rivers. It's hard to imagine a better place to live.

In addition to its parks and pathways, Rome has a rich history. Hernando de Soto is said to have visited the city in the 1500s. Rome's most famous citizen was Miss Martha Berry, the daughter of a wealthy cotton planter. Beginning in her own playhouse, she started a school for the poor mountain children in the area, which later became Berry College. If you're visiting with a friend, you can take turns walking the dog when you tour the Martha Berry Museum and her home, Oak Hill Plantation. Also, during the Civil War, John Wisdom, the "Paul Revere of the South," rode to warn the city that the Yankees were coming. Disaster was averted for a year, when Rome fell to Union forces.

When in Rome, stop in at the visitors center for a map of the area and other brochures on the north Georgia mountains. The visitors center is housed in a restored 1901 train depot. You can rent audio cassettes for a walking/driving tour of the historic districts while you and your pooch chat with the friendly natives. The visitors center is open Monday through Friday from 9 A.M. to 5 P.M., Saturday from 10 A.M. to 3 P.M., and Sunday from noon to 3 P.M. It's located at the corner of Riverside Parkway and Dogwood Street at 402 Civic Center Hill. To reach it, turn right onto Riverside Parkway from Broad Street as you come into town, then right onto Dogwood Street. Call (800) 444-1834 for more information.

The town is located about 65 miles, or an hour by car, from Atlanta. Take Interstate 75 north to exit 125 (Highway 20) and turn left. Turn left onto Broad Street at the sign for the historic district. You may want to park your car toward the end of Broad Street and head to the Clock Tower. The vintage Victorian homes in the Between the Rivers historic district are best admired from this side of the river. Be sure to bring something for scooping up after your pooch (plastic bags are best). Although there's no ordinance, it seems a shame to soil the gardens.

• **Heritage Park** 🐾🐾🐾🐾 *See* **㉗** *on page 192.*

Heritage Park extends down both the Etowah and Oostanaula Rivers. Be sure to leash your pet. The paved walkway along the Etowah River has little shade, but the breeze off the river offers cool comfort except in the middle of the summer. The walk along the Oostanaula River has plenty of shade and is beautiful, thanks to landscaping by two local garden clubs. At two miles each way, the trails are long and pleasant and give excellent views of the historic structures in the town. Stop at one of the many sandwich shops or bring your own lunch to picnic along the river. This is too pretty a place to hurry home.

Park hours are daily from 6 A.M. to 8 P.M. in the winter months, and 6 A.M. to 10 P.M. the rest of the year. To reach the park, drive down Broad Street and turn right on West First Street. Park in the lot on the left and walk across the Robert Redden footbridge, an old railroad bridge converted to a walking/biking trail as part of the Rails to Trails project. Continue down the path to the gazebo. Turn left at the gazebo to walk along the Etowah River, right to walk along the Oostanaula River. See page 220 for directions from Atlanta. (706) 291-0766.

• **Ridge Ferry Park** 🐾🐾🐾🐾 *See* **㉘** *on page 192.*

Ridge Ferry Park, set on the banks of the Oostanaula River, has paved trails along the river, large fields for relaxing in the sun, and wooded areas for great sniffing. All in all, this is a wonderful place to spend a day relaxing with your leashed pooch. The park also has a playground, picnicking areas, volleyball, badminton, rest rooms, and two trails. The trail along the river from the library to the Chieftains Museum (see page 222) is a mile and a half each way. At the museum, you can pick up the loop trail, which makes for a hike of a mile and a half round-trip.

Park hours are daily from 6 A.M. to 8 P.M. in the winter months, and 6 A.M. to 10 P.M. the rest of the year. The park is located on Riverside Parkway, past the visitors center. See page 220 for directions from Atlanta. (706) 291-0766.

DIVERSIONS

Chieftains Museum: If you drive into Rome on Highway 20, you'll pass numerous signs saying you're on the Chieftains Trail—the infamous Trail of Tears, the route of the forced march of the Cherokee Indians in 1838 that resulted in so many deaths. If you have a friend along, take turns walking the dog so you can both explore the Chieftains Museum (no pets allowed), which is housed in a nineteenth-century plantation house and has exhibits tracing life in the area from the Mississippian culture (ca. A.D. 700 to A.D. 1600), to that of the Cherokee Indians (ca. 1700 to 1838), and finally to plantation life and the Civil War. It's fascinating to see the complexity of life in the Mississippian period, and quite sobering to see how European-imported diseases wiped out the Indians. The Cherokee tried to adapt to European influence, developing an alphabet and even putting out a newspaper, but ultimately fell victim to greedy landowners. The museum is open Tuesday through Saturday from 10 A.M. to 4 P.M. Admission is $3 for adults and $1.50 for children. From Broad Street, turn right onto Riverside Parkway. 501 Riverside Parkway, Rome, GA 30162; (706) 291-9494.

SUMMERVILLE
PARKS AND RECREATION AREAS

• **James H. "Sloppy" Floyd State Park** 🐾🐾 *See* **29** *on page 192.*

Though it should come as no surprise to someone living in a state where Bubba is a common first name, the idea that a state representative would go by the name of Sloppy was more than I could imagine when I first noticed this park on my map. I just had to see the place named for this untidy gentleman, so the boys and I drove on over for a visit. I don't know what kind of legislator Sloppy was, but the park isn't at all exceptional. There are two trails, both easy walks on level ground along lakes and over streams. Leashes are required here. Bandit liked the park because of the water, but Laddie got hot and bored.

The campground has wooded sites that rent for $12 per night. All sites have water and electrical hookups. To reserve a campsite, call (770) 389-7275.

Hours are daily from 7 A.M. to 10 P.M. The park is located about 75 miles, or an hour and a half by car, from Atlanta. Take Interstate 75 north to the exit for U.S. 411/Highway 20 and turn left. Stay on U.S. 411 until you get to Rome, where you turn right on U.S. 27. About three miles from Summerville, turn left on Marble Springs Road and follow the signs to the park. (706) 857-0826.

PLACES TO STAY

James H. "Sloppy" Floyd State Park Campground: See James H. "Sloppy" Floyd State Park on page 222.

VILLANOW

PARKS AND RECREATION AREAS

• **Keown Falls** 🐾🐾🐾🐾 🔊 *See ③⓪ on page 192.*

Keown Falls can be very dramatic or little more than a trickle, depending on the rainfall that year. The best time to visit is in the early spring after a good rain. Your dog must wear a leash in the park. This waterfall is one of the few in Georgia where you can walk under and behind the cascade. When rainfall has been heavy, looking out through a wall of water is a real treat. My dogs seem to enjoy it, too, since there's usually plenty of spray in the air.

The loop trail to Keown Falls is 1.7 miles long. Along the way, you'll get a chance to see an unusual tree called the shagbark hickory, which sheds its bark in long strips. The trail is fairly easy except for the last ascent up stone steps to an observation deck.

The Johns Mountain Trail, which approaches the falls from the other direction and meets the loop trail at the observation deck, is 3.5 miles long and more strenuous.

Be sure you're wearing sturdy, thick lug-soled boots and are carrying water for you and your pooch, before attempting the hike.

The park is open 24 hours a day, all year. It's located approximately 110 miles, or a two-and-a-half-hour drive, from Atlanta. Take Interstate 75 north to the Resaca exit (Highway 136). Stay on Highway 136 heading toward LaFayette. A half mile before Villanow, turn left onto Pocket Road and follow the signs to Keown Falls or Johns Mountain. (706) 397-2265.

• **The Pocket** 🐾🐾🐾🐾 🔊 *See ③① on page 192.*

Even people who live near the Pocket have trouble giving directions to this scenic spot. And even if someone tells you they've been here, they may be referring to the *other* Pocket, about 25 miles away. As a result, this recreation area is not heavily used and is a wonderful destination for you and your leashed dog to spend a full day exploring the mountains. Your pup will love splashing in the streams, and you will enjoy the peace and quiet, since you might just be the only one here.

The Pocket is a nearly level horseshoe-shaped valley surrounded on three sides by steep mountains. The 2.6-mile Loop Trail leads from the picnic area through the woods and over two bridges. Numerous springs feed into Johns Creek here, with boardwalks over the wettest areas. Along the way, look for the rare pink lady's slipper orchid, which blooms in April. Other spring-blooming wildflowers include violets, toothwort, trillium, mayapple, spring beauty, and bluets. Trailside trees include the loblolly pine and dogwood.

The park is open 24 hours a day, all year, and is located about 110 miles, or two and a half hours by car, from Atlanta. Drive north on Interstate 75 to the Resaca exit (Highway 136). Stay on Highway 136 heading toward LaFayette, turning left on Pocket Road about half a mile from Villanow. The recreation area is about eight miles down Pocket Road. (706) 397-2265.

SOUTH GETAWAYS
BLAKELY
PARKS AND RECREATION AREAS

• **Kolomoki Mounds State Park** 🐾 🐾 🐾 🐾 👣
See ㉜ on page 192.

Seven Indian mounds, including one of the largest temple mounds in the country, are among the highlights at this fascinating state park. This area is believed to have been a major settlement for the Kolomoki Indians of the early Mississippian period (ca. A.D. 700 to A.D. 1300). Some of the mounds have been excavated and one of them is enclosed in the museum. One unusual feature of the site is that the mounds weren't all built at the same time or by the same culture. Carbon dating of one of the mounds puts it at about 500 B.C., so the Kolomoki may have been building their mounds where more ancient Indians had built before them.

Even if your leashed pooch isn't accustomed to hiking, she should have an enjoyable day at Kolomoki Mounds State Park, whether splashing in the lake or hiking on the trails. The terrain is flat and Laddie-approved, and the easy Wandering Water Trail is just over a mile in length.

Amenities for two-legged types include miniature golf and a swimming pool. The park also has a campground that is open year-round. Campsites (pooches stay for free) are equipped with water and electrical hookups and cost $12 per night. You can reserve a state park campsite by calling (770) 389-7275.

Like all other state parks in Georgia, a parking pass is required. You can purchase a day-use pass for $2 from one of the rangers or buy an annual pass for $25.

The park is open daily from 7 A.M. to 10 P.M. The museum is open from 9 A.M. to 5 P.M., Tuesday through Saturday, and from 2 P.M. to 5:30 P.M. on Sunday. The park is about 190 miles, or three and a half hours by car, from Atlanta. Take Interstate 85 south to Interstate 185. At Columbus, turn onto U.S. 27 South. The park is off of U.S. 27, six miles north of Blakely. Follow the signs to the park. (912) 723-5296.

PLACES TO STAY
Kolomoki Mounds State Park Campground: See Kolomoki Mounds State Park on page 224.

JACKSON
PARKS AND RECREATION AREAS
• **High Falls State Park** 🐾🐾🐾🐾 👣 *See ❸❸ on page 192.*

This scenic park about 45 miles south of Atlanta is a delightful place to spend a Saturday with your leashed pooch. It has three easy to somewhat moderate trails which total only about four miles, so you can easily do all of them in one day.

The falls are at a wide point on the Towaliga River, where it cascades over granite boulders. Ruins of a water-powered grist mill, burned in the Civil War but later rebuilt, can be reached via the Historic Ruins Trail. The path winds along a stone canal where you may spot river otters as well as waterbirds and wildflowers.

The Nature and Falls Trails provide an excellent view of the falls plus an opportunity for your pup to get his feet wet. Large muskrats live in the area, but you probably won't see any. Even if a leash law wasn't in effect, you'd want to keep your pup close by your side. The muskrats live in the bushes near the water and attack if provoked.

The Non-Game Trail is the longest, at a little over two miles, and is also the most fun for your pet. You'll cross several streams and have enough time for her to dry off before getting back in the car. In addition to spectacular ferns, the flowering redbud trees and dogwood trees and the abundant wildflowers make this trail beautiful in the spring. The trail starts in the Area 2 Campground.

Be sure to wear sturdy, thick lug-soled boots on these hikes and bring water for you and your pooch. As with all other state parks in Georgia, a parking pass is required. You can purchase a day-use pass for $2 from one of the rangers or buy an annual pass for $25.

The park is open daily from 7 A.M. to 10 P.M. It's located about 45 miles, or an hour by car, south of Atlanta. Take Interstate 75 south to exit 65 (High Falls Road) and turn left. The park is about two miles down High Falls Road. (912) 994-5080.

LUMPKIN

PARKS AND RECREATION AREAS

• **Providence Canyon State Park** 🐾🐾🐾🐾 👟
See **34** *on page 192.*

Providence Canyon State Park is quite a sight. Dubbed "Georgia's Little Grand Canyon," I would call it "Georgia's Little Bryce Canyon," since it has pink, yellow, and orange spires and cliffs like the canyon in Utah. It's also the best advertisement for kudzu that I know, as you'll see as you drive into the park entrance. Kudzu, the rampant weed that has taken over Georgia, was actually deliberately imported from Japan as an erosion control measure. Growing more than one foot per day, kudzu rapidly got out of hand and has become as much of a pest as water hyacinths in Florida canals. As recently as 25 years ago, you could buy kudzu seeds in nurseries in Atlanta. Now, of course, it's not only illegal to sell the seeds but it would be hard to find someone naive enough to buy them. I don't even trust buying things made of the dried vines. I see those dried vines on the roadways every winter, but they somehow come to life in the spring. I avoid the park during the late summer Kudzu Takeover Day (held in August). Since it appears that the kudzu has taken over long before Kudzu Takeover Day, I don't want to see what happens on that date.

You could argue that Providence Canyon is man-made, caused as it was by erosion due to poor farming practices. In the mid-1800s, runoff from a farm building created a small ditch, which continued to erode to the present depth of more than 150 feet in 15 canyons.

Several trails wind down into the canyons, all of them easy to moderate and all of them allowing access to shallow water at the bottom, which should please your leashed pup. The two main trails are the Canyon Loop Trail, which is three miles long, and the seven-mile Backpacking Trail. Numerous side canyons cut off from the Canyon Loop Trail, allowing you and your dog to spend as much time exploring as you'd like without going over the same ground.

Pick up a trail map at the visitors center, and be sure you're wearing hiking boots. Although the trails are not rocky, there's usually enough mud in places to make your footing somewhat unsteady.

Your dog, however, will be in her element as she races through slot canyons and splashes across shallow waterways. You may want to cover your car seats with towels before you begin your hike into the canyon, since your canine companion will almost certainly be muddy when you get back to the car. Remember to carry water for your dog, too.

Since this is a state park, a parking pass is required. You can purchase a day-use pass for $2 from one of the rangers or buy an annual pass for $25.

The park is open daily from 7 A.M. to 9 P.M. during the summer, and closes at 6 P.M. during the rest of the year. It's located about 120 miles from the south side of Atlanta, or a little less than three hours by car. Take Interstate 85 south to Interstate 185. At Columbus, turn onto U.S. 27 South. When you reach Lumpkin, turn west on Highway 39C. The park is approximately seven miles down Highway 39C. (912) 838-6202.

PLACES TO STAY

Budgetel Inn: Your small dog is welcome to join you at this hotel. Rooms are $55 to $60. 2919 Warm Springs Road, Columbus, GA 31909; (706) 323-4344.

Comfort Inn: Your pet can stay as a guest in your room for free. Rooms are $45 to $55. 3443B Macon Road, Columbus, GA 31907; (706) 568-3300.

MACON
PARKS AND RECREATION AREAS

• **Ocmulgee National Monument** 🐾🐾🐾🐾 👣
See ㉟ on page 192.

I've always been fascinated by Indian mounds, and these predate those at the Etowah Indian Mounds in Cartersville by thousands of years. Leashed dogs are welcome in the park, though not in the fine museum here. But if you visit with a friend, you can take turns checking out the museum and the 12-minute film.

Spring and fall are the best times to visit. My longhaired boys get too hot on the trails in the summer. All the trails are easy and flat, but several are too muddy to be attempted with a pooch. Except during dry periods, the River Trail, the Walnut Creek Trail, and the Opelofa Trail should be avoided because of the mud. All that goo is just too much of a temptation, and all the towels in the back seat won't be enough to keep the mess out of the car. The Loop Trail, at .3 miles, may be mud-free, but it's also far from the water, which doesn't make Laddie and Bandit too happy. My favorite trails are the human cultural trails, which pass by the prehistoric areas. They're also longer than the Loop Trail and a little more interesting, since I've seen more signs of wildlife here.

The park is open daily from 7 A.M. to dusk. It's located about 70 miles, or a little over an hour by car, from the south side of Atlanta. Take Interstate 75 south to Macon. Don't get on Interstate 475; stay on Interstate 75 until you pick up Interstate 16 South. Take exit 4 off of Interstate 16, turning east on U.S. 80. The park entrance is two miles down U.S. 80. (912) 752-8257.

PINE MOUNTAIN
PARKS AND RECREATION AREAS

• **Callaway Gardens** 🐾 🐾 🐾 🐾 🐾 ➤ *See* 36 *on page 192.*

Most Atlantans have been to Callaway Gardens for the spectacular Azalea Festival in the spring. When the thousands of azaleas are in bloom along the paths and around the 13 lakes of the 2,500-acre park, it's hard to imagine a prettier spot. And when you realize that everything you see was deliberately planted to restore land depleted by cotton farming, it seems like a miracle.

You and your leashed pet can view the flowers from a number of trails. The Bicycle Trail, which winds through the azalea, rhododendron, and holly gardens, is 7.5 miles round-trip, making for a good day hike. The shorter Azalea Trail is named for the more than 700 varieties of azaleas along it, and the Wildflower Trail has many rare varieties, including several kinds of trillium.

If you go during one of the special events, such as the Azalea Festival, your dog is allowed with you on the shuttle buses. You won't be able to take her into the buildings, however, including the must-see Cecil B. Day Butterfly Center, so bring a friend along to dog-sit while you take a look inside. The Butterfly Center is the largest glass-enclosed butterfly conservatory in North America, containing more than 1,000 free-flying butterflies from three continents. Bring your camera!

Hours are daily from 7 A.M. to 7 P.M. In the summer months and during special events, the park closes at 10 P.M. The park is about 70 miles, or a little over an hour by car, from Atlanta. Take Interstate 85 south to U.S. 27. Follow the signs to Pine Mountain and Callaway Gardens. There's a $20 per car charge for parking. (800) CALLAWAY.

• **Franklin Delano Roosevelt State Park** 🐾🐾🐾🐾 👣
See ③⑦ on page 192.

Located on Pine Mountain, the southernmost mountain in the state, this park is crisscrossed with 33 miles of trails ranging from easy to moderate for you and your leashed pup to explore. President Roosevelt's Little White House at nearby Warm Springs brought him to the Pine Mountain area many times. Dowdell's Knob, his favorite picnic spot, has a panoramic view of the surrounding country.

If your dog is a flat-trail lover like Laddie, you'll want to stick with the Mountain Creek Loop Trail, which starts at the nature lodge. An easy loop of 3.5 miles, it nonetheless winds through mountain laurel and magnolias, over several creeks, and by the ruins of a Civilian Conservation Corps fish hatchery.

The Pine Mountain Trail is 23 miles one way, but you can shorten the hike by hooking up with one of the connecting trails. The Delano Trail is a one-mile loop off the Pine Mountain Trail, while the Big Poplar Loop is almost eight miles. The main trail passes by several waterfalls and beaver dams. Because it crosses Highway 190 seven times, if you come with a friend in separate cars, you can park one of them at a convenient point along the road and experience part of the beauty of this trail without going the full distance. I consider 23 miles to be more of a backpacking trip than a day hike, but I suppose if you and your dog are in good enough condition, it could be done. Get your veterinarian's approval before making such a long hike with your pooch, though. And be sure to bring water for both of you, regardless of the length of the hike. Your pup can stay for free at the campground in the park. (You'll have to pay $12 for a site, though.)

As with other state parks in Georgia, a parking pass is required. You can purchase a day-use pass for $2 from one of the rangers or buy an annual pass for $25.

The park is open daily from 7 A.M. to 10 P.M. It's located about 70 miles, or a little over an hour by car, from Atlanta. Take Interstate 85 south to U.S. 27. Turn left on Highway 190 and follow the signs to the park. (706) 663-4858.

PLACES TO STAY

Franklin Delano Roosevelt State Park Campground: See Franklin Delano Roosevelt State Park above.

FESTIVALS

Azalea Festival: The Azalea Festival at Callaway Gardens (see page 228) is one of the most spectacular sights in Georgia in the spring. Your pooch isn't allowed on the beach or in the Cecil B. Day Butterfly Center, but the main attraction at this time of year is the garden. Rent a bicycle or walk with your pup through the acres of azaleas. There's even a lake where your pooch can cool his pads. The festival is held each year from the last week of March through the middle of April. For more information, call (800) CALLAWAY.

EAST GETAWAYS
GREENSBORO
PARKS AND RECREATION AREAS

• **The Oconee River Recreation Area** 🐾🐾🐾🐾 ◀▶ 🐕
  See ㊳ on page 192.

This way to dog heaven! Yes, your pup can run in leash-free bliss at the Oconee River Recreation Area. Laddie gives it an enthusiastic paws-up, due in no small part to the gently rolling terrain and lack of steep hills to climb. One word of warning: unless you want your dog to get really mucky, plan your visit for sometime after Easter; the entire area is a floodplain, and the Oconee River is highest during the winter and early spring, which could make for a muddy mess in your car.

If you're interested in prehistoric Indian cultures, you'll enjoy the Indian Mounds Trail. Since the Etowah Indian Mounds near Cartersville restricted dogs a few years ago, Laddie hadn't seen a mound until we came here. To be honest, he was unimpressed with the effort required to build the mound and I believe he was unaware that this was anything other than a natural feature.

He did enjoy the 1.5-mile round-trip trail out to the mounds. The white-blazed trail leads through a heavily wooded pine and hardwood area. If you come in the spring, you'll be dealing with some mud but you'll also see wildflowers, including the orange-colored flame azalea, one of our most spectacular native shrubs. The trail has plenty of shade and several small streams to cross along the way, which will be like heaven to your pup, especially since he'll be able to splash freely, off-leash!

There are two mounds about a quarter of a mile apart. Unlike the Etowah Indian Mounds, which are primarily in open country along the river, these are covered with trees, as is the surrounding land. The mounds here are approximately the same age as those at Etowah, from the late Mississippian period (ca. A.D. 1350 to A.D. 1540). The mound builders have possible ties to early Creek Indians.

The first mound you'll come to is called Mound B. It's the smaller of the two, at nine feet high and approximately 30 feet wide. The surrounding area is a floodplain, and you can see watermarks several feet up on the trees on top of the mound. It was excavated by the University of Georgia in 1982 and 1988. They found no bones, indicating it wasn't a burial mound. The current theory is that the mounds were used for ceremonies, with possibly a structure on top for the chieftain or religious leader.

Mound A is about a quarter of a mile farther down the trail, and is much higher, at 32 feet. It's about 30 feet wide at the top and twice that at the bottom, partly due to erosion and unauthorized digging, but partly because it was not built as flat as either Mound B or the mounds at Etowah.

Stay off the mounds to protect them. Although your pooch doesn't have to be leashed here, make sure he stays off the mounds as well.

The two-mile round-trip hike to the ruins of the Scull Shoals settlement is lots of fun for water-loving dogs. Not only does the trail follow along the bank of the Oconee, it also crosses several streams along the way, allowing plenty of opportunity for that wet dog smell we all love. This area is thick with mountain laurel and is beautiful in late spring. Also watch for spring beauty, star chickweed, and many varieties of violets.

The Scull Shoals community used to be truly on the frontier, and the settlers had a difficult time with the Creek Indians in the late 1700s. There were sporadic, bloody confrontations between them, and the name of Scull Shoals may have come from Indian skulls washing up during spring flooding. You won't have to worry about your dog finding any skulls, though, because the settlement was abandoned since the paper and cloth mills were shut down over a century ago. Be sure to keep your curious pooch away from the crumbling ruins.

The park is open daily from 7 A.M. to 10 P.M. all year long. Call the Forest Service before you go to check on the flood situation. Remember those watermarks on the trees! The park is about 75 miles, or a two-and-a-half-hour drive, from the intersection of Interstate 20 and Interstate 285. From Atlanta, take Interstate 20 east to the Highway 44/Greensboro exit and turn left. At Greensboro, turn left onto Highway 15. Turn right onto Macedonia Road at a sign for the Macedonia Church. Drive two miles and turn left onto Forest Service Road 1234, a dirt road. Two miles down, turn left onto Forest Service

Road 1231. Go half a mile and turn right on Forest Service Road 1231A. The road dead-ends about half a mile down into the parking area. Back on Forest Service Road 1231, the Scull Shoals Historic Area is half a mile past Forest Service Road 1231A. (706) 485-7110.

LINCOLNTON
PARKS AND RECREATION AREAS

• **Elijah Clark State Park** 🐾🐾🐾🐾 👣 *See* **39** *on page 192.*

This park is an incredible find, thanks to my friend Jim, who told me about it while I was doing research for this book. I asked what the park had to offer, and he matter-of-factly said there was a lake. Although I prefer more hilly terrain, since Laddie has entered my life I've done a lot more hiking around lakes where the ground is flat (for him) and the view is usually pretty with chances to see or at least hear wildlife (for me). Laddie doesn't enjoy going uphill, and it's hard to find hikes within driving distance of Atlanta that don't have at least some uphill sections. Jim estimated it would take Laddie and me about three hours to walk around the lake.

Bandit was just a new pup at the time, and Laddie seemed so tired of competing for my attention that I decided to leave Bandit at home, giving Laddie some sorely needed Mom time for a change. The two of us left early in the morning and headed east, arriving at the park about three and a half hours later. At first I couldn't see anything of interest, and was completely underwhelmed. Poor Laddie had endured a long, rough morning in the car, and I wasn't looking forward to a repeat performance anytime soon. We stopped at the park office and I went in to ask directions to the lake trail. The two rangers looked puzzled and told me there wasn't really a trail but I could walk along the shoreline because the water level was down. That sounded good for Laddie, so I decided things were looking up and it would be a great day after all. I was pretty sure that Jim's estimate of the length would be wrong, since he said the park was about a two-hour drive from home. I asked the rangers how long they thought it would take to walk around the lake. One of them looked puzzled again, but the other one said he had an estimate around somewhere. After flipping through some cards, he said the estimate was 30 days for eight hours a day. The other ranger mentioned that the lakeshore was approximately 1,200 miles long.

As it turns out, there's a huge, beautiful 76,000-acre lake at this park called the Clarks Hill Reservoir. If you and your pooch aren't up to the 1,200-mile hike (ha!), you can take the three-quarter mile nature trail instead. Even Laddie was happy with this choice. The trail is only slightly rolling and crosses a boggy area and a stream. Bandit would have been in heaven. Laddie likes to stand in streams and let the water cool his feet, so he was pretty content, too. A boardwalk crosses over the worst of the boggy section. The rangers had all but guaranteed that we would see deer on the walk, but no self-respecting deer would come by with Laddie around.

Pooches must be leashed (six-foot maximum) at all times while in the park, and they're not allowed on the beach. If you do decide to take the lakeshore trail—or part of it at any rate—your pooch can accompany you. Wait until at least Easter, however; in early spring the lake is too high to hike along the shore. Another nature trail is on the drawing table but hasn't been started yet.

Amenities include miniature golf, a playground, and picnicking areas. The lake has four boat ramps, and waterskiing is permitted. Because of its location, this isn't a heavily used park—something to keep in mind if you're tired of the summer crowds at lakes north of Atlanta.

Like all other state parks in Georgia, a parking pass is required. You can purchase a day-use pass for $2 from one of the rangers or buy an annual pass for $25.

The park offers both cottages and camping sites. Your pooch isn't allowed in the cottages, but the campground is particularly nice for dogs, with pines and hardwoods between the sites. I've found that Laddie needs a little screen between our campsite and the neighbors'. Otherwise, he's constantly agitated. The campground has 165 sites, about 115 of them on the water. If you're staying in the campground, you have to pay just one day-use fee for the length of your stay. All sites have water and electrical hookups and run $12 per night. You can reserve a campsite by calling (770) 389-7275.

The park is open daily from 7 A.M. to 10 P.M. It's approximately 145 miles, or three hours by car, from Atlanta. Take Interstate 20 east to exit 59 (Highway 78). Turn left onto Highway 78. After about three miles, turn right onto Highway 43 at the Pine Grove Baptist Church. Go 18 miles to Lincolnton, where Highway 43 ends at a traffic light. Turn left, then right onto U.S. 378. The park is seven miles down on the left. For more information about the park, call or write to P.O. Box 293, Route 4, Lincolnton, GA 30817; (706) 359-3458.

PLACES TO STAY

Elijah Clark State Park Campground: See Elijah Clark State Park on page 232.

MADISON

Bandit and I made our first trip to Madison when he was five months old with our friend Vickie and her Pomeranian, What. As we were wandering in and out of the shops downtown, Vickie asked how Bandit could see where he was going, since his long "bangs" hung over his eyes. She suggested I pin his hair up with a barrette, but we couldn't find any that were small enough. Finally, I found infant barrettes in a dime store and was able to secure his hair. With his eyes free of the constant veil of hair, Bandit's whole personality changed, and he spent the rest of the day turning his head constantly to look at everything. The following week I had his hair cut.

If you like antebellum homes or small town America, you're going to love Madison. When you add in its location, less than an hour from Atlanta and near several parks, you'll find it's hard to resist for a day trip or even a weekend. The residents are dog-friendly, and there's even a charming bed-and-breakfast, Burnett Place (see page 235), that welcomes both you and your pooch. During the Civil War, Joshua Hill, a Union sympathizer, went out to Sherman's camp to plead with him to spare the town. As a result, whereas most of the South was burned to the ground, nearly 50 of the wonderful old antebellum and Victorian homes in Madison still stand and can be toured today. A park on Main Street is named in Hill's honor. Be sure to explore the eclectic mix of antique and gift shops in town. Your pooch is almost always welcome to join you.

PARKS AND RECREATION AREAS

• **Hill Park** 😺 *See* ④ *on page 192.*

Named after Joshua Hill, this park has a large, grassy field with plenty of trees for shade, always appreciated by Bandit. For his human friends, there's a picnic shelter, tennis courts, and a children's play area, but the park is mainly just a comfortable place to spread out a blanket and enjoy a picnic. Leashes are a must.

The park is open daily from 7 A.M. to dusk. It's right on Main Street, also known as U.S. 441. From Atlanta, go east on Interstate 20 for about an hour (approximately 50 miles) to exit 51 (U.S. 441). Turn left at the exit. The park is down the road about three miles on the right. (706) 342-0588.

SHOPPING IN MADISON

Old Madison Antiques: Downtown Madison is full of delightful shops like this one. Open since 1975, Old Madison Antiques is the oldest antique store in Madison, and it's run by a group of partners who love dogs. Bandit was a little too rambunctious around the glassware for my comfort, though, so I carried him. The shop has a great selection of furniture dating from the 1840s. 184 South Main Street, Madison, GA 30650; (706) 342-3839.

Utterly Yours: Owner Ron Erwin specializes in products for garden, nature, and animal lovers, and, being all three, this is my kind of shop. I'm biased toward anyone fawning over my pets, but even Bandit, who was playing "shy boy" the day we visited, was smitten with Ron and his staff. Ron prefers that you carry your pooch through his two-story shop, but it's well worth it when you see the eclectic selection. Each of the rooms seems to specialize in something different, from Georgia-made gift oddities (such as cotton pod angels) to jewelry made from antique china and flatware. 183 South Main Street, Madison, GA 30650; (706) 342-9388.

PLACES TO STAY

Burnett Place: This circa 1830s home is on the National Register of Historic Places. Owners Ruth and Leonard Wallace love dogs, although their cats roam the grounds. If your pooch can avoid that temptation, he's welcome to stay with you and even join you in the dining room at mealtime. All of the rooms are furnished with antiques and have private baths; two have fireplaces. Rates are $65 to $75. 317 Old Post Road, Madison, GA 30650; (706) 342-4034.

FESTIVALS

Arts Festival: The Arts Festival, formerly the Theatre Festival, is held the last weekend in July each year in downtown Madison. Your leashed pooch will enjoy wandering among the booths of arts and crafts, but isn't allowed indoors for the concerts and plays. The festival is held at the cultural center. 434 South Main Street, Madison, GA 30650; (706) 342-4743.

Cotton Patch Craft Show: This arts and crafts show is held the second Saturday of October. You and your leashed pooch are welcome to wander among the booths and even into the auditorium. You can sample home-baked goods or get your pup's face painted. Sometimes the festival includes a pet costume contest, which is always fun if you can talk your dog into it. The festival is held downtown on the square and is sponsored by the Madison Women's Club. P.O. Box 524, Madison, GA 30650; (706) 342-4454.

Madison in Bloom: This flower show includes lots of activities to amuse your pet. Just imagine her expression as she watches the bed races with you. In case you've never been to a bed race, teams compete by putting wheels on beds and, while one member of each team lies down, four others push the bed rapidly down the street. If bed racing doesn't interest your pup, stroll through the lawn and garden show. Just be sure to keep a tight rein on the leash so she doesn't mark the flowers in the show! The festival is held on the square downtown in April, and it's sponsored by the Downtown Business Council. For more information, contact the council at P.O. Box 32, Madison, GA 30650; (706) 342-4454.

DIVERSIONS

Bless your little saint: Each October, on the Sunday nearest the Feast Day of Saint Francis, the Church of the Advent in Madison holds a Blessing of the Hounds. This tradition started in Virginia, where fox hunting was popular, and was a blessing for the hounds in the hunt. Fox hunting is not as prevalent as it once was, and the event has evolved into a blessing for all pets. Bring your pooch, but don't be surprised to see a variety of other animals at the church. In years past, cats, birds, turtles, and even snakes have received the blessing alongside dogs. The Episcopalian church is located at 338 Academy Street, Madison, GA 30650; (706) 342-4787.

RUTLEDGE
PARKS AND RECREATION AREAS

• **Hard Labor Creek State Park** 🐾 🐾 🐾 🐾 🐾
See ㊶ on page 192.

Located in Rutledge near the town of Madison, this park is a great place to go with your leashed pooch for an afternoon of mostly easy hiking on two trails. I always head to the Beaver Pond Trail, which is my favorite because I'm forever hopeful I'll see one of these creatures. Alas, with the boys along, all I've seen is evidence of the animals in the pond. The part of the trail that passes close to the pond is also supposed to be a good location for bird-watching. Be sure to look for the ducks in the nesting boxes that stick up out of the water on poles. When I asked a ranger how they got in, she explained that they hop up onto a perch and then crawl into the box.

A short path leads from the Beaver Pond Trail to the Brantly Trail. This trail is also easy and Laddie-approved. Although the trail is peaceful and pleasant any time of year, it can get pretty warm in the summer. If your pooch likes water, she can cool off in Hard Labor Creek or Lake Brantly.

As in other state parks in Georgia, a parking pass is required. You can purchase a day-use pass for $2 from one of the rangers or buy an annual pass for $25.

The park is open daily from 7 A.M. to 10 P.M. It's located about 60 miles, or an hour by car, from the intersection of Interstate 20 and Interstate 285. From Atlanta, take Interstate 20 east to exit 49 (Rutledge). Go through Rutledge and continue on Fairplay Road to the park, which will be on the right. (706) 557-3001.

WINDER
PARKS AND RECREATION AREAS

• **Fort Yargo State Park** 🐾🐾🐾 🦴 *See ⓸ on page 192.*

My passion for wildflowers was first sparked one spring at Fort Yargo State Park. Throughout the previous winter, my friend Betty had been describing the beauty of various wildflowers, but the flowers we saw on our first hikes in the spring had all been pretty ugly. I'd been anticipating wild *flowers*, like what I would plant in a garden. The first time she showed me flowers in the woods, I'd been disappointed to find, after several months of build-up, mere weeds. All that changed when we came to Fort Yargo State Park. As we were walking behind the fort, I spotted something bright purple on the ground and was amazed to find a wild violet as perfect and lovely as any of the African violets I so carefully nurture. When I pointed it out to Betty, she just grinned and gestured behind me. The entire bank was covered in the blooms.

My dogs, of course, don't give flowers any more respect than trees, but there's plenty to keep them happy here as well, including short, easy trails and a creek. Dogs must be leashed throughout the park. One trail leads to the blockhouse or fort that gives the park its name. Built by settlers in 1792 as protection against the Indians, it's well preserved but tiny. The entire structure could fit in the living room of my house, inhabited by one adult and two dogs. If you walk on past the fort, you'll reach the arm of the creek where I found the violets.

The two-mile trail by the lake is gorgeous in the fall, when the colorful trees are reflected in the water. It also gets less use than the trail to the fort, which makes it more enjoyable. Be sure to take in the wonderful view from the bridge over Marbury Creek.

The half-mile Birdberry Trail wanders by the north end of the lake and is specially graded and wide for wheelchair—and Laddie—access.

As in other state parks in Georgia, a parking pass is required. You can purchase a day-use pass for $2 from one of the rangers or buy an annual pass for $25.

The park is open daily from 7 A.M. to 10 P.M. It's located about 50 miles from Atlanta, and can be reached in less than an hour by car. Take Interstate 85 north to Highway 316 North. U.S. 29 will join up with Highway 316 near Lawrenceville. Stay on U.S. 29/Highway 316 until the intersection with Highway 81, and the park will be on the right. (770) 867-3489.

WEST GETAWAYS
CARROLLTON
PARKS AND RECREATION AREAS

• **John H. Tanner State Park** 🐾🐾🐾 🦴 *See ㊽ on page 192.*

With two lakes and two short and easy trails, this park pleases both Laddie and Bandit; boating, swimming, miniature golf, and camping, in addition to hiking, will keep any human tagalongs happy, too. A wide variety of waterbirds call the lakes home, so be sure to keep a tight grip on your pup's leash during the spring. Trixie had a run-in with swans at one of these lakes many years ago, through no fault of her own. (When swans are nesting, they're very aggressive.) If you or your pooch is new to hiking and not ready for anything too strenuous yet, the one-mile loop trail around the upper lake is a good start. There's also a short nature trail up at the northwest end of the lake.

You can't use your annual state ParkPass at this historic site. The charge is $2 for adults and $1 for ages six to 18. You can purchase an annual pass for $25 for the entire family. There's no charge for your pet.

The year-round campground here has 36 sites with water and electrical hookups. The camping fee is $12 a night. To reserve a campsite, call (770) 389-7275.

The park is open daily from 7 A.M. to 10 P.M. It's located about 40 miles west of the city, and the drive takes less than an hour. From Atlanta, take Interstate 20 west to exit 3 (U.S. 27) and turn left. Follow the signs to the park. (770) 830-2222.

PLACES TO STAY

Best Western of Bremen: Your pooch will cost an additional $5 per night, making the room rate $57 to $65 per night. 35 Price Creek Road, Bremen, GA 30110; (770) 537-4645.

Days Inn of Bremen: There's an $8 charge per night for your dog, plus your room rate of $40 to $60. 1077 Alabama Avenue, Bremen, GA 30110; (770) 537-3833.

Days Inn of Carrollton: Folks with pooches must pay a $20 refundable deposit. Rooms are $42 to $48 per night. 180 Centennial Road, Carrollton, GA 30117; (770) 830-1000.

John H. Tanner State Park Campground: See John H. Tanner State Park on page 238.

DALLAS
PARKS AND RECREATION AREAS

• **Pickett's Mill Historic Site** 🐾🐾🐾 👣 *See* **44** *on page 192.*

Pickett's Mill was the site of one of the bloodiest battles in the Civil War. The Union losses were so great and the humiliation so complete, that it wasn't even mentioned in Sherman's memoirs. With so many memorials and reminders of the war in Georgia, it's easy to become immune to the horrors of that time. But Pickett's Mill will bring a new perspective on just what a terrible rending our country faced at that time. The bulk of the battle lasted just two hours, yet left more than 2,000 men dead, more than three-quarters of which were Union troops. The visitors center has a 17-minute film that not only describes what occurred but includes excerpts from letters from some of the soldiers who lived through the carnage. While your dog can accompany you into the visitors center, she isn't allowed into the theater itself. If you go with a friend and take turns watching the film, position yourself so you can see park visitors as they enter and exit the theater. It's sobering to watch a lively, chattering crowd go in, and a silent, somber one come out.

There's an eerie quality on the trails as well, with most people quiet and introspective as they begin to hike. The site has changed little since the battle, and as you walk the trails, it's easy to imagine the difficulty the men went through in the heavy woods and deep ravine. There are three trails, blazed red, white, and blue. When you stop in at the visitors center, tell them which trail you plan to take and they'll loan you a laminated map and guide to sites along the way. The red trail is the longest of the three at 1.7 miles. The white, at 1.1 miles, and blue, at 1.5 miles, are less strenuous, although all are rated moderate. Allow about an hour and a half for any of the trails, to give you time to read the information. Though a creek runs through the ravine, you and your pooch won't be able to get to it since you have to stay on the trail to avoid damaging the site. You'll need to scoop anything your pup tries to leave behind as well, so throw some plastic grocery bags in your pack or stuff them in your pocket. Leashing is required, too.

Twice a month on Sundays, the park offers living history demonstrations. Civil War reenactors set up camps along the trails and show you just what life was like for the soldiers at that time. The demonstrations are of camp life and no battles are fought, so your pet will be quite comfortable taking in the sights. Don't visit with your pooch on the first weekend in June, when the soldiers demonstrate field tactics, drills, and charges. They fire their weapons and cannons during that time and it can get pretty loud, even though they don't reenact the battle itself. A night battle is reenacted in the fall during a candlelight tour of the battlefield, so avoid a visit with your pooch at that time, too.

Your annual state ParkPass won't get you into this historic site. The charge is $2 for adults and $1 for ages six to 18. You can purchase an annual pass for $25 for the entire family. You may want to call and ask about the next open house, when admission is free. There's no charge for your pet.

Hours are from 9 A.M. to 5 P.M. Tuesday through Saturday, and noon to 5 P.M. on Sunday. The park is closed on Monday. It's located approximately 20 miles from Atlanta, a 30-minute drive. Take Interstate 75 north to exit 120 (Highway 92) and turn left. Turn right on Due West Road, right on Mount Tabor Road, then right into the park. (770) 443-7850.

DOGGY
DIVERSIONS

PICK OF THE LITTER

Looking for the best scenic spots in Atlanta to take your favorite pooch? Interested in meeting other dog lovers like yourself? Or thinking about adopting another dog? On the following pages, I list some of the best places Atlanta (and, in some cases, Georgia) has to offer pooches and their people. Let me know if I've missed one of your favorites! And, by the way, within each list, the choices are given in alphabetical order.

BEST WATERFALL WALKS

I love waterfalls, and so do my dogs. Bandit likes to play in them, and Laddie likes to lie in them to cool off. I can't think of anything more restful than letting the rush of the water drown out the sounds of humanity, especially when you live in a large city like we do. When was the last time you didn't hear cars or planes or voices? Park yourself next to one of these and you'll hear yourself think, maybe for the first time in years:

- **Amicalola Falls State Park,** Blairsville/Dahlonega, page 194
- **Anna Ruby Falls,** Helen, page 213
- **Cloudland Canyon State Park,** Rising Fawn, page 217
- **Cochran Mill Park,** Fairburn, page 165
- **DeSoto Falls Recreation Area,** Blairsville/Dahlonega, page 196
- **Dukes Creek Falls,** Helen, page 214
- **High Falls State Park,** Jackson, page 225
- **High Shoals Falls,** Helen, page 215
- **Keown Falls,** Villanow, page 223
- **Panther Creek Falls,** Clayton, page 210

BEST PLACES TO MEET OTHER DOG LOVERS

Like parents who meet at the playground and exchange notes on potty training and tantrums, dog owners love to compare chewing and housebreaking stories. Few of us are immune to the social benefits of having a dog. It's easier to walk up to someone and strike up a conversation while you're admiring his or her dog than it is to approach a lone stranger. If you're interested in making new friends among other dog lovers in the Atlanta area, the following are *the* places to see and be seen:

- **Braelinn Ponds,** Peachtree City, page 113
- **Chattahoochee River Park,** Roswell, page 166
- **Cochran Shoals Unit of the Chattahoochee River National Recreation Area,** Marietta, page 58
- **East Roswell Park,** Roswell, page 167
- **Hidden Valley Park,** Ellenwood, page 181
- **Huddleston Pond,** Peachtree City, page 112
- **Kennesaw Mountain National Battlefield Memorial Park, Burnt Hickory Road entrance,** Marietta, page 61
- **Peachtree Battle Park,** Atlanta, page 153
- **Piedmont Park,** Atlanta, page 154
- **Stone Mountain Park,** Stone Mountain, page 90

BEST WILDFLOWER WALKS

If you and your pooch enjoy hiking together, you've probably come to the conclusion that the two of you operate on different speeds. For Laddie and Bandit, being in the Great Outdoors means a chance to stop and sniff every inch of ground and revel in the scents they just can't find in our backyard. Rather than getting frustrated (and bored) or frustrating them by forcing them to heel or keep up with me, I spend those moments admiring the wildflowers along the trail. With my dogs in tow, I rarely get to see many animals, but the plants can't get away from us. While the boys are investigating a tree, I can look at the violets that are blooming just inches away.

You can pick up a wildflower identification book so you'll have some idea of what you're looking at, or take my approach and cultivate friends who already know something about them. The knowledge does rub off eventually! Here are my favorite wildflower hikes:

- **Amicalola Falls State Park,** Blairsville/Dahlonega, page 194
- **Anna Ruby Falls,** Helen, page 213
- **Black Rock Mountain State Park,** Clayton, page 207
- **Cloudland Canyon State Park,** Rising Fawn, page 217
- **Coleman River Scenic Area,** Clayton, page 208
- **Fort Mountain State Park,** Chatsworth, page 205
- **Fort Yargo State Park,** Winder, page 237
- **Sosebee Cove,** Blairsville/Dahlonega, page 198
- **Sweetwater Creek State Park,** Lithia Springs, page 99
- **Vogel State Park,** Blairsville/Dahlonega, page 199

BEST PLACES TO ADOPT A DOG

Have you ever visited your local humane society? If so, you know first-hand that there's a significant overpopulation problem with dogs in Atlanta—and in this country. The Humane Society of the United States estimates that every year 10 million dogs and puppies are put to sleep because there just aren't homes for them all. When I decided to add a dog to my household, instead of going to any of the area pet stores, I checked out the following organizations. You'll feel good about adopting a dog from an animal shelter, since you truly are saving a life. Thousands of dogs are put to sleep each year in the Atlanta area alone because people don't spay or neuter their pets and allow them to breed even though they can't provide a home for the puppies.

Before I understood the enormity of this problem, I bred my American Eskimo dog, Trixie. Each of her puppies went to loving homes, or so I thought. Six months later, one of my puppies was the Atlanta Humane Society's featured "Pet of the Week" in the newspaper. I was shocked. The person who turned in my puppy to the pound had paid a small fortune for her and was told she came with a money-back guarantee, no questions asked. By the time I got down to the Atlanta Humane Society, my pup had been adopted. The kind folks there opened my eyes to the problem of too many dogs, even too many purebred dogs. (Call your local humane society for help in locating rescue groups that specialize in a particular breed of dog.) The following week, Trixie was spayed, and I started volunteering at the humane society in my county.

Please consider selecting your next pooch from one of the following agencies:

- **Adopt-A-Greyhound:** (404) 634-4883.
- **Atlanta Humane Society:** 981 Howell Mill Road, Atlanta, GA 30318; (404) 875-5331.
- **Clayton County Animal Control:** 7810 North McDonough Street, Jonesboro, GA 30236; (770) 477-3509.
- **Cobb County Animal Control:** 1060 County Farm Drive Southwest, Marietta, GA 30060; (770) 956-9739.
- **DeKalb County Animal Control:** 845 Camp Road, Decatur, GA 30002; (404) 294-2930.
- **DeKalb Humane Society:** 5287 Covington Highway, Decatur, GA 30035; (404) 593-1155.
- **Douglas County Animal Control:** 1755 Humane Society Boulevard, Douglasville, GA 30134; (770) 942-5961.
- **Fayette County Animal Control:** 140 Stonewall Avenue West, Fayetteville, GA 30214; (770) 487-6450.
- **Fayette County Humane Society:** Leave a message at (770) 487-1073 and your call will be returned within 48 hours.
- **Fulton County Animal Control:** 860 Marietta Boulevard, Atlanta, GA 30318; (404) 794-0358.
- **Gwinnett County Animal Control:** 632 High Hope Road, Lawrenceville, GA 30246; (770) 339-3200.
- **Henry County Animal Control:** 46 Work Camp Road, McDonough, GA 30253; (770) 954-2100.

BEST POOCH-PLEASING OUTDOOR ACTIVITIES

People walk, jog, bicycle, skate, play ball, and more for fun and fitness. So why not get your pooch involved in his very own activity that'll help keep his tummy trim and offer him a howling-good time? Dogs, like humans, can benefit from outdoor activities or hobbies that increase their self-confidence, which in turn can make for a happier and more well adjusted pooch. Best of all, the following activities require your involvement, too:

1. Hiking. This book offers a wealth of information on where to hike with your pooch in the Atlanta area and beyond. Where you hike is really a matter of personal preference. My boys and I like trails that take us far away from civilization. But you may prefer hikes that are short, sweet, and closer to home.

The Sierra Club, which sponsors hikes throughout the state, is a great place to meet others with kindred hiking spirits. Although dogs aren't allowed on officially scheduled hikes and backpacking trips, dog lovers in the group often plan hikes where they can take their pets along. Contact the Sierra Club at (404) 888-9778.

Recreational Equipment, Inc. (REI) carries a full line of hiking supplies. It is located on the access road to Interstate 85, between Clairmont Road and North Druid Hills Road, at 1800 Northeast Expressway, Atlanta, GA 30329, and can be reached at (404) 633-6508.

Petsmart stores have backpacks for dogs. Check the index in this book for the Petsmart nearest you.

If you plan to tackle anything significantly more strenuous than your dog is accustomed to, such as backpacking, your veterinarian can tell you if your pooch is up to it or needs a slow but steady fitness routine at first.

2. Lure Coursing. Usually performed by what are known as sight hounds such as greyhounds or whippets, lure coursing is a race where dogs chase a plastic lure around a track. Several organizations sponsor training and trials, including the Coursing Hounds Association of the Southeast (also known as CHASE). One of the best ways to get information on lure coursing is through the Adopt-A-Greyhound organization: (404) 634-4883.

3. Agility Training. Like lure coursing, agility training has gained quite a following throughout the Atlanta area, and classes and trials are held frequently. Agility training involves an obstacle course, where dogs are trained to climb an A-frame, crawl through a conduit pipe, and jump hurdles. Agility training can be done for fun or competitively, and at a local or national level. For more information on this sport, contact the Atlanta Recreation and Fun Club for Dogs at (770) 961-2435, Canine Capers at (770) 448-5204, or the Collie Club of Georgia at (404) 875-5913.

4. Herding. Some breeds of dogs have an instinctive herding ability to round up animals such as sheep. If you want to take advantage of your pup's natural instinct, several organizations throughout the metropolitan area are devoted to herding classes and trials. For more information, contact the Dogwood Rottweiler Club of Metro Atlanta at (770) 928-6159, the Georgia Herding Dog Association at (770) 435-9763, or the Shetland Sheepdog Club at (770) 445-6915. You'll even find sheep farms inside the Perimeter, where groups work their dogs with sheep each week.

5. Frisbee. Playing Frisbee with a pooch is great fun for everyone. Well, almost everyone. My brother taught his 120-pound pit bull, Butch, to play Frisbee. We were throwing the disc from person to person, person to dog, when Butch decided it was his turn. Next thing I knew, I was lying on the ground, surrounded by family and friends. Butch was so intent on catching the Frisbee that I don't think he even noticed he had knocked me out.

The key to teaching a dog how to play Frisbee is in the way you introduce your pooch to the toy. Whatever you do, don't start off by slinging the disc at your dog's face. Try using the disc as a bowl for treats or sliding it along the floor—anything to make your dog more comfortable with the object before trying to make him catch it. Laddie always looks insulted if I try to get him to catch something. He also hasn't caught on to the idea of play as an end in itself. If an activity doesn't involve food, he's amazed that Bandit or I would want to get him to do it. Bandit, on the other hand, sees any moving object (or stationary object, for that matter) as a potential toy, whether it's a disc shooting across the floor or my feet in socks.

The Greater Atlanta Dog and Disc Club holds demonstrations all over the city to show people how much fun this sport can be. The best way to learn how to play the game with your pooch is by contacting that organization at (770) 386-6184. Start yourself off right by calling them before you begin.

6. Obedience Training. Obedience commands, such as sit, stay, down, come, and heel, are used to train your pooch to be a well-behaved and socialized companion. Behavior problems are the most-cited reason for turning in a dog at an animal shelter. Training your dog to obey basic commands will not only make him more fun to live with, but you never know when you may need your dog to react instantly to a life-threatening situation. Besides, when your dog is under your voice control, you'll be able to take him to the off-leash parks in Forsyth County and let him have the time of his life! For more information about obedience training, contact the Atlanta Obedience Club at (770) 457-5717.

7. Tracking. When a dog is tracking, she's following a scent laid on the ground. Although I'm not aware of a tracking club currently in the Atlanta area, some members of the Atlanta Obedience Club teach tracking and can help point you in the right direction. The Atlanta Obedience Club can be reached at (770) 457-5717. They can also help you find out about upcoming obedience shows, where you and your pooch can compete for glory.

8. Fly Ball. You probably know from the name that this sport is great fun for you and your dog. It reminds me of a relay race. The first dog jumps over hurdles to get to the fly ball box. When she presses the slanted side of the box, a tennis ball is ejected. The dog catches the ball, jumps back over the hurdles, and brings the ball to her owner. The owner grabs the ball and the next dog in the relay takes off. Fly ball can be played for fun or competitively, at a local or national level. Call the Atlanta Obedience Club at (770) 457-5717 for more information.

RESOURCES FOR ROVER

CHEROKEE COUNTY

- **Cherokee County Humane Society:** Leave a message at (770) 928-5115. All calls are returned within 48 hours.
- **Cherokee County Recreation and Parks Department:** 7545 North Main Street, Building 200, Woodstock, GA 30188; (770) 924-7768.

CLAYTON COUNTY

- **Clayton County Animal Control:** 7810 North McDonough Street, Jonesboro, GA 30236; (770) 477-3509.
- **Clayton County Parks and Recreation Department (Jonesboro office):** 101 Lake Jodeco Road, Jonesboro, GA 30236; (770) 477-5797.
- **Clayton County Parks and Recreation Department (main office):** 2300 Highway 138 Southeast, Jonesboro, GA 30236; (770) 477-3766.
- **Clayton County Parks and Recreation Department (Riverdale office):** 7208 Church Street, Riverdale, GA 30296; (770) 997-5945.

COBB COUNTY

- **Austell Parks and Recreation Department:** 2716 Broad Street Southwest, Austell, GA 30001; (770) 944-4329.
- **Cobb County Animal Control:** 1060 County Farm Drive Southwest, Marietta, GA 30060; (770) 499-4136.
- **Cobb County Humane Society:** Located adjacent to the Cobb County Animal Shelter at 1060 County Farm Drive, Marietta, GA 30060; (770) 482-5678 or (770) 422-8874.
- **Cobb County Parks, Recreation, and Cultural Affairs Department:** 1792 County Farm Drive, Marietta, GA 30060; (770) 528-8800.
- **Kennesaw Parks and Recreation Department:** 2529 J.O. Stephenson Avenue, Kennesaw, GA 30144; (770) 422-9714.
- **Marietta Parks and Recreation Department:** 205 Lawrence Street, Marietta, GA 30063; (770) 528-0615.
- **Smyrna Parks and Recreation Department:** 200 Village Green Circle, Smyrna, GA 30082; (770) 431-2842.

DeKALB COUNTY

- **Decatur Parks and Recreation Department:** 231 Sycamore Street, Decatur, GA 30030; (404) 377-0494.
- **DeKalb County Animal Control:** 845 Camp Road, Decatur, GA 30002; (404) 294-2930.
- **DeKalb County Recreation and Parks Department:** 1300 Commerce Drive, Room 200, Decatur, GA 30030; (770) 371-2631.
- **DeKalb Humane Society:** 5287 Covington Highway, Decatur, GA 30035; (770) 593-1155.

DOUGLAS COUNTY

- **City of Douglasville Recreation Department:** 8830 Gurley Road, Douglasville, GA 30133; (770) 920-3007.
- **Douglas County Humane Society:** 1755 Humane Society Boulevard, Douglasville, GA 30134; (770) 942-5961.
- **Douglas County Parks and Recreation Department:** 2105 Mack Road, Douglasville, GA 30135; (770) 920-7130.
- **Douglasville Kennel Club of Georgia:** (770) 920-8315.

FAYETTE COUNTY

- **Fayette County Animal Control:** 140 Stonewall Avenue West, Fayetteville, GA 30214; (770) 487-6450.
- **Fayette County Humane Society:** Leave a message at (770) 487-1073 and your call will be returned within 48 hours.
- **Fayette County Recreation Department:** 140 Stonewall Avenue West, Fayetteville, GA 30214; (770) 461-9714.

FORSYTH COUNTY

- **Forsyth County Parks and Recreation Department:** 1950 Sharon Road, Cumming, GA 30131; (770) 781-2215.
- **Hall County Parks and Recreation Department:** 711 Green Street, Gainesville, GA 30504; (770) 535-8280.
- **United States Army Corps of Engineers Parks:** Lake Sidney Lanier, P.O. Box 567, Buford, GA 30518; (770) 945-9531.

FULTON COUNTY

- **Atlanta Humane Society:** 981 Howell Mill Road, Atlanta, GA 30318; (404) 875-5331.

- **Atlanta Parks, Recreation, and Cultural Affairs Department:**
  675 Ponce De Leon Avenue Northeast, Atlanta, GA 30303;
  (404) 817-6752.
- **Doraville Recreation Department:** 3037 Pleasant Valley Drive,
  Doraville, GA 30340; (404) 765-1080.
- **Fulton County Animal Control:** 860 Marietta Boulevard,
  Atlanta, GA 30318; (404) 794-0358.
- **Fulton County Parks and Recreation Department:** 1575
  Northside Drive Northwest, Suite 375, Atlanta, GA 30318;
  (404) 730-6200.
- **Hapeville Recreation Department:** 3444 North Fulton Avenue,
  Hapeville, GA 30354; (404) 669-2136.
- **Pets Are Loving Support (PALS):** PALS provides care for pets
  belonging to people with AIDS, keeping patients and their pets
  together as long as possible. 1438 West Peachtree Street North-
  west, Atlanta, GA 30309; (404) 876-7257.
- **Roswell Recreation and Parks Department:** 38 Hill Street,
  Roswell, GA 30075; (770) 641-3765.

GWINNETT COUNTY

- **Gwinnett County Parks and Recreation Department:**
  75 Langley Drive, Lawrenceville, GA 30245; (770) 822-8840.
- **Humane Services of Metro Atlanta:** 4051 Highway 51,
  Suite C-102-258, Lilburn, GA 30247; (770) 662-4479.

HENRY COUNTY

- **Henry County Animal Shelter:** 46 Work Camp Road, McDonough, GA 30253; (770) 954-2100.
- **Henry County Humane Society:** P.O. Box 941, McDonough, GA 30253; leave a message at (770) 914-1272 and a volunteer will return your call.
- **Henry County Recreation Department:** 100 Windy Hill Road, Suite A, McDonough, GA 30253; (770) 954-2039.

ATLANTA GETAWAYS

- To reserve a campsite at a state park, call (770) 389-7275.
- To request a state park rate and reservations booklet, call (800) 869-8420.
- **TLC Humane Society of Dahlonega:** P.O. Box 535, Dahlonega, GA 30533; (706) 864-2817.

CANINE CALAMITIES

You may never experience any of the following problems with your
dog (except for the occasional tick), but it's a good idea to be prepared if and when an emergency strikes. The information in this
chapter, while not intended to be all-encompassing or to replace a
first aid guide, will help get you through most situations you might
encounter in the woods or even in your own backyard.

I consulted with Dr. Jan Egins of the Fair Oaks Veterinary Clinic
for many of the useful tips you'll find on the following pages. I can
give no higher praise than to tell you that Dr. Egins and her col-
leagues have provided warm, loving care for my pets for more than a
decade. Laddie isn't comfortable with too many people, but he loves
Dr. Egins—and loves going to see her. I recommend the clinic highly
if you're looking for a vet in the Marietta/Smyrna area. The clinic is
located at 2142 Austell Road, Marietta, GA 30060; (770) 432-7155.

TICKS AND LYME DISEASE

It's hard to escape ticks in Georgia. They're most commonly found in wooded areas, but then so are my dogs and I. Removing ticks can be tricky. If you don't have tweezers, Dr. Egins suggests using a napkin or your fingers. The important thing is to get as close to your pup's skin as you can, and then pull the tick straight out. If the head is left in the skin, it can cause an infection, like any other foreign body. If you can't grasp the tick close to the skin, try twisting it counterclockwise, "unscrewing" the tick's head. Frequently they will let go. Disinfect the area before and after removing the pest.

Lyme disease is a serious ailment that can result from a tick bite. Arthritis, with swollen and painful joints, is the number one symptom in dogs. Other symptoms include general malaise, elevated temperature, and irritation at the site of the tick bite. Dogs don't get the bull's-eye rash that people do, but there's a blood test to help your vet make the diagnosis. While dogs can now get a Lyme disease vaccine, a good bit of controversy surrounds the extent of its effectiveness. Still, Dr. Egins has used the vaccine for about four years on her patients. The vaccine's merits lend some peace of mind against the disease in high-risk areas, so many owners choose to use it. While Atlanta is not considered a high-risk area, the mountains of north Georgia are tick country.

The disease is usually spread by the deer tick, which is about half the size of the dog ticks you'll typically find on your pooch. But other types of ticks (as well as fleas) are now suspected of spreading the disease, though the dog tick has yet to be implicated.

So, what do you do? I choose to vaccinate my dogs because we're in the mountains frequently. Even if the vaccine isn't 100 percent effective, it does provide some protection. If there were a vaccine available for me, I would get it in a second.

PLANTS AND OTHER FOREIGN BODIES

Cockleburs, beggar's-lice, and foxtails are all names for plant material designed to latch onto any hair (or socks) that brush by, thereby distributing the plant's seeds. They're generally just an annoyance, both to you and your pooch, but can cause a problem if they aren't removed, since hot spots can develop under matted dog hair.

These aren't the only plants that can cause trouble. Trixie once managed to stab herself in the eye with a stick in our front yard. I didn't even try to remove the object myself. As it turns out, my squeamishness was the right approach. Dr. Egins recommends an immediate trip to the nearest vet or animal hospital if your dog has impaled herself. You can cause additional damage by tugging on the stick or bone.

A more common problem is caused by long blades of grass. Dogs (and cats) somehow manage to inhale or stab themselves in the nose with grass, which can cause a nasal discharge and all the symptoms of an upper respiratory infection.

Sticks and bones lodged crossways inside a dog's mouth are also not unusual. The funny thing is that dog owners often don't notice these things. Dr. Egins says she finds many of these problems during annual exams.

Poison ivy can make you miserable, but your pooch probably won't be bothered by it. See the introduction on page 18 for information on how to keep this problem plant from spoiling your trip.

WATER PROBLEMS

Giardia is a nasty parasite that pups—and people—can get from drinking out of a stream or creek. While it's difficult to keep a thirsty dog from wetting his whistle, Dr. Egins recommends carrying water for your dog so he has options other than the Chattahoochee River or a mountain stream. Dogs do build up some sort of immunity to the parasite, just as humans do, but they can get pretty sick in the meantime. Dr. Egins says she sees three to four cases a year with severe, persistent diarrhea. Young dogs and those with suppressed immune systems (from a recent illness or even allergies) are the most likely to get sick.

SKUNKS, SNAKES, AND OTHER ANIMALS

While my boys and I have seen skunks in campgrounds in Georgia, we've never encountered one while hiking in the woods. If your pooch does happen upon a skunk who decides to defend himself, your dog (and you) will come out the loser. Dr. Egins suggests washing your dog with Dawn dish detergent, one of her favorite general remedies. Dawn is also readily available in the areas where you're most likely to have a run-in. Other options include soaking in an acid-based juice such as tomato or lemon juice, followed by shampooing with Dawn.

In almost a decade of practice, Dr. Egins says she has seen only two cases of dogs with snakebites. (Many dog owners assume that two marks on a dog indicate a snakebite and rush their pups to the vet, says Dr. Egins, but in most cases a snake wasn't the culprit.) Georgia is home to various kinds of snakes, but only a few of these reptiles are poisonous. I'm wary of all snakes, poisonous or not. I've never been bitten, but I carry a snakebite kit in my pack, just in case of an emergency. Most of the snakes my boys and I have encountered have been near water.

If your dog is bitten by a snake, you should be able to see the two holes where the bite occurred. Always assume it was a poisonous snake unless you're able to make an exact identification. Immediately begin washing the wound with water and soap, if you have it. Carry your dog to the car, if possible, as all movement helps to spread the venom through her system. Let someone else drive, and continue washing the wound right up until you arrive at the emergency clinic. Don't let your pup drink any fluids. She may go into shock, or start vomiting or convulsing. Keep her as warm as possible by wrapping her in a blanket, which will also help to prevent injury from seizures. Hold her on her side, with her feet slightly elevated, and hurry!

BROKEN BONES

Dogs are pretty resilient, but they do occasionally break one of their bones. Trixie broke a toe once when she ran into a speed bump. Although she seemed barely capable of lifting her cast when I was around, I caught her running through the house and leaping up on the couch several times. If your dog is limping, check the affected pad and in between the toes for a burr, stick, or stone. If you don't find anything, let your veterinarian take a look. Whether your dog suffers from a broken bone, a sprain, or a strain, you'll need to have it checked.

In case of a compound fracture, where the broken bone is sticking out through the skin, wrap your dog securely in a blanket. If the break happens on a trail, you'll need to carry the injured pup back to your car.

The only time you shouldn't pick your dog up is in the case of spinal injuries. Just as with people, moving an animal with a spinal injury can cause permanent paralysis. How do you know if there's a spinal injury? Dr. Egins says that the main symptom is paralysis in the hind legs. If you have someone else with you, send him or her for a stretcher. Otherwise, you'll have to make a judgment call on leaving the dog while you go for help, or carrying him out as best you can.

BLEEDING

If your dog is bleeding profusely, apply pressure with a clean cloth or piece of gauze. You can wrap the gauze or cloth around the limb or affected area, but don't twist it too tight or you may cut off the circulation. When you're applying pressure, push your hand against the cloth or gauze, but don't constrict the area by circling it with pressure. For example, if your dog's leg is bleeding, press the gauze against the wound. Don't hold the gauze on with your hand wrapped around his leg. Again, the main danger is cutting off the circulation to the rest of the extremity.

While Dr. Egins recommends against making a tourniquet yourself (most people do it poorly and cause more tissue damage), if you're convinced your pup will bleed to death before you get her to help, you may *have* to make one. To do so, place clean gauze just above the cut. Wrap it around the limb, tying a stick into the wrap. Twist the stick slowly until you see the bleeding has stopped, and tape it in place. While you're transporting the dog to the veterinarian, loosen the bandage at least every few minutes and check for bleeding. If the wound is no longer bleeding, remove the tourniquet.

Use the water you've carried along to clean the wound. Hydrogen peroxide can also be used, although it will sting. Never clean a wound with rubbing alcohol, or your injured dog may take off for the next county.

CONTROLLING AN INJURED DOG

An injured dog, even a calm, loving friend, can be dangerous. You can improvise a muzzle with a strip of gauze, a shoelace, or a leash. Wrap it repeatedly around your dog's nose to keep her mouth closed, and don't be afraid of cutting off the circulation to the nose and lips. If you have a gauze strip, tie it in a bow, slip it over your dog's face, and tighten. If the dog is having trouble breathing, don't put a muzzle on her. You can still protect yourself by immobilizing her neck by making a thick collar with a towel or a blanket.

HEATSTROKE

Leaving your dog in a car with the windows rolled up isn't the only way he can get heatstroke. Dogs try their best to please their owners, even when they're uncomfortable. A client of Dr. Egins was out jogging with his dog when he noticed the pup was breathing heavily. He immediately carried the dog home and drove to the clinic, but the dog couldn't be saved. Pooches will literally run until they drop. Even if you're just walking, dogs need frequent water stops and rest in extreme temperatures, just as people do.

If your dog becomes affected by the heat, pour water over him. Don't use ice water, which would be too much of a shock to his system. Your water bottle can be used to help cool him down. If you have alcohol in your first aid kit, use it to rub the insides of his ears, between his toes, on the pads of his feet, and on his stomach. Then, immediately get to an emergency clinic if you're far from your vet. You don't have time to waste.

SHOCK

If your dog has a severe injury or is bleeding internally, she could go into shock. The symptoms of shock include pale gums, shallow, rapid breathing, and a listless attitude. Wrap her in a blanket and elevate her feet. Then lay her on her side, with a pillow placed under her legs.

BEE STINGS

If your dog is allergic to bee stings—which you may not discover until he's stung—seconds count. The danger with allergic reactions is that the neck and face frequently swell, regardless of where the bite occurred, which can cut off his breathing. Dr. Egins recommends Benadryl as a safe treatment. Check with your vet about the dosage for your dog, and carry the dosage in your first aid kit at all times.

EMERGENCY MEDICINE

Other than Benadryl, Dr. Egins doesn't recommend giving your pet *any* over-the-counter medicine for first aid. Tylenol should *never* be given to a dog or cat, and ibuprofen is nearly as deadly. Aspirin causes a much more severe reaction in a dog's stomach than it does in a person's, so it should be given only under the direction of your pet's doctor, and always with food.

GENERAL ADVICE

In terms of general advice on keeping your best pal healthy, Dr. Egins offers the following tips. Always have water available for your pooch to prevent dehydration and heat stroke and to clean a wound. Keep your dog up to date on all of his vaccinations. He can be exposed to parasites and viruses by simply sniffing at the remains of another dog's dinner, so keep him away from dog messes whenever possible. If your dog has been sick recently, suffers from allergies, or is less than a year old, he'll be more susceptible to picking up diseases in the woods or along the street.

Finally, if your dog is injured when you're a couple of hours or more away from your vet, go directly to the nearest vet under the following circumstances: if your pooch is bleeding profusely, in convulsions, has labored breathing, has swelling about the face or neck, is unconscious, has white gums, or if you suspect a spinal injury.

EMERGENCY VETERINARY CLINICS

I used to work with a woman named Suzy who had four boys, and every Monday morning we would compare weekend stories. Suzy's always involved a trip to an emergency room. I couldn't understand how she could be so calm as she talked about Michael's broken arm or Scott's dislocated shoulder.

During the 14½ years that Trixie was with me, we had a midnight visit to an emergency veterinary clinic once. I'm not necessarily saying it has something to do with being a boy, but once Laddie joined my household, we visited the emergency clinic often enough for the staff to recognize us on sight.

Odds are that you're going to need to at least talk to a veterinarian at some time during your dog's life when your vet's office is closed. Petsmart stores throughout the Atlanta area have full-service vet clinics on site, open Monday through Friday from 9 A.M. to 8 P.M., Saturday from 9 A.M. to 6 P.M., and Sunday from noon to 6 P.M. Consult the index in the back of this book or a phone book for the store nearest you. The following emergency clinics can also be called upon in a pinch:

COBB COUNTY

- **Cobb Emergency Veterinary Clinic PC:** The clinic is open from 6 P.M. to 8 A.M., Monday through Friday, from noon Saturday to 8 A.M. Monday, and 24 hours on holidays. 422 Roswell Street Northeast, Marietta, GA; (770) 424-9157.

DeKALB COUNTY

- **Briarcliff Animal Clinic and Hospital:** The clinic is open from 7:30 A.M. to 7 P.M. Monday through Thursday, 7:30 A.M. to 6 P.M. on Friday, 7:30 A.M. to 5 P.M. on Saturday, and 1 P.M. to 5 P.M. on Sunday. Seven days a week, a doctor is on call from the time the clinic closes until 9:30 P.M., and will return your call. After 9:30 P.M., an answering machine will direct you to an emergency clinic. 1850 Johnson Road Northeast, Atlanta, GA; (404) 874-6393.
- **DeKalb-Gwinnett Animal Emergency Clinic, Inc.:** The clinic is open from 6 P.M. to 8 A.M. Monday through Friday, from noon Saturday to 8 A.M. Monday, and 24 hours on holidays. 6430 Lawrenceville Highway, Tucker, GA; (770) 491-0661.

- **Dogwood Hospital for Animals:** The clinic is open from 8 A.M. to 7 P.M. Monday through Friday, and from 8 A.M. to 5 P.M. on Saturday. During the clinic's off-hours, a doctor will be paged and will call you back. 2647 Buford Highway Northeast, Atlanta, GA; (404) 636-0363.
- **Emory Animal Hospital:** The hospital is open from 7:30 A.M. to 7 P.M. Monday through Friday, from 8 A.M. to 5 P.M. on Saturday, and from 1 P.M. to 5 P.M. on Sunday. Seven days a week, including holidays, a doctor is on call until 10 P.M. After 10 P.M., patients are referred to the DeKalb-Gwinnett Animal Emergency Clinic, Inc., 1226 Clairmont Road, Decatur, GA; (404) 633-6163.

FULTON COUNTY

- **Animal Emergency Clinic PC:** The emergency clinic is open from 6 P.M. to 8 A.M. Monday through Friday, from noon Saturday through 8 A.M. Monday, and 24 hours on holidays. 228 Sandy Springs Place Northeast, Atlanta, GA; (404) 252-7881.
- **Atlanta Animal Hospital:** The clinic is open from 7:30 A.M. to 7 P.M., seven days a week. An answering service will page a doctor to come in to the hospital outside of normal business hours. 5005 Kimball Bridge Road, Alpharetta, GA; (770) 475-0600.
- **Atlanta Emergency Center of North Fulton:** The hospital is open from 6 P.M. to 8 A.M. Monday through Friday, and from noon Saturday to 8 A.M. on Monday. 900 Mansell Road, Roswell, GA; (770) 594-2266.
- **Veterinary Medical Center:** The clinic is open from 7 A.M. to 9 P.M. seven days a week, and closed on holidays. After normal clinic hours, an answering machine directs patients to an emergency clinic. 8750 Nesbitt Ferry Road, Alpharetta, GA; (770) 998-8450.

GWINNETT COUNTY

- **DeKalb-Gwinnett Animal Emergency Clinic, Inc.:** The clinic is open from 6 P.M. to 8 A.M. Monday through Friday, from noon Saturday to 8 A.M. Monday, and 24 hours on holidays. 6430 Lawrenceville Highway, Tucker, GA; (770) 491-0661.

INDEX

ACKNOWLEDGMENTS

This book could not have been written without the enthusiastic support and unselfish assistance of my boys, Laddie and the Bandit. I would like to express my deep gratitude also to David Herlache for his assistance in researching this book; to his helpers, Cricket, Bruno, and Tiffany, for making it fun; to Elaine Coe, without whose expert navigational advice I would never have found my way around the Perimeter; to Betty Baker for always being there to provide moral support and whatever help was asked for; to all of the park rangers who patiently answered my gazillion questions, and especially Connie Vogel-Brown; to Dr. Jan Egins for her expert veterinary assistance; and to Cindy Goodman for her help with breed questions. And finally, thanks to Trixie, who started it all.

CREDITS

Editor-in-Chief	Rebecca Poole Forée
Senior Editor	Jean Linsteadt
Production Manager	Michele Thomas
Associate Editor	Karin Mullen
Assistant Editor	Aimee Larsen
Production Assistant and Map Design	Alexander Lyon
Proofreader	Annelise Zamula
Acquisitions Editor	Judith Pynn
Series Editors	Maria Goodavage, Lyle York
Cover (The Phoenix) and Interior Illustrations	Phil Frank

Special thanks to Maria Goodavage, who graciously contributed material to the introduction.

ABOUT THE AUTHORS

Laddie (pictured at left) is an American Eskimo dog who doesn't like to be called a spitz. He doesn't want to have anything to do with other dogs or people, believing they just want to mess with him. He loves to walk on flat surfaces and around lakes, and can detect a two-inch grade in an instant. A typical day for him includes eating breakfast, napping, and dreaming about dinner (trying to telepathically communicate that his bowl is empty), eating dinner, begging for snacks, and dreaming about breakfast. Puppy **Bandit** is a lovable fellow of mixed heritage, namely Llasa apso and bichon frise. Bandit was supposed to weigh no more than 12 to 15 pounds, but Laddie is beginning to wonder if he'll ever stop growing. The boys share their home with **Marilyn Windle,** a writer recently promoted from the lofty title of Door Person because she installed a dog door.

BOOKS BUILDING COMMUNITY

Foghorn Press is pleased to support environmental and social causes nationwide. In an effort to create an awareness of and support for these worthy causes, the Books Building Community program unites Foghorn's media, bookstore, and outdoor retail partners with nonprofit organizations such as the:

atlanta humane society

The Atlanta Humane Society and Society For Prevention Of Cruelty To Animals, Inc., founded in 1873, is a private, nonprofit organization that serves as a regional sanctuary for the needs of animals, pet owners, and the community at large concerning animal welfare issues and problems. The AHS operates the only full-service charitable veterinary hospital in the Southeast, providing medical care for in-house animals, animals adopted from the Shelter, and animals of the financially disadvantaged. The Society is not an affiliate or branch of any other agency and is an autonomous organization. The AHS receives no federal or local governmental support or United Way funding. Society programs and services are complemented by a strong and dedicated volunteer base.

The Atlanta Humane Society is dedicated to hands-on care of animals. The Shelter and Clinic comprise 48,000 square feet of state-of-the-art animal husbandry. All animals are accepted at no charge. There are no time limits on the animals awaiting adoption, and the AHS has one of the highest animal adoption rates in the country.

Support services include, but are not limited to: advocacy, law enforcement, cruelty investigation, rabies control, mobile adoptions, 24-hour PE+AID ambulance service, lost-and-found services, companion pets for the elderly, obedience programs, Mend-A-Heart grief counseling, rescue services, disaster rescue, Pet Facilitated Therapy programs for the institutionalized, programs in conjunction with social service agencies, and a Food Bank program for other animal welfare agencies.

The Atlanta Humane Society represents a haven of hope. We speak for those who can't speak for themselves.

For more information, contact the Atlanta Humane Society, 981 Howell Mill Road Northwest, Atlanta, GA 30318-5562; (404) 875-5331.

FOGHORN OUTDOORS

Founded in 1985, Foghorn Press has quickly become one of the country's premier publishers of outdoor recreation guidebooks. Through its unique Books Building Community program, Foghorn Press supports a variety of community environmental issues such as park, trail, and water ecosystem preservation. Foghorn Press is also committed to printing its books on recycled paper.

Foghorn books are sold throughout the U.S. Call 1-800-FOGHORN (8:30–5:30 PST) for the location of a bookstore near you that carries Foghorn Press titles. If you prefer, you may place an order directly with Foghorn Press using your Visa or MasterCard or visit our Web site at www.foghorn.com. All of the titles listed below are now available, unless otherwise noted.

THE DOG LOVER'S COMPANION SERIES

Foghorn's Dog Lover's Companion series is for travelers who want to bring their canine companions along for the ride. Readers will find regional listings of pet-friendly restaurants, hotels, parks, walks, and hikes that will keep their dogs' tails wagging.

THE BAY AREA DOG
LOVER'S COMPANION
352 pp., $13.95

THE CALIFORNIA DOG
LOVER'S COMPANION
720 pp., $19.95

THE SEATTLE DOG
LOVER'S COMPANION
256 pp., $17.95

THE FLORIDA DOG
LOVER'S COMPANION
552 pp., $19.95

THE BOSTON DOG
LOVER'S COMPANION
416 pp., $17.95

THE ATLANTA DOG
LOVER'S COMPANION
288 pp., $17.95

THE COMPLETE GUIDE SERIES

The Complete Guides are the books that have given Foghorn Press its reputation for excellence. Each book is a comprehensive resource for its subject, from *every* golf course in California to *every* fishing spot in the state of Washington. With extensive cross-references and detailed maps, the Complete Guides offer readers a quick and easy way to get the best recreational information available.

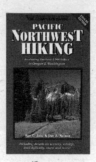

ALASKA FISHING
640 pp., $19.95

CALIFORNIA GOLF
896 pp., $19.95

PACIFIC NORTHWEST HIKING
808 pp., $18.95

SOUTHWEST CAMPING
544 pp., $17.95

BAJA CAMPING
296 pp., $12.95

CALIFORNIA BEACHES
640 pp., $19.95

CALIFORNIA CAMPING
848 pp., $19.95

CALIFORNIA FISHING
832 pp., $19.95

CALIFORNIA HIKING
856 pp., $18.95

TAHOE
704 pp., $18.95

WASHINGTON FISHING
528 pp., $19.95

CALIFORNIA BOATING AND WATER SPORTS
552 pp., $19.95

CALIFORNIA IN-LINE SKATING
480 pp., $19.95

PACIFIC NORTHWEST CAMPING
720 pp., $19.95

THE EASY SERIES

The Easy books are perfect for families, seniors, or anyone looking for easy, fun weekend adventures. No special effort or advance planning is necessary—just head outdoors, relax, and enjoy.

EASY BIKING IN NORTHERN CALIFORNIA
224 pp., $12.95

EASY CAMPING IN NORTHERN CALIFORNIA
240 pp., $12.95

EASY HIKING IN NORTHERN CALIFORNIA
240 pp., $12.95

THE NATIONAL OUTDOORS SERIES

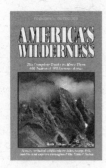

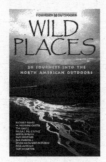

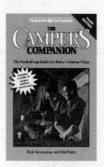

AMERICA'S WILDERNESS
The Complete Guide to More Than 600 National Wilderness Areas

592 pp., $19.95

WILD PLACES
20 Journeys Into the North American Outdoors

350 pp., $15.95

THE CAMPER'S COMPANION
The Pack-Along Guide for Better Outdoor Trips

458 pp., $15.95

AMERICA'S SECRET RECREATION AREAS
Your Recreation Guide to the Bureau of Land Management's Wild Lands of the West

640 pp., $17.95

EPIC TRIPS OF THE WEST
Tom Stienstra's Ten Best

208 pp., $9.95

OUR ENDANGERED PARKS
What You Can Do to Protect Our National Heritage

224 pp., $10.95

THE GREAT OUTDOOR GETAWAYS SERIES

For outdoor adventure, nothing beats Foghorn's Great Outdoor Getaways guides. Full of terrific ideas for day trips or weekend journeys, these books point you in the right direction for fun in the Great Outdoors.

GREAT OUTDOOR GETAWAYS TO THE BAY AREA & BEYOND
632 pp., $16.95

GREAT OUTDOOR GETAWAYS TO THE SOUTHWEST
448 pp., $16.95

A book's page length, price, and availability are subject to change.

For more information, call 1-800-FOGHORN, visit our Web site at www.foghorn.com, or write to: Foghorn Press, 555 DeHaro Street, Suite 220 San Francisco, CA 94107

Foghorn Press

BOOKS BUILDING COMMUNITY™

ATLANTA AREA
CHAPTER REFERENCE MAP

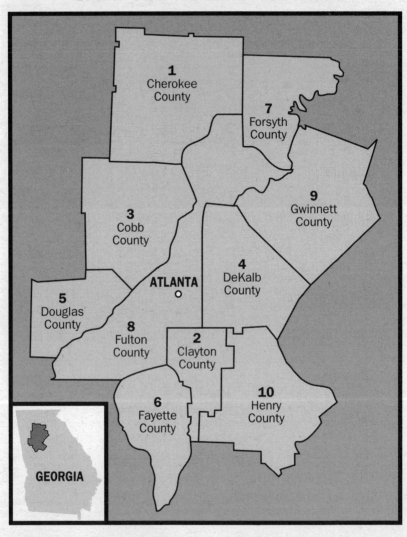